Praise for *Solving for Why*...

Solving for Why provides an eye-opening view of mathematics interventions that are teacher-friendly with student-centered results!

—*Melony M. Brady, Principal, Annie Fisher STEM Magnet School,*
Hartford, Connecticut

We all remember that special student, the one who struggled so hard to learn math concepts and procedures. We all remember trying strategy after strategy, with varying degrees of success. And, we all remember the questions we used to guide our thinking about helping that child: *Why did the youngster struggle? How can we "get under the hood" to better understand that child's thinking? How can we best intervene to promote success for that child and for all diverse learners in ways that are both effective and efficient? Solving for Why* addresses these concerns with concrete, specific, and actionable strategies that support teachers of mathematics, coaches, learning specialists, and school leaders in closing the achievement gap in mathematics in every classroom in every school in ways that are both insightful and impactful. By focusing on interventions to support *each* child, Tapper's book is an excellent guide for supporting *all* children and the dedicated teachers who serve them.

—*Maryann Marrapodi, Chief Learning Officer, Teachscape*

My prediction is that *Solving for Why* will become a much-referenced guide in how to authentically address the complex mathematical needs of our students. As a math coach, a question I hear daily is, "How do we know what we need to know and then what do we do about it?" John Tapper provides approaches that are explicit and clear. The result is a warm and, sometimes, humorous way to begin to find our own answers to many of our most persistent questions about mathematical thinking.

—*Veronica May Sampson, math coach,*
Windham Southeast Supervisory Union,
Brattleboro, Vermont

Solving for Why is a must-have resource for math teachers, general educators, and special educators who are seeking ways to help their struggling students become successful math learners. The powerful and practical assessment approaches help teachers get to the heart of why their students are struggling in mathematics. By gaining insights into their students' math difficulties, teachers will be able to plan effective interventions and differentiated lessons that address their students' specific learning needs. The extensive classroom examples and helpful suggestions provide a wealth of ideas for teachers to apply with their students.

—*Amy Brodesky, project director, Addressing Accessibility in Mathematics,*
Education Development Center (EDC)

John Tapper has developed a valuable and engaging resource for teachers of struggling math learners, filled with classroom anecdotes and written in a clear, teacher-to-teacher voice. Grounded in research on mathematics education, his approach helps teachers understand each student's thinking as an entry point to promoting deep understanding of rigorous content.

—*Eliot Levine, University of Massachusetts and author of*
One Kid at a Time: Big Lessons from a Small School

Solving for Why is a must-read for anyone who works with struggling mathematics learners. Dr. Tapper's thirty years of experience working with elementary school students and teachers along with his solid grasp of the research base on the teaching and learning of mathematics have resulted in a book that is wise, practical, and engaging. The book's organization, conversational style, and rich classroom examples make this an enjoyable and insightful read. I highly recommend this book to novice and veteran educators alike, who are searching for strategies for how to understand, assess, and best meet the needs of their struggling learners.

—*Jean McGivney-Burelle, Associate Professor of Mathematics and Director of the Secondary Mathematics Education Program, University of Hartford, W. Hartford, Connecticut*

In *Solving for Why*, John Tapper has developed a system to support teachers as they strive to understand all students' mathematical thinking. The process of collaborative study allows and encourages teachers to create hypotheses about students' mathematical understandings and test those hypotheses with the support of colleagues. This resource should be in the professional library of all teachers, special educators, mathematics coaches, and administrators who work with struggling mathematics students.

—*Elizabeth Petit Cunningham, doctoral student and former classroom teacher, University of Nebraska–Lincoln*

Solving for Why is the book our mathematics teaching profession has been long waiting for! John Tapper has provided classroom teachers, special educators, mathematics coaches and school leaders an invaluable resource for helping struggling students deeply understand mathematics. Tapper combines foundational research and principles of effective mathematics instruction for struggling math learners with meaningful classroom vignettes to create a resource that explores specific strategies at both the teacher-student and school levels. *Solving for Why* should be in the hands of every educator who wants all K–8 students to succeed in mathematics.

—*Bob Laird, Vermont Mathematics Initiative and co-author of*
A Focus on Fractions: Bringing Research to the Classroom

GRADES
K-8

Solving for Why

Understanding, Assessing, and Teaching Students Who
Struggle with Math

John Tapper

Math Solutions
Sausalito, California, USA

For my students, who have made teaching math
such a wonderful adventure

Math Solutions
One Harbor Drive, Suite 101
Sausalito, California, USA 94965
www.mathsolutions.com

Math Solutions is a division of Houghton Mifflin Harcourt.

MATH SOLUTIONS® and associated logos are trademarks or registered
trademarks of Houghton Mifflin Harcourt Publishing Company. Other company
names, brand names, and product names are the property and/or trademarks of
their respective owners.

ISBN-13: 978-1-935099-33-8
ISBN-10: 1-935099-33-7

Editor: Jamie Ann Cross
Production: Denise A. Botelho
Cover design: Jan Streitburger
Interior design and composition: Denise Hoffman, Glenview Studios
Cover and interior images: © iStock (cover); pp. 3, 6, © Shutterstock

Printed in the United States of America.
10 11   0014   22 21 20 19 18 17
4510003870

Contents

Acknowledgments

A publication, I now understand, is like a small town where people contribute to the experience in a wide variety of ways. There are many people who have contributed knowledge, support, or their experiences to help me make this book. First and foremost are the teachers who participated in the Math for Struggling Learners courses, particularly, Veronica Sampson, Liz Cunningham, Chris Farnham, and Jen Patenaude. Without their contributions there would be no book. I'm also grateful to Jean Ward and Casey Murrow for supporting these courses over several years.

A most sincere and appreciative thank you to Jamie Cross and the people at Math Solutions for being open-minded, skillful, and encouraging. Your efforts have made this a much better resource.

My conversations about how children learn math began with my experiences in the Westminster Primary Program. Judy Coven was the best mentor and partner a young teacher could have. She has inspired many children and new teachers with her skill and insight. Some of the vignettes in this resource are from our work together. My firm belief that children, rather than content, are the heart of the curriculum comes mainly from Judy.

I am lucky to have been part of the Vermont Math Initiative; it gave me the opportunity to work with teachers at all grade levels both as learners and as colleagues. I was particularly lucky to have the chance to work with Bob and Judi Laird, who are among the best math teachers I know. Sandi Stanhope and Fran Huntoon were an important part of my VMI experience, and their support and insights have contributed to this manuscript.

P.S. 363 (the Neighborhood School) in Manhattan was the place where some of the early ideas about understanding the wide variety of learners' thinking began for me. There is truly no better experience for a teacher than working in an excellent urban school. Judith Foster and Milo Novelo were, and are, outstanding education leaders who supported my efforts to work with struggling learners. My work benefitted from conversations with Milo Novelo and with Grace Chang and Barbara Fraiser, two gifted teachers with special skill as teachers of mathematics.

Acknowledgments

I am grateful for the support of my colleagues and students at the University of Hartford who continue to inspire me and make the work of teaching mathematics more fun than it has any right to be. David, Megan, Kim, and Melissa were supportive at the beginning of this enterprise and now I can acknowledge them in print.

My extraordinary children, Brianna, Ben, Ian, Isaac, and, now, Kelsey and Zach, have had to live with growing up with a father who is constantly bothering them about mathematics. I've tried out so many activities on them, probed their thinking, and made them solve problems. I am so appreciative of their patience and love. Brianna, who has been an urban educator and is now entering the world of research, has become a colleague. Her work with English language learners has helped me further my own thinking about the role of language in math learning.

My wife should really be the coauthor of this book. Her expertise with math and science professional development, her reading and editing of the manuscript, her constant love and encouragement made it possible for me to write this. I am so very grateful for her, and for her help on this book.

How to Use This Resource

Why This Resource?

Solving for Why: Understanding, Assessing, and Teaching Students Who Struggle with Math, Grades K–8 blends current research on ways to understand and identify the math with which learners struggle with practical, mainstream classroom practice. The gap between those who learn math with relative ease and those who struggle creates inequities in opportunities for higher education and for the workplace. *Solving for Why*'s research-driven, practical, friendly approach supports educators in narrowing this achievement gap. The contents are primarily focused on learning about struggling students and assessing student knowledge and understanding to guide intervention aimed at student success. This focus, on *understanding the mathematical thinking of struggling learners* and using that knowledge to design instruction for their success, is remarkably different from recipe-type approaches that assume the same solution applies to learners with similar struggles. Rather, the solution to mathematical struggles is often revealed from a rich understanding of each individual learner.

Who Is This Resource For?

Solving for Why is a resource for anyone who teaches mathematics, grades K–8. It is useful for classroom teachers, resource room teachers, special educators, math leaders (curriculum specialists, math coaches, etc.), and principals. These professionals have reported benefits from the perspectives, assessments, and approaches to remediation shared in this resource.

> "It is estimated that, for every two years of school, children who struggle with math acquire only one year's worth of mathematical proficiency . . . struggling learners who are not subjected to early intervention may reach a learning plateau by middle school and acquire the equivalent of one year of mathematical proficiency during grades 7–12 . . . the disparity between those who learn math with relative ease and those who struggle with math disabilities is widening at an alarming rate."
>
> —PBS, "Difficulties with Mathematics"

My Story

The Louder and Slower Approach

One of my own struggles as a classroom teacher—and one of the most helpful experiences I've had as a teacher—is finding ways to help students who have difficulty understanding the math I am teaching. There seems to be a broad range of student difficulties. Some students grapple with remembering math facts. Some have difficulty with problems. Others seem to learn something one day and forget it the next.

Whenever I researched how to help these students, or asked one of the school's learning specialists for help, I frequently seemed to get the same response: Take it slower. Practice longer. Don't expect too much understanding. I have come to call this method the "louder and slower approach."

Louder and slower is similar to how my friend Michael approaches speaking to locals when he's traveling in another country. When the person he's trying to speak with doesn't understand what he's saying, Michael reverts to talking louder and slower. He makes it seem like the person he's talking to is deaf, not that they simply don't share the same language.

If we stretch this analogy, we can imagine Michael, a native English speaker, trying to speak to Joan in another country who, rather than having no understanding of English at all, has learned a few phrases:

Michael: Hi. Do you speak English? Do you know where the ATM is?

Joan: Good day. Pleased to meet you.

Michael: Pleased to meet you, too. Do you know where . . .

Joan: Thank you. Pleased to meet you.

Michael: DO YOU K N O W W H E R E . . .

Being a struggling learner, it turns out, can be a lot like being a foreigner when your teacher is Michael. Teaching a struggling learner can be a lot like being Michael. We want to communicate but we only have an instinct for louder and slower. When I was a new teacher I had a discouraging conversation with a colleague in which he urged me not to spend too much time helping a fourth-grade student understand multiplication. His view was (this was, and still is, *very* common) that this student did not have the capacity and/or time to learn what multiplication was and how it worked. His prescription was to drill the algorithm and facts and hope for the best. At the time I deferred to his judgment, though it felt like putting up a white flag. I remember feeling that a ten-year-old was too young for us to give up on. (Are they ever old enough for that?)

What's called for is understanding. After years as a math specialist in rural and urban schools, and hundreds of hours reading others' research and conducting my own, I've learned that there are alternatives to louder and slower. I feel we, as a community of educators, are at the beginning of what will be a productive period of research and exploration of mathematical difficulties. This resource represents an effort to bring together research and classroom practice and to create a model for instruction that recognizes the importance of conceptual understanding, of understanding our students, and of helping them gain access to important mathematical ideas in appropriate ways. We do this, to return to my foreign-language metaphor, by learning the language of the students whom we teach. Rather than shouting slowly, we must try to understand how our students think, how they make sense of mathematical ideas (if they do), and how to create a learning environment for them that allows them to do their best work.

> "We must try to understand how our students think, how they make sense of mathematical ideas (if they do), and how to create a learning environment for them that allows them to do their best work."

Solving for Why represents a new set of tools for teachers—something beyond louder and slower. As more teachers test these ideas in the field, and as empirical research on their effectiveness grows, we will develop better and better ideas of how to serve our students who struggle with mathematics. If you've chosen to read this resource and apply its principles, congratulations— you are now part of the process.

What Is the Research?

This resource is centered around what I call the Math for Struggling Learners (MSL) approach. MSL is the marriage of research and practice in what researchers sometimes call "design research." What that means is that I used whatever I could glean from current literature and research and had teachers try it out and help me make it better. I worked with about two hundred teachers over four years to develop and hone these ideas. Each group tested assessments, gave suggestions and feedback on the nitty-gritty details of how to administer them, and shared their insights into how developing theories for instruction helped them teach struggling learners.

The teachers whom I worked with (in professional development settings) represent the full range of classroom experience. Teachers from kindergarten through high school have tested and worked with the ideas in this

What Is RTI and Does This Resource Address It?

Response to Intervention (RTI) is an approach to identifying special needs that relies on creating and using research-based interventions to support struggling students and to gain information about their understanding. The RTI approach uses increasingly focused forms of intervention to address student needs. The goal is to serve students in the least restrictive and most appropriate environment.

Solving for Why takes a similar approach to supporting struggling learners. The idea is to "solve for why"—to gain insight into student understanding—through frequent assessment and communication with students. These insights into student thinking help inform instruction and create an evolving intervention to meet student needs. This is the kind of focused instruction that RTI calls for.

This resource also makes use of several instructional formats that allow for the development of problem-solving skills. It addresses the development of conceptual models, focused practice, and feedback with those models during strategy development, as well as the development of procedural skill with algorithms. Part 3 shares a lesson plan format that allows teachers to practice both inclusion and differentiation to meet the needs of a wide variety of learners. Practitioners of RTI will find *Solving for Why* to be a resource that informs both the evaluation of struggling math students and the creation of effective instructional plans for these students. ■

resource. The work of the kindergarten teachers in the MSL courses helped me realize how the MSL approach should be modified for early childhood. The high school teachers articulated the numerous connections between their work and the work in earlier grades. They helped me understand how important conceptual models are, even for students in higher math.

Many special-education professionals have also helped refine what I have come to think of as "our thinking" about teaching struggling learners. One particular teacher stands out. She taught a self-contained classroom for profoundly challenged learners. I was unsure whether she would be able to apply our assessments and thinking in such a difficult setting. By knowing her students well, and by adapting the activities, she showed me that a skillful teacher can have meaningful mathematical interactions with her students, even when they have significant challenges.

One particular MSL class was noteworthy in that there were several teachers who exclusively taught children with behavioral/emotional difficulties. They helped me to appreciate how important affect is to developing mathematical understanding. These professionals gave me a great deal of insight into the importance of setting and pace in conducting clinical interviews with volatile learners.

How Is This Resource Organized?

This resource is organized into three parts: "Understanding Why Students Struggle," "Three Assessment Strategies to Identify Why Students Struggle," and "Supporting Students Who Struggle." These parts can be read in any order, though I suggest starting with Part 1 because it is a good foundation for the underlying concepts that inform the text. I encourage the reader to avoid the temptation to skip to Part 3 in order to find quick fixes for everyday issues in instruction. The reference lists in Chapter 9 for teaching struggling students are only worthwhile if you understand each student's thinking. The tools for achieving this make up the heart of the resource, Parts 1 and 2.

Part 1 identifies what to look for in student understanding, and why uncovering understanding is so important. It explores some of the definitions currently used for struggling learners and presents three frames (learner, content, instruction) for understanding their thinking. It shares how supporting struggling learners is an iterative process that requires the development of theories rather than prescriptions. Part 1 forms the conceptual basis for the assessments and remediations introduced in Part 2.

Part 2 shares well-tested assessments for uncovering student thinking. It explores the three assessments that were developed in MSL classes:

Concrete–Representational–Abstract (CRA), Collaborative Study, and Student Interviews. While all teachers who take the MSL class learn to use all three assessments, they find that continuing to use particular assessments after the course is a product of their role as math educators.

Part 3 offers suggestions for supporting the struggles you uncover. It features a chapter on supporting students with cognitive challenges, a chapter exploring a main lesson—menu lesson plan (which gives practitioners a lesson structure that supports both inclusion and differentiation), and a chapter of resources for students who struggle with specific math concepts (to address these in depth is the scope of several more resources; I've chosen instead to identify the resources on the market that excel in doing this already). The suggestions in these chapters come from the experiences of teachers in the field and are closely linked to the general approach outlined in Part 1.

Part One

Understanding Why Students Struggle

Who Is a Struggling Math Learner?

1

The Big Ideas

- The term *struggling learner* captures the difficulty that many students experience temporarily (general or typical struggles), as well as describing students who have persistent conceptual difficulties (learner-specific challenges) that make mathematics more difficult to learn.

- While difficulties in learning to read are extensively researched and documented, research on supporting math learners who struggle is less so.

- Math struggles are strongly associated with three factors: environmental, learning challenges, and quality of instruction.

Chapter Outline

Defining a Struggling Math Learner

Researchers and practitioners have had difficulty creating accurate vocabulary and precise definitions for the variety of ways children struggle with mathematics. *Math disability*, *mathematical learning disabilities*, *mathematical difficulties*, and *developmental dyscalculia* are all terms that are applied to children whose mathematical development differs from that of the general population (Mazzocco 2007). The term *mathematical difficulties* covers the most ground, being used in research to identify students with poor achievement for any of a number of causes (Gersten, Jordan, and Flojo 2005; Hanich, Jordan, Kaplan, and Dick 2001). Given the confusion about what to call children who have trouble with math, I think the term *struggling learner* is most appropriate. Allsopp, Kyger, and Lovin (2007) use this term to identify students with a variety of cognitive and social challenges related to low math achievement. *Struggling learner* also captures the difficulty that many students experience temporarily (general or typical struggles), as well as describes students who have persistent conceptual difficulties (learner-specific challenges) that make mathematics more difficult to learn.

Comparing Math Research to Reading Research

Why do some students struggle with mathematics and how can we help them to be successful? While difficulties in learning to read are extensively researched and documented, research on supporting math learners who struggle is less so. In the past twenty-five years, less than fifty studies on students who perform at low levels in mathematics have been completed, as compared to over eight hundred for reading (Baker, Gersten, and Lee 2002). Mathematical difficulties share some similarities with, and contain some differences from, more broadly researched reading difficulties. As reading research explores both skills and the complexity of linguistic development, mathematics also draws on a wide variety of cognitive skills that increase in complexity as the student grows older.

Unlike reading, however, mathematics touches a broad range of dissimilar content domains (Mazzocco 2007). While reading skill continues to develop throughout elementary and secondary education, there is a "top of the hill": once a learner can read fluently, refining her skill is a subtler enterprise. This is not the case with mathematics. In some sense, math is "prelinguistic." It deals with conceptual topics that can be understood without words, although framing a concept with words is almost always helpful. Math concepts grow and develop throughout a student's education. Some would argue that math gets more and more "difficult" as students get older. We'll explore this a bit more in later chapters.

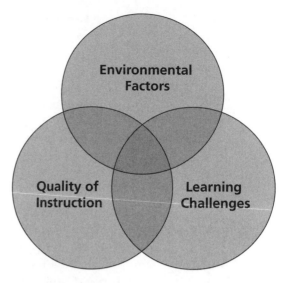

Figure 1.1 Three main factors associated with student difficulties in mathematics

Three Main Factors of Math Struggles

Math struggles are strongly associated with three factors. It would be inaccurate to suggest that these are *causes* of math struggles. Rather, research about these factors suggests a strong correlation with mathematical difficulties. These factors can be thought of as three intersecting categories (see Figure 1.1).

Environmental Factors

Environmental factors that influence learners include language, culture, race, parent education, and socioeconomic status (Blanchett, Mumford, and Beachum 2005; Baker, Gersten, and Lee 2002; Tate 1997). The National Assessment of Educational Progress (NAEP) has identified achievement gaps in these areas for more than twenty years. Gaps in math performance include significant differences between ethnically diverse and white students. Gaps also exist between English language learners (ELLs) and those students whose native language is English, as well as between students living in poverty and those from the middle class (National Center for Education Statistics 2006).

Cognitive Challenges

Cognitive challenges, as described here, are neurologically based differences that can make learning mathematics more difficult. Students in this group are those who struggle with math disability (Fuchs, Fuchs, Prentice et al. 2004), memory issues, attention deficits, sequential and spatial organization difficulties (Levine 2002), and physical challenges (like blindness). These students require specialized instruction matched to their particular learning needs. This is the group that, far and away, receives the most Louder and Slower instruction (see page x), and needs much more. Chapter 7 focuses on some of these challenges.

Sometimes it's difficult to know whether a learner struggles because he is working with cognitive challenges or because he has gaps in his mathematical understanding. Memory difficulties, for example, might have more to do with instruction than with a student's memory. A math concept needs to be connected to other information stored in memory or it will be almost impossible to retrieve. We all have experiences of this. We learned some mathematical formula for the test on Friday, even though we had no idea what it meant. We passed our test and promptly forgot all about the formula. If you doubt this, ask yourself, "What does the quadratic formula mean?" You spent a lot of time learning this formula and working problem sets with it in high school. Unless you are a high school math teacher or a professional mathematician, you have probably forgotten most of the meaning for the quadratic formula.

On the other hand, if you *are* someone who uses math (an engineer, for example) you probably remember a lot about the quadratic formula. It has meaning to you, so you don't struggle with it. Learning a procedure without understanding is a common reason for students to struggle with math. These lapses in concept development present themselves as "gaps" in students' learning, and sometimes masquerade as "memory issues" or other cognitive challenges.

My Story

Leah's Cognitive Challenges

When I was teaching in Manhattan I encountered a student who struggled with *both* memory and attention challenges. Leah had trouble with focus after about ten minutes in any lesson. She did not regulate her attention and effort well (often a characteristic of Attention Deficit Disorder [ADD]) and, as a result, her mental resources thinned out quickly. Leah also had retrieval difficulties with long-term memory. Once her attention was gone she was unable to remember much of what we'd done during the lesson or to retrieve anything from previous lessons. It took me weeks to figure this out. I had a ten-minute window to work with, to help Leah construct new understanding. After that, she needed a significant break or our work together would be unproductive.

Quality of Instruction

The last category, *quality of instruction*, describes students whose difficulties with learning mathematics are related to a mismatch between the learner and the instruction. Usually learner difficulties are the cumulative result of a mismatch between what the teacher thought she or he was teaching and what the student actually learned. An example of this, perhaps the most common for struggling learners, is when math taught in school has no personal, real-world meaning for the student.

Some students' difficulty comes from the their emotional state and its relationship to math learning. One teacher I was working with reported that he had two students who were belligerent whenever they became frustrated with mathematics problems. This teacher developed a theory about his students' frustration that suggested their reaction was to the meaninglessness of the work he gave them. When he allowed the students to gather data on the traffic patterns around the schools, he reported that they "were sorry when they had to stop." In engaging his students with meaningful mathematical work, he found them much less resistant.

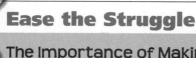

Ease the Struggle

The Importance of Making Meaning from Mathematical Ideas

Struggling math learners are the kids in virtually every classroom who are stuck. For a wide variety of reasons they cannot make sense of the math they are trying to learn. Creating personal meaning—making sense—is key to knowing and doing mathematics (Allsopp, Kyger, and Lovin 2007; Tapper 2010). When students create meaning from a math concept, they are connecting it to what they already know and making it available for further use in new situations (Kilpatrick, Hoyles, Skovsmose, and Valero 2005). When math concepts are personally meaningful they can be generalized to new situations and used to build more complex concepts.

Struggling learners have difficulty creating this personal meaning—connecting new learning to prior knowledge, and/or organizing it in ways that make it accessible. Sometimes the sense-making difficulty is the result of gaps in their mathematical understanding. Sometimes students have trouble creating mathematical meaning because they have to overcome cognitive challenges with memory or attention. And sometimes students get stuck because they don't think of math as meaningful. For these students math is only something they're supposed to do in school when the teacher asks. ■

Sara's Meaning of Math

I once conducted a Student Interview with a seventh-grade student who exemplified how important making meaning of school mathematics really is. She was on an Individual Education Plan (IEP) for mathematics because she was performing more than two years behind her grade peers. Her teacher—one of the Math for Struggling Learners (MSL) teachers I'd worked with—asked me if I'd do a Student Interview with her to "see what she is capable of learning." He had tried a variety of approaches with her and hadn't had much success with any of them. He felt the way I'd felt (and still feel sometimes) when a student had great needs and there seemed to be little to do to help them.

I asked questions about the student's interests, strengths, and some of her perceived difficulties. Since she was operating far below her grade level, I prepared a number of problems representing fourth-grade standards and a few more up through the seventh-grade expectations. I went to the school and met with the student for about an hour to find out about her math thinking.

The student, Sara, presented herself as consummately bored. She slouched into the small room where we were talking and gave me an "Oh, another one of these" looks that told me she was no stranger to testing. I felt for her. When kids have difficulty with anything at school, it seems, people are always asking them to demonstrate their difficulty. It must feel like having a broken leg and being asked to show where it hurts—over and over.

Sara and I talked a bit about her Guster tee shirt and about the music she liked. I started the math part of her interview off with a problem about buying MP3s for her iPod. The problem asked, *How much would five songs cost?* She gave me a pleading look and said, "Do I add? Subtract? Multiply?" I told her to think about it. She shrugged and wrote

$0.99 on the paper, then 5. Then she wrote $0.94. I asked her why she thought the answer was $0.94 and she told me that money problems meant that you were spending and that spending was subtraction. Though there was some logic in her answer, I was beginning to see why her teacher was concerned.

I wasn't sure where to go next in the interview, so I looked at my notes and noticed that Sara was a gamer. I asked her what her game system was and which games she liked. Her entire affect changed. She chatted away telling me she had *two* systems and giving me a long list of titles she enjoyed. I commented that it must have cost her a lot to get so many games. She said that she often bought them at yard sales for five to ten dollars. I couldn't resist asking a math question:

"If you bought a box of seven games for five dollars each, what would you expect to pay?"

She didn't even hesitate, "Thirty-five dollars."

I was shocked. "How did you know that?"

"Well," she said, "there's seven of 'em and they're five bucks a piece. That's thirty-five dollars, isn't it?"

"What about if there had been nine of them?" I asked.

"That's another ten bucks," Sara informed me. "So it'd be forty-five dollars."

It turns out that Sara had almost no idea that the mental computation she could do with money (the example here is just one of many, most are more complex) "out in the real world" had anything to do with math. For Sara, the math she did at school was a school activity without any personal meaning. Sara was one of many children I've met with a similar disposition to math. She was unusual in the development of her "outside of school" math, but she shared the characteristic that her struggle showed that math was not personally meaningful.

Looking Ahead

In order to help struggling students learn mathematics we need to first understand how they think and then to develop theories about what might be causing them difficulty. Aside from environmental factors, we must discern whether the struggles learners face come from learning challenges or from the quality of instruction. The following chapters focus on ways students develop mathematical understanding, methods for understanding student thinking, and techniques for developing theories to help us teach them.

Reflection Questions

1. What are your ideas about why students in your class struggle? How might these be related to their past experiences? To cognitive challenges? To the math instruction they've received?

2. What makes math meaningful to you? Why do you do it? How could you make the mathematics you teach more meaningful to your students?

3. Think about the students you've taught who were struggling math learners. How would their lives be different if they were good at mathematics?

Three Frames
for Understanding
Student Thinking

The Big Ideas

- Three important frames for understanding student thinking are the *Learner*, *Content*, and *Instruction Frames*.

- In the *Learner Frame*, there are two main types of understanding: procedural and conceptual.

- In the *Math Content Frame*, special demands are placed on both teachers and students; specifically, math content is conceptually expansive and covers a wide variety of content domains.

- The *Instruction Frame* is based on three stages in the development of understanding: models, strategies, and algorithms.

> "The vast amounts that have been written about teaching math might give the impression that all of the difficulties encountered by math students are caused by teachers, and it is always the teacher's responsibility to sort out the student's problems. This is, of course, one of the things teachers are paid to do, but there is some onus on the student as well. You need to understand how to learn."
>
> —Ian Stewart, *Letters to a Young Mathematician*

Chapter Outline

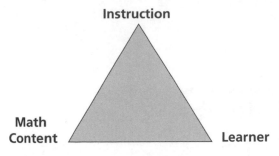

Figure 2.1 Three frames for understanding student thinking

Three Frames for Understanding Student Thinking

If we want to reach all our students, especially those who struggle, we need to first develop a deep and personal understanding of their learning. To start, this chapter focuses on student learning through three frames: the learner, math content, and instruction (see Figure 2.1).

Frame 1: The Learner

The *Learner Frame* focuses on the student—how she or he understands important concepts, whether the concepts rely on useful models, and whether the concepts are organized by cognitive schema. To deepen our understanding of the learner, we need to consider the types of understanding he or she may be acquiring.

Two Types of Learning: Procedural and Conceptual

Mathematics learning can be described as either *procedural* or *conceptual*. There is a difference between knowing the steps to solve a problem (procedural) and understanding the big mathematical idea (conceptual). Many people, for example, know how to calculate a mean, or average (procedural).

Ease the Struggle

Standards

Standards give teachers a road map for the development of mathematical content. Standards help us see which mathematical ideas are most important at a particular age or grade level, how concepts build on one another, and where to go next with our instruction. Unfortunately, no one gave us a map of our students' brains. Despite our best efforts and our clearest reasoning regarding cognitive development, students learn the way they learn, not the way we expect them to learn. For this reason we can use mathematics content and standards as an important component in our work as teachers, but if we want to reach all our students, especially those who struggle, we need to understand how a student thinks about mathematics, how he understands an idea, and how he can use it in a new situation. ■

My Story

What's Going On in Heather's Mind?

I was beginning a unit on probability with first and second graders. I decided to first find out what thoughts they already had about the subject. We played a game called *Likely/Unlikely*. I gave the students a number of scenarios and they told me whether the situations were *likely* or *unlikely* to happen. I asked them whether it was likely that they'd have to get up to go to school tomorrow, that they'd see a dinosaur in school, or that their parents packed only cake and ice cream for lunch. The game was fun and we all had a good laugh. Students had no trouble deciding which events were likely or unlikely.

To begin our formal investigation of probability, I showed the group a six-sided die. I had one for each of them and (to their delight) a small plastic cup they could use to shake the die and roll it. I asked students if they knew how dice worked (they did) and whether they had ever used them (they had). I decided to introduce the investigation by asking students for predictions on their first roll. Heather was sitting closest to me on the rug, so I asked her my opening questions:

"Heather, I'm going to roll this die. Do you have any idea what number I'll roll?"

"Yes, I know what number you'll roll."

"Do you mean you know what number I'm *likely* to roll?" (I purposely made a connection to our initial game.)

"No, I *know* what number you'll roll."

"You *know* the number I'll roll?"

"Uh-huh. You're going to roll three."

Heather's sureness was one of many times when I realized I had no idea what was going on in a student's head. "OK," I said. "How do you *know* I'm going to roll a three?"

"Because," Heather said patiently, "it's my lucky number."

Far fewer actually understand what a mean is, and what it can tell us about a group of measures (conceptual). This dichotomy between *knowing* the steps and *understanding* the steps (the broader view) is a little like having a list of directions to get where you're going versus having a map of the entire area.

Let's put this in the context of navigating through New York City. You may choose to walk or ride a bicycle, using a city map as guidance; this is an experiential method for "learning" the city. Through finding your way from one place to another—including making mistakes—you construct a good mental picture of where things are in the city.

However, perhaps you choose to rely on subway directions from friends instead (New Yorkers are famous for their subway directions). Your friends scribble down a series of steps in list form; you then follow this list step-by-step. The written directions help you solve your immediate need to get from one point to another, but they don't give you a broader perspective (a map) of the city. In addition, if the directions are wrong or misunderstood, you are bound to get frustrated and lost!

Math learning is much like these two circumstances: when learning math, does it make sense to have a broad experience or follow a precise set of directions? Ideally we first and foremost want all our students to have a broad *conceptual* perspective. We want students to see connections between mathematical ideas, to notice the multiple ways to solve problems, and to have flexible thinking when it comes to going from one point to another.

If the learner understands a mathematical concept, not just a procedure, it becomes a tool for her—a gateway to deeper mathematical ideas. When a concept becomes a tool, the student can generalize it and apply it to a wide variety of problem-solving situations. By contrast, when a mathematical

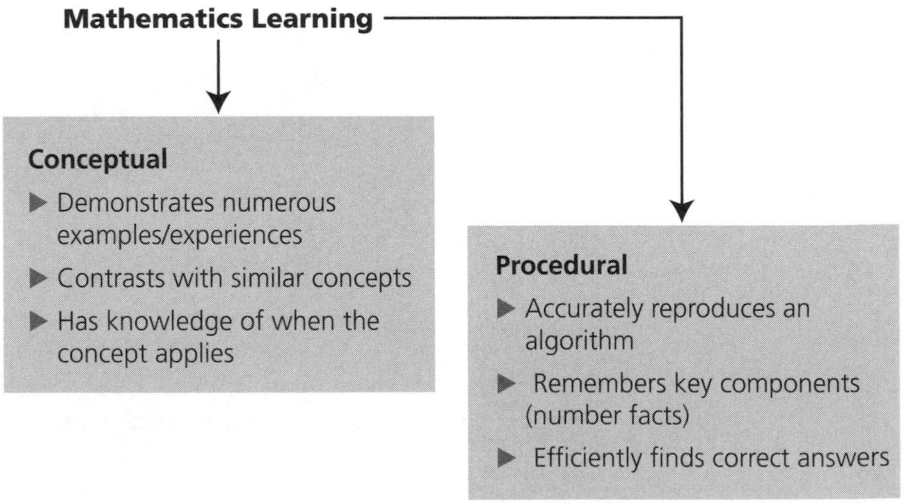

> "[W]hen learning math, does it make sense to have a broad experience or follow a precise set of directions?"

Mathematics Learning

Conceptual
▶ Demonstrates numerous examples/experiences
▶ Contrasts with similar concepts
▶ Has knowledge of when the concept applies

Procedural
▶ Accurately reproduces an algorithm
▶ Remembers key components (number facts)
▶ Efficiently finds correct answers

Figure 2.2 The differences between conceptual and procedural knowledge

idea is understood only as a procedure—a series of steps resembling a list of directions—the idea is likely used only in familiar situations or in situations in which it was practiced (see Figure 2.2).

When teaching students who struggle, whether their difficulty is temporary or a more ongoing challenge, we need to let go of the idea that learning math is about memorizing a set of steps. Concepts develop when students make personal meaning through experience and reflection. In the earlier analogy about maps versus directions, traveling around New York City on foot or by bicycle can help someone to understand a bigger view of the city. With enough experiences, a traveler can even make his or her own map. Experiences that build mathematical concepts can help learners create a similar kind of "math map." These experiences include exploring materials, finding patterns, sorting objects or ideas, solving problems, and having mathematical conversations. A key to providing these experiences is the use of mathematical models.

Ease the Struggle

Mathematical Models

A map of New York City is a model for the city itself—a representation of the island of Manhattan. New York is far too complex for us to keep all of it (wholly) in our minds; a map provides an accessible image to help us find our way around. Mathematical models work just the same way.

Mathematical models are mental constructions that we all use to understand complex ideas (Schoenfeld 1994). Without models on which to ground our mathematical thinking, we may only attain the kind of knowledge that comes from practicing every kind of mathematical procedure we might ever need. This understanding is not flexible; rather, it is bound to particular contexts. We can see this with our students when they are only able to solve problems that are matches for the instruction they've just received. They can, for example, solve problems with multidigit multiplication, but only after they've just practiced it. Without a model to ground mathematical understanding, students are unlikely to generalize what they know (Ryan and Williams 2007). ∎

Ease the Struggle

What It Means to Generalize— and to Overgeneralize

If students had to learn every concept as something brand-new, humanity would probably still be living in caves and lighting our homes with fire. What accelerates all learning is our ability to transfer what we learn in one setting to another. When students learn to skip-count by twos and fives, they quickly learn that they can skip-count by any number because they *generalize* what it means to skip-count—to count on by a particular number. This ability to use what we've learned and apply it in new ways is critical to learning mathematics.

Sometimes, though, students apply something they've learned to a new situation in an inappropriate way. When learning about decimals, for example, students will sometimes think that 0.28 is greater than 0.9 because, "Twenty-eight is bigger than nine." In this instance the transfer of understanding doesn't appropriately fit the new circumstances. When this happens it is referred to as *overgeneralizing*. ∎

Ease the Struggle

Schema

The framework or structure of ideas in our minds is what psychologists called *schema* (Piaget and Cook 1977). Schema are mental structures that connect information. By creating these structures we organize information to make it easier to find. The organizational structures connect concepts in a variety of ways, often by finding similarities and differences.

We know, for example, that addition and subtraction share the quality of using two (or more) smaller groups that are part of a larger group. This is their similarity. On the other hand, when we join groups we call what we do "addition" and when we separate them, we call it "subtraction."

Having schema for additive reasoning—joining and separating—helps us to understand the operations of addition and subtraction. Schema give us an organizational structure to use when retrieving information. ■

What if we tried to get around New York City without a map (a model) for it? If our brains could produce step-by-step directions without the need for mental models, our thinking would generate a series of steps to get anywhere in the city we might want to go (much like GPS systems!).

For better or worse, our brains don't work that way. Our minds organize information according to its characteristics and connections to other information (Colvin 2008). This organization is what helps us recall and use what we've learned. When information is organized well, it's relatively easy to retrieve. The way learners often learn new vocabulary, for example, is to make associations with ideas or words they already know and to use the syntax of English as an organization scheme. The new words being learned are connected to other words with similar or different meanings and then fit into the learner's existing organizational structure of English syntax. If learning new vocabulary were based *only* on practicing, we'd probably have to repeat all the words and phrases we know regularly or we'd forget them. The structure of our knowledge is what helps us remember, even when we haven't used an idea for a while.

Frame 2: The Math Content

Understanding how the learner understands math concepts is critical to helping struggling learners. Almost as important is understanding the special demands that math content places on both teachers and students. Specifically, math content is conceptually expansive and covers a wide variety of content domains.

Math Content Is Conceptually Expansive

As an early elementary teacher I taught reading for many years. Reading instruction has its own challenges, but it also has a clear end goal: independently reading text and understanding what's being read. This goal is elusive or difficult for some readers, but it is, nonetheless, a clear goal. When a student in elementary school is able to read a book with good comprehension, she is well on her way to becoming an expert reader. She will need to expand her vocabulary, develop the use of inference, and accommodate a variety of literary genres. However, once she is reading independently with good comprehension, much of the further skills can be learned on her own.

A clearly articulated goal, like independent reading, doesn't really exist in mathematics. When students reach one conceptual understanding, there is always another beyond. This is because the field of mathematics is *conceptually expansive*. Like all content areas in elementary and middle school, the *content* grows as children mature and are expected to know more facts and information about math. But in mathematics, the *conceptual demands* also grow. In math, students are not only expected to know more information, they are expected to *think differently* as they move up through the grades.

An example of this expectation is the way students move from additive, to multiplicative, to proportional reasoning. When students learn to reason additively, they begin to understand the joining, separating, and partitioning of groups. As they move into multiplicative reasoning, students must think differently. The groups they count with must have the same number of members. Finally, as students develop proportional reasoning they begin to look beyond the numbers themselves to the relationships between numbers.

> "[I]n mathematics, the conceptual demands also grow. In math, students are not only expected to know more information, they are expected to think differently as they move up through the grades."

Math Content Covers a Wide Variety of Domains

One of the difficulties, as well as advantages, of learning mathematics is that so many different kinds of thinking and knowledge fall into the category of "math." The National Council of Teachers of Mathematics (NCTM) has identified five content strands for K–12 students. These include: number and operations, algebra, geometry, data analysis and probability, and measurement. Each of these presents particular challenges to both teachers and students. The challenge for students is to make connections between the content they learn in different domains. The challenge for teachers is to develop the math content knowledge to be able to support students in such a wide variety of knowledge domains.

Vocabulary that crosses between math domains can be a way to make conceptual connections. When exploring shapes that are congruent, for example, students will often use language that indicates the ways in which the shapes are congruent:

"I can put one of the trapezoids on the other and cover it completely."

"They (the shapes) match perfectly."

"The sides and angles are the same."

"They are equal."

Describing congruent shapes as "equal" represents an interesting conceptual connection between mathematical content areas. "Congruent" and "equal" mean different things. Congruent means having the same size and shape.

Equal means having exactly the same quantity. "Sameness" is a quality that carries over from one content area, or domain, to the other. It's our responsibility as teachers to understand these important connections in order to help students build connections—and understanding—from one content area to another.

In another example, many fourth graders are taught the concepts of area and perimeter at the same time they are learning about multiplication.

Ease the Struggle

The Importance of Content Knowledge for Teacher Effectiveness

Fennema, Carpenter, Peterson, and others investigated the relationship between the amount of math a teacher knows and the influence this knowledge has on teaching (Carpenter, Fennema, Peterson, and Carey 1988; Fennema and Franke 1992). In the 1980s researchers investigated whether taking more math courses would make a teacher more effective with students. There was not a strong relationship between these two factors. Interestingly, how far a teacher progressed in his mathematical career (whether he took calculus or linear algebra, for example) is much less relevant to his success with students than how well he knows the math at the level he teaches. While this finding might seem counterintuitive (wouldn't people who have had more math understand—and teach—it better?), it makes sense when we think about math content in light of all the other factors that go into successful math teaching—like understanding the learner and using pedagogy well. *Doing* a math course is not the same as *knowing* the math. Finishing a high school math course doesn't mean that you understand the content deeply. Usually, deep understanding comes from multiple experiences with concepts. The understanding necessary for teaching is a kind of deconstructed knowledge that means you've made extensive connections with concepts in a variety of contexts.

What seems to be needed, from a content perspective, is that teachers understand the content they teach *at their grade level*. A second-grade teacher must understand second-grade math really well. She must understand additive reasoning, geometry, measurement, data and probability, and algebraic thinking *appropriate to her grade level and curriculum* to be effective with students.

This idea gains validity when considering successful teachers from upper-elementary grades who are moved to lower-elementary grades during their careers. Often it takes a year or two for these teachers to achieve the same level of student success at the lower-grade level that they enjoyed at the upper-grade level. Why would this be? Surely the math content in sixth grade is more challenging than the content in first or second grade? The difference lies in the deconstructed understanding of mathematics at each grade level. Math is rich at every level; each concept has many facets and connections to other ideas. Knowing these connections and understanding the variety of ways a concept can be explored mathematically is what makes for strong instruction, particularly for struggling learners. Being a sophisticated mathematician may be difficult. But knowing the math content deeply from a particular level of elementary school is something every teacher can do.

Possessing deep knowledge of mathematical content means that teachers can pose good problems, ask good questions, and guide students to understanding by knowing where they want students to be. By understanding a variety of ways to get there (see "Frame 3: The Instruction") teachers can help students take the journey from their current thinking to more sophisticated mathematical understanding. ■

While area is a way to measure the amount of flat space occupied by an object, it is also an excellent method for understanding, modeling, and conceptualizing multiplication. Finding the area of rectangles engages students in several mathematical domains simultaneously, and teachers need to help students carry understanding from one category of ideas (measurement) to another (multiplication). Students who can make the connections between these important concepts (measurement, geometry, and number) will be more successful with all of them.

Frame 3: The Instruction

In addition to understanding the learner and the math content, to support both struggling and non-struggling learners we need to understand how we instruct. The *Instruction Frame* is based on three stages in the development of understanding: models, strategies, and algorithms. These stages inform us about concept development and guide us toward meaningful instruction.

The Use of Models in Instruction (Stage 1)

Earlier in this chapter we took a closer look at models from the learner perspective (see "Ease the Struggle: Mathematical Models," page 15). Models are a cognitive structure that a student uses to understand a mathematical

Ease the Struggle

Pedagogy

Pedagogy has its roots as a Greek word related to *pedagogue* and to *paidagogos*. The contrast between these two interpretations of pedagogy says a lot about the different ways teaching has been approached over time.

A *pedagogue* is an especially strict teacher. This is the image of teaching we often get from the early parts of the last century: a stern taskmaster who calls forth remembered knowledge from the front of the room. This, for better or worse, is the image of pedagogy that many of us still have today. This model for teaching subtly shows up when teachers spend all their math lessons "explaining," "demonstrating," and "going over" content, rather than structuring experiences and conversations for students to do the important work of learning mathematics.

Paidagogos, on the other hand, can mean "a person who accompanies a child to school." I like the idea of this image because the companion has no direct power over the child. Yet this paidagogos companion guides directly without demanding and gets the child to her destination.

For the struggling learner, it's hard to imagine a more compelling contrast between pedagogue and paidagogos. If you are struggling with mathematics, who would you rather work with? ■

idea. We can use models *instructionally* to help develop these ideas. We can also use models *diagnostically* (or formatively) to tell us something about the way a student thinks about concepts.

A mathematical model can be a concrete, representational, or abstract analogy for an important concept. A model's requirements for use with math concepts are:

▶ the learner has, or can easily acquire, experience of it,

▶ it can be manipulated (mentally or physically) to adapt to new situations, and

▶ it has important properties of the mathematical concept itself. (Schoenfeld [1994] offers more information on the connection between model use and conceptual understanding.)

Base ten blocks, for example, are excellent mathematical models. They are common in most elementary classrooms. They are easily manipulated and they have the same regrouping properties as base ten numbers: 10 ones can be linked or traded to make a ten; 10 tens can make a hundred. Base ten blocks can also serve as models for other complex ideas. They can "stand in" for money (pennies, dimes, dollars) and for decimals (ones, tenths, hundredths).

Another common mathematical example of a model is the use of a "machine" as an analogy for how linear functions work. Most learners have experience with machines. You put bread in a toaster. The toaster does something to the bread, and toast comes out. You put laundry in a washing machine, it does something to the clothes, and the clothes come out. The experience that many learners have with machines is that you put an object in it, the machine does something to it, and a result comes out. This satisfies the first requirement for a model: *the learner has experience with machines.*

The kind of mathematical machine that we use for functions is easy to manipulate. We simply use new rules for what to do for numbers as they pass through. This makes it *easy to manipulate.* Finally, function machines can be made to "stand in" for the big idea that functions of x are related to outcomes (y). In the function $y = 2x + 4$, we can think of x's as raw materials we put into the machine. The y's are what comes out. If you were to put a "3" into the machine, the machine would multiply by two and then add four (see Figure 2.3).

By using the idea of a machine to simulate the way a function works, a learner can apply the idea of functions in new situations. The function machine, for example, doesn't have to only work for the equation $y = 2x + 4$. It can work for any linear function. Our thinking about functions is organized and facilitated by the model. In this case, we used the familiar idea of a machine to facilitate our understanding.

Similarly, when we introduce the ideas of addition and subtraction, we help students construct an understanding of additive reasoning by providing them with models that represent the key concepts of joining and separating.

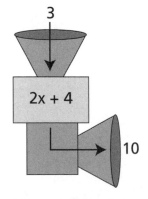

Figure 2.3 Using the idea of a machine to simulate the way a function works

We have children add one pile of blocks to another and find the total. We have them make "trains" (a combined length) with different lengths of "cars." We ask students to move position on a number line. All these activities are models for the actual concepts of adding and subtracting quantities. They all are relevant to learner experience, are easy to manipulate, and have strong connections to mathematical ideas.

A model can be understood as a mental lens, or prism, through which a learner understands a concept (see Figure 2.4). Choosing a model that will serve an individual learner well can allow her to "see" the concept and make use of it in a wide variety of contexts.

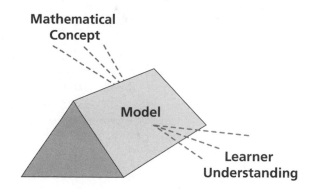

Figure 2.4 A model as a mental lens, or prism, through which a learner understands a concept

The Use of Strategies in Instruction (Stage 2)

A strategy is more complex than a model; a strategy uses models in a specific context to solve a problem. Problem-solving strategies are familiar to most math teachers: *Make the problem simpler*; *work backward*; *draw a picture*, and so on. When strategies are well connected to context and make meaningful use of models, they help students develop a repertoire of generalizable approaches to mathematical problems. When they are practiced without connections to models or contexts, strategies become another list of directions that students find difficult to transfer to new situations.

Often curricula (and teachers) focus a great deal of attention on developing strategies to help students learn new approaches to problem solving. Teaching students how to make a tree diagram and then giving them a problem or two for practice is a common example. It seems logical that students would learn the skill and then apply it to new situations. Unfortunately, very few students actually apply skills to problems this way, and when they do it is usually in an "I'm following a recipe" way. Although it can seem illogical, students learn best by exploring a concept first and then practicing skills that come from it. An example from swimming can help us understand why.

In the 1950s and '60s it was fairly common to teach the strokes for swimming outside of the pool before having students actually get in the water to practice them. There were even special tables at some pools (they looked like ironing boards) that would allow a student to lie on her stomach and practice making the appropriate strokes with her arms. These students were practicing the *skills* of swimming in order to learn how to swim.

As you could probably guess, when skills-first students entered the water, they failed to assume the correct posture and begin making the measured strokes they had practiced. Rather, they did anything—no matter how contrary to the skills they learned—to stay afloat.

Similarly, sometimes teachers tell young students that they are not allowed to count on their fingers when solving a difficult problem. What

> "Although it can seem illogical, students learn best by exploring a concept first and then practicing skills that come from it."

will most students do? They put their fingers under the desk, scratch their heads with all five fingers, and generally find numerous surreptitious methods for counting, even though they know they shouldn't. Why? When we are thrown into the water we use whatever strategy we can think of to stay afloat. *Strategies don't really make sense until you have a reason to need them.*

Consider this common problem: *There are 8 people at a party. If they shake hands with each other once—and only once—how many handshakes will there be in total?*

To solve this problem, we could teach students how to make a tree diagram and then have them apply the strategy. If we do that, though, we are teaching them strokes outside of the pool. They will apply the strategy and, while some students will make the connection between the problem and the strategy, many struggling learners will not. What some children will take away from an exercise for practicing tree diagrams is, "When I'm doing handshake problems, I use a tree diagram."

What if we placed the students in the water first, by asking them to simply solve the problem using models to help them develop strategies for solving? We could have the students explore the problem using their own bodies or "stand-ins" for their bodies, like cubes or tiles. When the students have created some solutions, we could then ask them to share their work and their thinking with the class. Often the tree diagram strategy will come up naturally at this point. Students don't always have a name for the strategy, but they demonstrate it. If no student solves the handshake problem using a tree diagram, it makes sense for us to then share the strategy. There is context. Students understand the important elements of the problem (accounting for all the handshakes). They've been in the water. Now, sharing a sophisticated strategy makes sense. Students can make the connections between the strategies they've shown one another and the tree diagram being shared. In this way we create meaning for a strategy and not simply a new set of steps to be followed.

Strategies are ways students can use models to access problems, whether they are brand-new problems or problems that are familiar. The models create the access and strategies develop as ways to use them to solve these problems. Once students have adopted a specific strategy and consistently apply it in certain types of situations, it becomes algorithmic and algorithms emerge (usually invented). Over time these algorithms refine and become, or approximate, standard algorithms.

The Use of Algorithms in Instruction (Stage 3)

Algorithms are the shortcuts—the procedures—we use to do something efficiently over and over. Starting addition problems in the ones place and regrouping as you move up in place value is an example of a common algorithm. Once we learn an algorithm we practice it until we develop procedural fluency—until we can do it automatically.

While we often de-emphasize algorithms in pedagogy (because teachers tend to rush into them before students have developed concepts fully), they are important tools in the doing of mathematics. Having a quick and accurate method for solving common problems allows you to approach more complex work more easily. Creating algorithms that are based on deep conceptual understanding represents a final step in the development of mathematical ideas. In thinking about our teaching of algorithms, let's consider how algorithms develop and whether there are "right" algorithms that struggling learners should learn.

Strategies are the gateway to algorithms. As students share their approaches to common problems, and develop connections to contexts and elements of these problems, the efficiency

Ease the Struggle

Heuristic or Algorithmic?

In mathematics (and other fields) we can think of work as either *heuristic* or *algorithmic*. Heuristic work is conceptual and involves solving problems. In the analogy we used early in the chapter (see page 14), heuristic work is mapmaking. Algorithmic work, by contrast, is the work of following steps to reach an efficient and accurate result. Following written directions is algorithmic. ■

of certain strategies becomes more and more obvious. An algorithm can be thought of as an accurate and efficient strategy that works all the time.

Let's consider this example of how algorithms can develop from strategies. To begin, successful instruction always focuses on concepts within meaningful contexts. For subtraction, many teachers use place-value blocks as a kind of money, and the operation of subtraction as an exchange. Consider the equation:

$$
\begin{array}{r}
232 \\
- 117 \\
\hline
\end{array}
$$

The equation can be framed as, *"You have 232 but you owe me 117. Pay up!"* Students start with place-value blocks: 2 hundreds flats, 3 tens rods, and 2 ones (see Figure 2.5). Most children will start "paying" the teacher by handing over one of the hundreds flats and one of the tens rods. Then, when reminded that they need to pay 7 ones—and students realize they don't have enough ones—they make the trade of a tens rod for 10 ones and pay what they owe (7).

Over time, as children continue to work with the place-value model for subtraction, they begin to anticipate trades ahead of time. With practice,

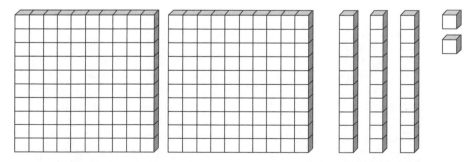

Figure 2.5 Place-value blocks to help solve *"You have 232 but you owe me 117. Pay up!"*

Ease the Struggle

The Adding-Up Algorithm for Subtraction

Since algorithms are the result of students' developing more and more efficient strategies, to understand the adding-up algorithm we have to look first at its origins in using the number line model for subtraction. (Chapter 9 examines this model extensively.)

One strategy for subtraction is to use an open number line with the minuend at one end and the subtrahend at the other. So *400 – 284* = would look like:

The idea is that we are trying to discover the difference between 400 and 284. We start the strategy by asking what a simple jump from 284 *toward* 400 might be. In this case, a jump of 6 is easy. A student could even count on to find out where the jump ended up.

Next we take another "easy" jump, from 290 to 300.

And, finally, we take the last jump to 400.

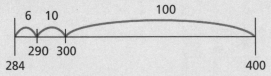

When we add all the jumps together we get 116, the difference between 400 and 284.

Since this is a strategy, there are many ways to go from one number to the other. While one method might be more efficient, as long as students can

find the distance from 284 to 400, their strategies are workable. If fact, different approaches can be beneficial. Conversations among students about which strategies are "fastest" often lead to insights that allow them to find the distance more efficiently.

When students have extensive practice with this strategy, they can be introduced to the adding-up algorithm as an option to efficiently reproduce the steps in the number line strategy. Consider:

$$
\begin{array}{r}
500 \\
- 127 \\
\end{array}
$$

The first thing I look for, when using the adding-up algorithm, is an easy jump. A jump of 3 will get me to 130.

$$
\begin{array}{r}
500 \\
- 127 \\
\hline
3 \qquad 130 \\
\end{array}
$$

Next I know that another 70 will get me to 200.

$$
\begin{array}{r}
500 \\
- 127 \\
\hline
3 \qquad 130 \\
70 \qquad 200 \\
\end{array}
$$

Finally, 300 more and I'm at 500.

$$
\begin{array}{r}
500 \\
- 127 \\
\hline
3 \qquad 130 \\
70 \qquad 200 \\
300 \qquad 500 \\
\hline
373 \\
\end{array}
$$

With practice, students can streamline this process even further and leave out the numbers on the right that keep track of the count and the addition to add up the jumps. These students simply keep track in their heads and write the answers as they go: 3, 73, 373.

If a teacher is used to the traditional "borrowing" algorithm, it can be a bit disconcerting to watch a student using the adding-up algorithm. Yet this approach is very successful with many struggling learners and gives them a conceptually based algorithm that is easy and efficient. ∎

many children will look at the problem and know before they start that they need more ones. They will only take 2 tens rods and ask for 12 ones. They have developed a strategy that saves them a step. This is the ideal time to introduce an algorithm for subtraction; students have demonstrated an understanding of both subtraction and place value *and they've begun to make their own strategies more efficient.* To such students an algorithm for subtraction is sensible and useful. They will not use it in place of understanding but to enhance their efficiency.

> "An algorithm is a shortcut that is not useful unless a student conceptually understands why it works."

Not all algorithms that students use are what adults would recognize as the "right" algorithm (the ones traditionally learned in school). The right algorithm depends on your understanding. While there is a *standard*, or accepted, algorithm for most operations, any algorithms that get you to the correct answer accurately and (relatively) efficiently will do for a struggling learner. There are different "standard algorithms" across the world. The situation in each country is the same, though. An algorithm is a shortcut that is not useful unless a student conceptually understands why it works. See the "Ease the Struggle" parts of this section for two examples of

Ease the Struggle

Partial-Products Algorithm for Multiplication

The partial-products algorithm can begin as a strategy to find the area of rectangles using decomposition. For example, 23×45 can be decomposed into $23 \times 45 = (20 + 3) \times (40 + 5)$.

We can use an area model for this equation:

45

23

Using the decomposition strategy with the area model, we turn this rectangle into smaller rectangles:

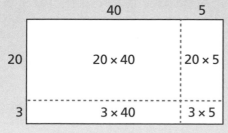

Now we have four partial products that will give us an answer to the original equation. Over time, students will dispense with the area strategy and simply use the partial products that come from the equation. They internalize the model and simply use the strategy to efficiently calculate an answer:

$$
\begin{array}{r}
23 \\
\times\ 45 \\
\hline
15 \\
100 \\
120 \\
800 \\
\hline
1{,}035 \\
\end{array}
$$

15	3×5
100	5×20
120	40×3
800	40×20

While this isn't the standard algorithm that many of us were taught in school, it is an efficient method for computing accurate answers to multidigit multiplication equations. If students streamline this approach, they can even use the standard algorithm with understanding and accuracy. ∎

algorithms that have become more common but are different from what are often called the "standard algorithms" for subtraction and multiplication: the adding-up algorithm for subtraction, and the partial-products algorithm for multiplication.

Reflection Questions

1. Consider the math that you teach. How do you prepare for the specific needs of the learners in your classroom? What content do you find most difficult for students to understand? How do you use models, strategies, and algorithms to help students learn concepts?

2. What connections can you make between the algorithms that students at your grade level learn and the development of strategies to support them?

3. Should students be required to learn the "standard" algorithm? Why or why not?

Developing Theories for Why a Learner May Be Struggling

The Big Ideas

- A theory is a possible explanation for a student's understanding of a specific mathematical concept.

- It's important to create multiple theories about student thinking; these honor the idea that there is some logic in student thinking and help us find a way to understand it.

- There are many approaches to creating theories including: using the three frames for understanding student thinking, recognizing patterns in student work, using student confidence scores, and using flexible interviews.

- After creating theories, it's crucial that we test them out.

Chapter Outline

What Is a Theory About Student Understanding?

Theories are possible explanations about student thinking that can lead to instructional choices to support struggling math learners. The term *theory* has lots of meanings in a wide variety of contexts. For our purposes, a theory is a possible explanation about what might be going on in a student's mind in relation to a specific mathematical concept. A theory can usually be articulated with the sentence, "I think what the student might think is _____, because _____." A theory gives one possible explanation for the thinking/logic related to a student's struggle.

When working with struggling math learners we base our theories on observable evidence. While this sounds obvious, I have found that sometimes we base our ideas about learner struggles on inferences that are not based on observation. I've had teachers tell me, for example, that a student struggles because "She's used to school being easy and she doesn't know how to persevere when it's hard." Though there might be some truth in this assertion, we seldom have direct evidence to support such a theory. For this reason, when developing theories we stick to what we can observe and/or measure and what those observations and measurements might tell us.

There is room for some inference in the development of theories. We infer, for example, that when a student is fidgeting, looking around, and asking off-topic questions, he is distracted. These actions provide physical or behavioral evidence. Inferences should be based on observed behavior rather than a general sense of what the student might be doing. Theories must rely on evidence we can *observe*.

Ease the Struggle

Theories Versus Prescriptions

Unlike the work done to analyze cueing systems when reading, prescriptions for supporting struggling math learners simply don't (reliably) exist. The need for theories, rather than prescriptions, for understanding student difficulties arises from two premises: having only one idea limits the possibilities for us to understand student thinking and can be more thoroughly understood if we look at it from a learner, content, and instruction point of view. ■

When Do We Use Theories About Student Understanding?

As we work with struggling learners, our theories progress from identifying more general difficulties to learner-specific struggles. As explained in Chapter 1, there are (generally speaking) two kinds of struggling learners in most classrooms: those who have a temporary difficulty with a new concept (general or typical struggles) and those who have persistent conceptual difficulties (learner-specific difficulties). I find it most useful to assume that all students' difficulties are temporary—at first. If our assumption is right, a minimal amount of remediation will usually put a student back on a successful conceptual trajectory—a path toward greater understanding.

On the other hand, there are some students who have persistent difficulties. These students require more detailed assessment and analysis. Both kinds of struggles—general and learner-specific—require that we develop theories about the students' thinking. In the case of general struggles, these theories are based on common misconceptions, content gaps, and other more easily remedied difficulties. Learner-specific struggles require a deeper exploration of student thinking, such as a Collaborative Study or a Student Interview (both of these techniques are covered in detail in Part 2).

Ease the Struggle

The Response to Intervention (RTI) Model

The Response to Intervention (RTI) model is commonly used to address learner difficulties in a variety of subjects. RTI is designed to address the specific differences in the ways that students struggle and the way students respond to efforts to help them. The approach taken in this resource embraces RTI; we first look for patterns of learner thinking that will respond to classroom interventions. If we test theories and find that we still don't understand student thinking, we use more learner-specific approaches for assessment and analysis. Our goal is to understand student thinking and to act on this understanding as quickly as we can. ■

How Do We Create Theories About Student Understanding?

The development of theories is straightforward: as we approach the task of understanding student thinking, we need to create multiple possible explanations for why a student might be doing what she's doing. Students almost never do things randomly. Even if their thinking is convoluted, complicated, or just wrong, there is almost always an underlying logic to it. The creation of multiple theories about student thinking honors the idea that there is some logic in student thinking and helps us to find a way to understand it. Starting from a perspective that students should be engaged with their ideas—rather than corrected for "wrong thinking"—creates a very different dynamic for working with struggling learners.

> "The creation of multiple theories about student thinking honors the idea that there is some logic in student thinking and helps us to find a way to understand it."

Four Means of Creating Theories

▶ Using the Three Frames for Understanding Student Thinking to Create Theories

▶ Recognizing Patterns in Student Work to Create Theories

▶ Using Student Confidence Scores to Create Theories

▶ Using Flexible Interviews to Create Theories

Using the Three Frames for Understanding Student Thinking to Create Theories

In Chapter 2, we identified three frames through which to understand student thinking: the learner, math content, and instruction. The three frames can help to create theories about what might be going on for a specific learner. These points of view can also help to illuminate possible remediation, once a theory has some evidence to support it.

Ease the Struggle

The Importance of Multiple Theories

Empirical research on the success of specific mathematics interventions is growing but not conclusive. Since we don't have a vast array of proven interventions to use when we diagnose particular struggles, we can't know for sure what might work. When it's easy to be wrong, it's safer to develop several potential theories and look for evidence to support one of them.

Consider the child who raises his hand seconds after reading a word problem. Almost every teacher has had the experience of chorally reading a problem with the class only to have a student immediately raise his hand and exclaim, "I don't get it." What's going on when that happens?

The answer is, potentially a lot! The student could have difficulty with understanding English. Many learners of English who have proficient *social* language are still struggling with *academic* language. The math problem might contain language that the student doesn't fully understand.

On the other hand, the student who raises his hand immediately might be practicing "learned helplessness"—the disposition that he needs help immediately every time he struggles at all with a problem. These students sometimes overuse the help of classroom assistants and don't ever develop the disposition of working on a problem before giving up.

The student might also have a short-term memory challenge. If this is the case, the student will have difficulty "clumping" relevant information as it arrives so that he can begin to unravel the problem with his working memory.

Another theory to consider is that the student might have attention difficulties, in which case he might not have focused on the important details of the problem and raising his hand is his way of letting you know this.

As you can see, if we jump to a quick conclusion about the student—rather than developing several theories—we can easily miss what's really going on. As we discussed in Chapter 2, to support a struggling learner we must first understand what's going on inside her head. Looking at student understanding, as we did in the last chapter, can do much to make student thinking clearer.

The following pages explore several approaches for creating theories for student thinking. Note that Part 2 of this resource introduces three assessments (Concrete–Representational–Abstract, Collaborative Study, and Student Interviews) that also address the development of theories. ■

To explore the potential the three frames have for creating theories, let's consider another common struggle—difficulties with regrouping during addition and subtraction. The frames provide different perspectives on the same struggle. Any of the theories that arise from these three perspectives might be right. Alternatively, the solution to helping the student might lie in considering some or all of the frames together.

Difficulty Regrouping:
The Learner Frame Perspective

Learners may have difficulty with regrouping for a variety of reasons. The most common is that they do not have a flexible model with which to conceptualize their thinking about place value. A theory about a student's struggle with regrouping from the *learner* perspective focuses on whether the student is able to demonstrate the connection between a model for place value—base ten blocks or money, for example—and the base ten number system. Struggles with place value may suggest that a student has no model on which to ground his understanding of tens and one or that he has "proceduralized" work with place value models.

Sometimes repeated work with models such as base ten blocks becomes routine. In such a scenario students move blocks around and make trades of tens for ones because they are following a step-by-step procedure, and not because they understand the grouping/regrouping involved. This sometimes happens when students play "trading games" without fully understanding them. For these students, the moving of blocks becomes a series of steps to be followed, like the set of directions (instead of a map) in our New York City analogy in Chapter 2 (see page 16). Whether students have proceduralized the use of manipulatives, or simply have not developed clear models for thinking mathematically, the result is that their understanding is limited. A theory about a student's struggle that focuses on the lack of effective models for understanding is an example of a theory about struggle from the Learner Frame perspective.

Difficulty Regrouping:
The Math Content Frame Perspective

Theories that focus on struggles from the Content Frame are informed by content gaps or important missing concepts. In our example of a student who has difficulty with regrouping, we could hypothesize that the student never developed the key concepts of place value. For such a student the *sameness* and *difference* between 2 and 20 would not be obvious. Both of these quantities are *two* of something. However, the important mathematical idea is that the group that each two represents (2 ones, or 2 tens) is different in power or magnitude. Several researchers have noted that magnitude is a critical concept for success with addition and subtraction (Booth and

Siegler 2008). If the child has not mastered math content around counting, magnitude, and place value, regrouping for addition and subtraction may be impossible because the prerequisite concept was not in place. A theory from the Math Content Frame will identify these important prerequisite gaps in key mathematical knowledge as a source of struggle.

Difficulty Regrouping:
The Instruction Frame Perspective

Theories about struggles that result from instruction come from the belief that the approach the teacher is using might limit the student's development of key concepts. For example, in my work with struggling math students, I've sometimes found that when I switch models from base ten blocks to money for place value and regrouping, my results are much better. In these cases I need to match the most appropriate model (Learner Frame) with the key mathematical idea (Content Frame). One of the theories I developed in working with a specific group of students who were having trouble with place value was that my instruction didn't match their needs. This later proved to be true when, trying out the theory, I had much greater success with regrouping by using money rather than base ten blocks.

The Instruction Frame is a lens on what the teacher does. This frame covers a broad range of classroom and instructional practices that might hinder a student's learning. The pace of instruction might not be right for an individual student. The opportunities that students have to explore concepts might not be sufficient. The teacher's use of the curriculum might not afford particular learners the most helpful learning experiences. All these types of difficulties can result in learner struggles and may be the most pervasive cause of such. While some might suggest that this could be construed as a criticism of math teaching, I encourage us to think of theories about learner struggles that come from instruction as opportunities. Ultimately, since teachers have control over their own classroom practices, struggles that come from instruction may be the easiest to remedy.

> " I encourage us to think of theories about learner struggles that come from instruction as opportunities. "

Recognizing Patterns in Student Work to Create Theories

Raffaella Borasi (1996) and Robert Ashlock (2010) have done extensive work on what they call "error analysis." Much of this work (though not all) is focused on analyzing the particular patterns of mistakes that students make when they misapply an algorithm. While I encourage us to be most interested in a student's understanding of the concept behind the algorithm, the approach of looking for patterns in student work is a good one for developing theories about students' struggles.

My Story

Isaac's Habit of Subtracting Numbers

I once worked with a second grader, Isaac, who subtracted numbers like this:

$$\begin{array}{r}{}^{4}\!\!\!\not{5}\,{}^{1}\!\!2\,{}^{1}\!\!1 \\ -389 \\ \hline 42 \end{array} \qquad \begin{array}{r}{}^{2}\!\!\!\not{4}\,{}^{1}\!\!8\,{}^{1}\!\!6 \\ -274 \\ \hline 1912 \end{array} \qquad \begin{array}{r}{}^{5}\!\!\!\not{7}\,{}^{1}\!\!0\,{}^{1}\!\!0 \\ -426 \\ \hline 184 \end{array}$$

When I shared Isaac's work with a few other teachers, they felt that Isaac didn't understand the algorithm for regrouping. They suggested that I re-explain to Isaac how the algorithm worked and/or demonstrate the algorithm using base ten blocks.

When I carried through with my colleagues' suggestion, I quickly realized that simply re-explaining the algorithm was not going to work with Isaac. (I've since learned that when we look at student struggles from the perspective of applying a set of rules, we almost never get at the underlying reasons for the struggle.)

Isaac's case is an example of why developing theories can be invaluable for understanding where students are struggling. Going with our first guess (re-explain the subtraction algorithm) may not remedy the problem. In Isaac's case, I needed to identify more possible explanations—theories—about what was going on before trying to fix the problem.

From the perspective of the learner, I asked myself why Isaac chose to borrow even when it was unnecessary. One theory from this perspective was that Isaac didn't understand the relationships that are critical to place value. In Isaac's work he seemed to distribute amounts from the minuend as though all place values were equal. This indicated a misconception about how the place value system works and how tens and hundreds are regrouped. Since the distribution of numbers (regardless of value or magnitude) seemed consistent, I saw this approach as a pattern of mathematical misunderstanding.

When working with Isaac without the benefit of knowing his prior experience, I wondered, "Where did he come up with this?" I wondered what

continued

My Story continued

classroom experiences might have led to his highly idiosyncratic approach to subtraction with regrouping. Perhaps he was taught the algorithm without really understanding how it worked? If this were the case, I'd need to find out how much he actually understood about the underlying concepts in regrouping. Did he have experiences with base ten blocks? Number lines? Money? Finding out the ways Isaac had responded to his prior instruction would give me clues about how I might approach deepening his understanding.

In looking for patterns, I was able to identify three reasonable theories with which to begin supporting Isaac:

1. The student doesn't have good models for understanding subtraction with regrouping.
2. The student doesn't understand place value and/or magnitude of numbers.
3. The student may have been instructed in the algorithm for subtraction before understanding fundamental concepts of place value.

These theories helped me explore Isaac's understanding and subsequently resolve his difficulty much more thoroughly than showing the error he made and re-explaining the correct approach to the algorithm.

Using Student Confidence Scores to Create Theories

Another method for developing theories about a student's understanding is to consider a student's confidence in his own understanding. To do this, we can compare the correctness of a student's solution to the confidence he expresses in explaining it. This approach is based on the idea that students who have good conceptual understanding are both *confident* and *correct*.

To help us assess students' understanding, we should always ask them to explain their thinking. As much as possible, we want students to show us what they're thinking using words, numbers, and representations. However, even with all these means of explaining we can sometimes fail to see whether a student is confused or simply making a minor mistake. For this reason, when students are solving a problem (in class or on an assessment) we can ask them to put a *confidence score* on their work. A confidence score is a number from 1 to 10 that students use to show how confident they are about their answer. If a student is very confident that her answer is correct, she should give herself a 10 as a confidence score. If she has no idea what she's doing, she should give herself a 1 for confidence. The more confident a student is, the higher the score she'll record.

Most of the time, the confidence scores students give themselves fall in the middle range (a score of 4–7). Sometimes, however, students express either low confidence in their answers (a score of 1–3) or high confidence (a score of 8–10). These scores provide a window into students' conceptual understanding. The scores tell us if a student's confidence is based on reality (really knowing why her answer is correct) or if there might be a misconception. The idea for reality scores was developed by Dr. Stephen Hegedus at the Kaput Center for Research in STEM Education at the University of Massachusetts, Dartmouth. Dr. Hegedus invented this score as part of an intervention study that made use of dynamic models to help students understand algebra.

In a research setting, these confidence scores are helpful in identifying trends in students' confidence on particular categories of problems. In using confidence scores with students in class, I've combined them with the correctness of the solution to create four profiles that in turn help me develop theories:

Four Profiles Based on Student Confidence and Correctness

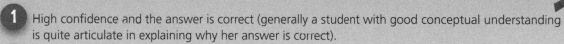

1 High confidence and the answer is correct (generally a student with good conceptual understanding is quite articulate in explaining why her answer is correct).

2 High confidence and the answer is incorrect (this is often the profile of a student with a misconception; a student is confident because he has applied the algorithm correctly but he does not understand why his solution doesn't make sense).

Possible theories: the student has a misconception about the concept, is using procedures without the underlying understanding, and/or is not looking for meaning in the computation.

3 Low confidence and the answer is correct (students who match this profile vary more than any other group; this could be the profile of a learner who has low confidence in general, or doesn't want to risk being wrong; more often the student has only an emerging understanding).

Possible theories: more work needs to be done with practice, communication, and reflection to create deeper understanding and more confidence.

4 Low confidence and the answer is incorrect (these learners are struggling with a concept; they tend to have a good sense of reality—they don't appear to understand the concept and they know it).

Possible theories: More information is needed from this learner to develop theories about why she's having trouble. The best tool for this is the flexible interview (see the following section).

The Garage-Building Problem

In class one day I gave students the *Garage-Building Problem: If it takes 6 carpenters 3 days to build a garage, how many carpenters will you need to build a garage in 1 day?* This problem probes students' conceptual understanding of proportional reasoning. It asks students to consider an inverse proportion. Many of the students relied on a procedure like cross multiplying and consequently got the wrong answer, suggesting that it takes just two carpenters to finish the project:

$$\frac{6}{3} = \frac{x}{1}$$

$$6 = 3x; \quad x = 2$$

I realized that students were not asking themselves, "If it takes six workers to build a house in three days, how could *fewer* workers do it in *less* time?"

This is one of many instances when I realized I needed to find out if students actually understand a problem or if they're just throwing formulas at it; I decided to have students give themselves a confidence score.

Using Flexible Interviews to Create Theories

A user-friendly tool for developing theories about student struggles is a quick, focused interview. Since the format for these interviews is unstructured and the time allotted for them can be as short as one question during math class, I call these "flexible interviews." Flexible interviews resemble short conversations. (Note that Part 2 of this resource explores a more in-depth approach to interviewing called Student Interviews.) A flexible interview has three basic parts: posing the problem, listening to student response, and testing your emerging theories. Ask good questions as a student works on the problem; this allows you to think about potential theories for why she is doing what she is doing. Following is a list of questions that we've found particularly helpful during flexible interviews.

To illustrate a flexible interview, let's consider the *Garage-Building Problem* (see "My Story: The Garage-Building Problem," above). When solving this problem one of my students, Megan, used the cross-products algorithm but gave herself a confidence score of 2—low confidence and an incorrect answer. Megan seemed to know that her answer was wrong, even though she used an algorithm. To understand what was going on, I needed a little more information. I decided to conduct a flexible interview with Megan:

Key Questions to Ask in Flexible Interviews

▶ Why did you do that?

▶ How did you come up with that?

▶ I noticed you paused just now, what were you thinking?

▶ Why did you change your mind just then?

> *Teacher:* You only gave yourself a 2 for confidence. You're not sure about your answer?
>
> *Megan:* No, well, I'm not sure.
>
> *Teacher:* What bothers you about your answer?
>
> *Megan:* We've been doing the multiplying across thing for these problems but I'm not sure I did it right.
>
> *Teacher:* What do you think might be wrong?
>
> *Megan:* I don't think I did it right because I don't think the answer makes sense.

This flexible interview gave me important information about Megan's thinking. This information can inform other theories, or can be used immediately to engage Megan in deeper thinking about proportional reasoning. When taking into account the three frames for understanding student thinking (see Chapter 2, page 12), I still don't know whether Megan is confused about the difference between direct and inverse proportions (the Math Content Frame), was taught the cross-products algorithm without understanding how it works (the Instruction Frame), or hasn't developed a model for proportions (the Learner Frame). Each of these theories could be tested further by asking more questions or looking at more of Megan's work.

Ease the Struggle

Three Questions to Support the Development of Theories

Ask yourself three key questions to help in the creation of a theory:

1. Is there a recognizable pattern in the student's work?

2. How realistic is the student about his understanding? (Does his competence match his confidence?)

3. What don't I understand about what the student has just done? ■

Testing Theories

After creating theories (mentally or in more formal ways, like writing them down), we need to test them out. Our goal, as a reminder, is to help identify why a student is struggling and move that student along a trajectory that will serve him in the future (we spend more time on this in Part 3, which focuses on specific tools for helping students develop greater understanding).

The theories we develop from formative settings such as a flexible interview, can often be tested immediately.

How can you test a theory you've developed? The process involves two questions (see left).

In the Garage-Building Problem (see "My Story: The Garage-Building Problem," page 36), I developed three theories to suggest why Megan gave an incorrect answer (and did not have confidence in it). These theories are:

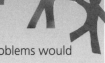

Two Questions for Testing a Theory

1 What questions and/or problems would help me test my theory?

2 What would the student's work/behavior look like if my theory were correct?

1. The student has no model for proportional relationships to draw on when thinking about the problem.

2. The student doesn't understand the difference between direct and inverse proportions.

3. The cross-products algorithm was taught before the student understood its meaning.

To test my theories, I need to give Megan another problem or two. In this case I choose two less complex problems:

Problem A
My dog eats 4 cups of food a day. If I dog-sit 3 more dogs just like him, how many cups of food will they eat in a day? A week?

Problem B
It takes Tom 3 hours to paint a fence. If Huck helps him, how long will it take? What if 2 friends help him?

These problems are helpful because they are focused on my theories. Before asking Megan to solve the problems, I need to ask what she notices about the problems. How are they similar or different? Next I'll ask her how she will approach them (how she will think her way through them). Finally, I'll ask her to solve them and to *think aloud* as she goes. I'll pay particular attention to places where she stops or changes her mind. At those points I'll ask her to tell me what she's thinking.

Megan's responses to my inquiries will tell me a great deal about her thinking. I can probe her approach to the problem to develop a better idea of how she is working on them. From her answers I'll get a sense of whether she has models "to think with," whether she can see the difference between the two types of problems, and whether she knows why the cross-products algorithm works.

Testing theories for general difficulties (misconceptions, content gaps, etc.) is usually a short process that yields information a teacher can use immediately. In the RTI model, this is known as a Tier 1 approach.

Ease the Struggle

Understanding RTI and Its Tiers

Response to Intervention (RTI) is an approach for supporting struggling students and identifying students with special needs. It is built on student responses to interventions and supported with research. The RTI approach is rooted in the idea that students should be supported in the least restrictive (and least invasive) environment. There are three stages, or *tiers*, to the RTI system that provide progressively greater amounts of support for math learning.

Tier 1

In Tier 1 of RTI, all students in a class are screened to identify those students who might be at risk for failure. As a result of screening, those students identified as needing support can benefit from early intervention that is provided in the regular classroom.

Tier 2

Tier 2 intervention is for students who continue to demonstrate weak assessment results and/or do not respond well to whole-class interventions introduced in Tier 1. These students will receive more intensive small-group instruction four to five times per week, often for twenty minutes or more. Small-group instruction is targeted at specific math content and student performance is carefully monitored.

Tier 3

Students who receive Tier 3 interventions are often (but not always) eligible for special services. Tier 3 intervention generally takes place in a one-on-one setting and often outside the regular classroom. Instruction may be given by a wide variety of learning specialists outside of the regular classroom teacher. ■

Concrete–Representational–Abstract (CRA) Assessments

4

The Big Ideas

- The CRA assessment is an assessment that's used with the whole class rather than just with students who appear to be struggling. It's a way to get a look at *everyone's* thinking.

- A CRA assessment asks students to solve a set of problems by demonstrating their thinking using three different models: a concrete, or physical model; a representational, or drawn model; and an abstract model, or equation.

- By comparing the way students use each type of model in a CRA, teachers can get a good view of students' understanding. With this information, teachers can plan more effectively to teach *all* the students in their classes.

Chapter Outline

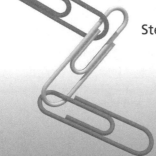

What Is a CRA?

Tier 1 of RTI calls for intervention that takes place within the regular classroom and is informed by data. The most common assessment used to find out what and how a student is thinking (and subsequently why a student may be struggling) meets both these criteria. It's called a Concrete–Representational–Abstract assessment, or CRA for short. The CRA assessment is used with the whole class rather than just with students who appear to be struggling. It's a way to get a look at *everyone's* thinking. Although students do individual work, every student will take part in this assessment. This assessment was first described by Allsopp, Kyger, and Lovin (2007) in their book *Teaching Mathematics Meaningfully: Solutions for Reaching Struggling Learners*. Over the years I've tested the usability of CRAs, receiving feedback from many teachers. This chapter explores the CRA based on these experiences.

Ease the Struggle

Understanding RTI and Its Tiers

Response to Intervention (RTI) is an approach for supporting struggling students and identifying students with special needs. It is built on student responses to interventions and supported with research. The RTI approach is rooted in the idea that students should learn in the least restrictive (and least invasive) environment. There are three stages, or *tiers*, to the RTI system that provide progressively greater amounts of support for math learning.

Tier 1

In Tier 1 of RTI, all students in a class are screened to identify those students who might be at risk for failure. As a result of screening, those students identified as needing support can benefit from early intervention that is provided in the regular classroom.

Tier 2

Tier 2 intervention is for students who continue to demonstrate weak assessment results and/or do not respond well to whole-class interventions introduced in Tier 1. These students will receive more intensive small-group instruction four to five times per week, often for twenty minutes or more. Small-group instruction is targeted at specific math content, and student performance is carefully monitored.

Tier 3

Students who receive Tier 3 interventions are often (but not always) eligible for special services. Tier 3 intervention generally takes place in a one-on-one setting and often outside the regular classroom. Instruction may be given by a wide variety of learning specialists beyond the regular classroom teacher. ■

The CRA represents the most general pass at understanding student thinking among the suite of assessments (CRAs, Collaborative Study, and Student Interviews) focused on in this part of the book. Each assessment can be thought of as a filter for understanding, a way to identify children having struggles so they can be supported. The CRA is the coarsest filter, though the easiest to implement. For this reason the CRA might be classified as a *screening* rather than a diagnostic assessment like Collaborative Study (Chapter 5) and Student Interviews (Chapter 6). In follow-up studies of assessments, teachers report they use the CRA more consistently than the other two assessments.

A CRA assessment asks students to solve a set of problems by demonstrating their thinking using three different models: a concrete, or physical model; a representational, or drawn model; and an abstract model, or equation. Models (see Chapter 2, page 19) are the mental constructs— the analogies, maps, or prototypes—that we think with. For the purpose of a CRA we examine the way students use concrete models, representational models, and abstract models to get insight into how they think about a mathematical concept.

Three Different Models Used in CRAs

1. A concrete, or physical model
2. A representational, or drawn model
3. An abstract model, or equation

Each of these models demonstrates a particular understanding of a mathematical concept and can be used to better understand student thinking. Taken together, they give a snapshot into how a student thinks about a particular concept. When students are finished, teachers sort students' solutions by looking at the models, strategies, and algorithms used; the understandings and misconceptions; and the potential areas of concern.

In Chapter 2 we looked at why models are important for understanding student thinking. A good part of solving for why is understanding which models a student uses, how she uses them, and what it means. When we use a CRA, we let our students show us the models they are using to solve problems around a particular concept.

The teachers with whom I've worked have consistently found that the most common cause of math struggles is the application of a procedure without understanding its underlying concept and usually points to an undeveloped (or missing) conceptual model. The bright-line distinction for whether students possess conceptual understanding tends to be their use of a model. If a model for thinking isn't present, a student doesn't really understand a concept (Ryan and Williams [2007] and Petit, Laird, and Marsden [2010] have reached the same conclusion).

The CRA is a particularly useful tool for looking at the presence of models, since it makes use of three different contexts to solve similar problems—all of which demand the demonstration of model use. The way a student uses models in each of these contexts gives the teacher good clues about the student's conceptual understanding.

My Story

A CRA Using the Necklace Problem

While working with a class of third and fourth graders in lower Manhattan, I was interested in their understanding of multiplicative reasoning. We were about to begin a unit on multiplication and I wanted to know what they knew about grouping and sharing. I used the following problem as part of a CRA:

The Necklace Problem

Maria wants to make necklaces for her friends. She has 4 friends.

Each necklace needs 10 beads.

Maria buys 3 bags of beads.

If each bag has 17 beads, will Maria have enough beads to make all her friends a necklace?

Ease the Struggle

What Is a Station?

A *station* (sometimes called a *center*) is a work area where a specific task or activity takes place. In CRA assessments the *concrete station* is simply a table (or tables) where concrete materials (cubes, tiles, beads, etc.) are provided for students to solve the assessment problem. Likewise, drawing materials are provided at the tables that house the *representational station*. The *abstract station* is a table containing copies of the assessment problems and reminders that students should use equations in the solving process that transpires there. For more on working with stations, see "Step 2: Administer the CRA," page 56. ■

I created stations—tables with materials and copies of the problem—where students could work: the *concrete* station had a variety of materials (cubes, tiles, beads, etc.), the *representational* station asked students to create a mathematical representation (picture, organized list, chart, graph, table, etc.), and the *abstract* station asked students to solve the problem with an equation. At each station I anticipated that the students would demonstrate a slightly different understanding of both problem solving and a math concept— in this case, multiplicative reasoning.

At the concrete station, Zach solved the problem using cubes. Zach explained his thinking as follows:

"Each cube is a bead. I started with three stacks of seventeen because she has three bags of seventeen beads."

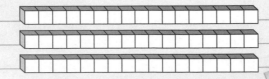

"Then I put those beads into stacks of ten because each necklace is supposed to have ten beads in it."

"I found out you could make five necklaces! So four is no problem."

At the representational station Lola created a chart to support her thinking. She explained, "I found out that there are fifty-one beads in all three bags. That would make five necklaces."

Bags	Beads	Beads	Necklaces
1	17	10	1
2	34	20	2
3	51	30	3
		40	4
		50	5

Some students at this station chose other models to support their thinking; Reese drew a picture of the work he did, Willy used a table, and Connor created an organized list.

At the abstract station Jordan solved the problem using equations and explanations:

$$17 \times 3 = 51$$
$$10 \times 4 = 40$$

51 beads – 40 beads for necklaces = 11 beads left over

"I timesed the seventeen times three because there's three bags of seventeen. I timesed the ten times four because there's four necklaces with ten beads. Fifty-one beads is what you have and forty is what you need."

At each station students had the opportunity to demonstrate their understanding—and their use of conceptual models.

Ease the Struggle

Comparing Student Work in a CRA

Analyzing the variety of ways students respond to the CRA can give a teacher insight into their thinking. See *The Necklace Problem* in the "My Story" section on page 46.

Kelsey's Work: Only Equations (No Model)

Consider the CRA of Kelsey, who wrote only equations for her work at the abstract station:

$$4 \times 10 = 40$$
$$17 \times 3 = 51$$

The equations indicate a certain level of understanding, even without an explicit solution. They seem to show that Kelsey knows she has to multiply to solve this problem. Looking at these two equations, we might assume that Kelsey understood the problem but forgot to fully answer it (Will she have enough beads?). The CRA is a combination of *three* problem solutions with models, however. The strength of this assessment is that we won't make any conclusions about Kelsey's understanding until we've looked at her work at all three stations.

Kelsey's Work: Beads as Placeholders

The same student, Kelsey, tried to answer the problem at the concrete station by making a pile of three beads and then a pile of seventeen beads (3×17) to show that she is multiplying three and seventeen:

A concrete model like this shows that Kelsey knew the numbers in the equation, but there is no evidence of equal groups, a cornerstone of multiplicative reasoning. Kelsey doesn't appear to be using the model as anything more than a placeholder for the numbers in the problem. This is a very common approach when someone thinks procedurally but not with understanding. They see only the numbers, but not how to work with the operation. With data from both these stations, would we still make the assumption that Kelsey could reason multiplicatively? Kelsey seemed to have procedural fluency with multiplication, but one theory for this performance is that she doesn't know what multiplication means (groups of a common number). If this is indeed the case, in later years, Kelsey will most likely demonstrate difficulty when solving problems involving multiplicative reasoning. CRA results like this warrant further investigation to see why a student was unable to create an adequate model. A flexible interview (this is explored later in this chapter on page 68) will often give us that information.

David's Work: Only a Model (No Equations)

Often a CRA will show the opposite result; David demonstrated an adequate model using materials or representations, but was not able to show equations to solve. As with Kelsey's examples, this is also good information. If the CRA is given prior to instructing a concept, having a model but no abstract way to represent it is a perfect place to be, since instruction is often aimed at giving students the symbols and procedures to efficiently express their conceptual understanding. Since David knows that three groups of seventeen means:

the procedures for computing the total number are sensible and don't take away the necessary understanding for problem solving. What this tells us about David is that he has the models "to think with" about multiplication, but does not yet have algorithms to compute with efficiently. He is at the place in instruction where he can begin to develop these.

The way students use models shows how well they understand a concept. By comparing the way students use each type of model in a CRA, teachers can get a good view of students' understanding. With this information, teachers can plan more effectively to teach *all* the students in their classes. ■

> "By comparing the way students use each type of model in a CRA, teachers can get a good view of students' understanding. With this information, teachers can plan more effectively to teach all the students in their classes."

Three Steps to Implementing a CRA Assessment

There are three main steps to implementing a CRA: plan, then administer, then analyze the results. The planning step requires teachers to choose a time and focus for the assessment, select an appropriate series of problems, and gather materials. In the administering step, teachers must make decisions about how to manage the class during the assessment (there are options). The analyzing step is where teachers look at student work to inform their instruction. Let's look at how to successfully tackle each step in the context of CRAs conducted by classroom teachers.

Step 1: Plan a CRA

Planning a CRA requires that you choose a time to do so, a clear mathematical focus for the assessment, and problems for each station that will give you insight into student thinking about that focus.

Three Steps to Implementing a CRA Assessment

▶ **Step 1:** Plan a CRA.

▶ **Step 2:** Administer the CRA.

▶ **Step 3:** Analyze the results.

Choosing When to Administer the CRA

Administering a CRA usually takes about one class period. Most teachers use CRA assessments at the beginning of a unit, though this is by no means the assessment's only use. The reason for using a CRA as a pre-assessment is to get a sense of how students understand a concept before teaching it. In this way a CRA can help to inform instruction.

Ease the Struggle

Defining a Clear Mathematical Focus

What if students already understand what you are supposed to teach? How will you identify misconceptions? I've always found it curious that more curriculum materials don't insist on this kind of inquiry before teaching a unit. Defining a clear mathematical focus and then assessing your students' understanding should be standard practice in all math teaching. ■

Choosing a Mathematical Focus

A crucial step in planning a CRA is to establish a clear mathematical focus for the assessment. What concept do you want to investigate for student understanding?

The more specific a mathematical focus can be, the more useful the assessment data will be. Deciding that your mathematical focus is "addition," for example, is too broad to be useful for instruction; there are many concepts related to addition—whether students understand the joining quality of addition, regrouping, counting all or counting on, to name a few. Instead, narrow your focus. Creating a CRA with a focus on "addition with regrouping into the hundreds place" offers more specific information that can directly affect how you approach instruction. Following are examples of teachers' thinking in determining the mathematical focus for a CRA. Consider each one. How would you state the mathematical focus being considered without making it too broad?

Examples of Teachers' Thinking in Determining the Mathematical Focus for a CRA

Kindergarten: "My first idea for a CRA was number sense, which is way too big. I focused my assessment specifically on counting how many things are in a set, and that when counting a set of objects the last word in the counting sequence names the quantity for that set. I know that counting involves being able to say the counting words in order and connect the sequence in a one-to-one manner. If children only know the order without one-to-one correspondence they won't be really counting. Children usually learn this way of counting before they learn that the last count word shows the amount of the set, or its cardinality."

Fifth Grade: "I think students should be able to divide and determine that a problem does or does not have a remainder. I also think they need to understand the meaning of the remainder. They should know if it's necessary to incorporate the remainder into the problem, or if can it be set aside. I would like the students to acknowledge that there is a remainder as well as state whether the remainder can be ignored in the solution to the problem or if it is a part of the solution. In fifth grade we review the concept of division with remainders and expect students to have a clear understanding of that concept."

Special Education: (This teacher worked with four students who had substantial learning challenges as part of a life-skills program. She identified the needs of this group by saying, "All students in this program qualified for special education, with handicapping conditions including learning impairment, emotional disturbance, and autism. All students had also been diagnosed with an attention deficit hyperactivity disorder." This educator focused her work on concepts with money.) "I designed the items for my CRA as a pretest for a unit on money. Money is a practical model that I think would serve my students well. I wanted to see what they remembered, and where I had to 'fill in the gaps.' Since a major component of the students' IEPs required them to plan purchases, develop a budget, and purchase the necessary supplies at local stores, a facility for money handling, as well as a good understanding of the value of money, was necessary. I chose to assess my students' understanding of place value with money when they were regrouping with addition."

In each case the teacher is looking for information about student understanding *of a particular concept:*

▶ that counting tells how many are in a set and the last number counted gives you this information

▶ what remainders mean and what you do with them

▶ how to regroup when using money

Within each CRA's mathematical focus, you will be probing student use of models, strategies, and algorithms. You can use the assessment to identify common understanding, and begin to articulate ways students might grow in relation to the identified concept. The teacher will use the assessment to identify common understandings in his class and to begin to articulate the ways students might grow in relation to the identified concept: What problems or activities might help further student understanding? What misconceptions need to be confronted?

> "Within each CRA's mathematical focus, you will be probing student use of models, strategies, and algorithms."

Choosing Problems

Once an appropriate mathematical focus has been identified for the CRA, we need to choose problems that are representative of that focus. The problem(s) chosen for the CRA should be at an instructional level—not overwhelming

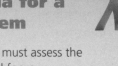

Key Criteria for a CRA Problem

1 The problem must assess the mathematical focus.

2 The problem must have context.

3 The problem should be solvable using common classroom models.

but not easily solved. The problem should take no more than ten to fifteen minutes to solve at any one of the stations. These problems can come from a wide variety of sources. Many teachers use problems from their end-of-unit tests. Others get problems from online sources like Problems of the Week (see The Math Forum at Drexel, http://mathforum.org/pows/). Some teachers create their own problems for use on the CRA. All of these can make for an excellent assessment. Be sure that the problem meets three key criteria.

CRA Problem Criterion 1: The Problem Must Assess the Mathematical Focus   Earlier in this chapter we looked at the importance of choosing a mathematical focus in planning a CRA. In turn, the CRA problems one chooses need to be related to and assess the mathematical focus.

CRA Problem Criterion 2: The Problem Must Have *Context*   Problems selected for a CRA should feature a familiar, meaningful situation that allows students to think about the problem in a variety of ways. Familiar contexts provide an entry point for all students. Problems might be grounded in games, experiences, or even popular culture. For example, a teacher might make use of her students' knowledge about trading baseball cards—something the children in her class do frequently (see examples of these problems on page 54). When students have a familiar context to work from they will usually find their way to a solution, even if the solution involves using a concrete model and "counting all."

Ease the Struggle

Conceptual Versus Procedural Understandings in Assessments

Sometimes we use assessments to check in on student *skills*. These kinds of assessments are fine, but they don't work well for a CRA. A CRA is an assessment that looks at student *conceptual* understanding. For this reason, arithmetic practice, fact recall, and so on, which tend to focus on *procedural* understandings, are inappropriate for a CRA. ■

One common misconception is that, for math problems to be meaningful, they must connect to the cultural experience of the students. Such a view suggests that Chinese students, for example, should solve problems that use Chinese names and situations. While problems that are framed to be culturally relevant can be meaningful, not all meaningful problems need to be culturally relevant. A colleague of mine who was studying the reading habits of Puerto Rican boys in the South Bronx said that the boys were often less interested in books about Puerto Rican boys than they were about Harry Potter. In her work, it seemed that the level of engagement depended on the story, not necessarily on its racial and cultural context. The same can be true about math problems.

CRA Problem Criterion 3: The Problem Should Be Solvable Using Common Classroom Models   Ideally, all problems in a CRA should be solvable with the kinds of manipulatives and representations (like number lines) that are readily available in the classroom. The idea is that students can demonstrate their mathematical thinking with tools they usually use. Consider the two problems below. For Problem A, students can use actual stickers, plastic tiles, or interlocking cubes to model the problem concretely. Since these materials are readily available in most classrooms, this problem would meet Criterion 3 for a CRA problem. On the other hand, the amount of money in Problem B makes it tricky if no play money (or real currency) were available to use as a model. Problem B is certainly a good problem, but it may not be a good choice for a CRA since creating a concrete model will be difficult. It's possible for students to model this problem using place-value blocks—but students often have difficulty regrouping both dollars *and* cents. In Problem B a thousands cube would have to serve as ten dollars. This is something students are unlikely to figure out.

Problem A

Jimmy left for school in the morning with stickers in his sticker book. At school his teacher gave him 6 more stickers to add to his book. When he got home he had 14 stickers in his book. How many stickers did Jimmy have when he went to school that morning?

Problem B

Maria took $40 shopping. She bought some shoes for $34.99. How much change will she get back?

Ease the Struggle

The Same or Different CRA Problem for Each Station?

In addition to the criteria for choosing problems, one needs to decide whether to use exactly the same problem at each of the three stations (concrete, representational, and abstract) or to use a slightly different problem. Teachers who have used CRAs are somewhat divided on this issue. In general, I've found that the data I gather are better when the problems are not identical at every station. Changes between problems don't need to be drastic. For the youngest children (grades K–2), often only changing the numbers is necessary (see the problems below, left). Other times, a small change in context will create a slightly different problem that addresses the same math concept (see the problems below, right).

Many teachers find that creating small differences between the problems helps their students to treat each problem as "something new." When the same problem shows up at all three stations, students sometimes bring knowledge from a previous station to help them. In most math situations we would encourage this kind of transfer; however, since the goal of a CRA assessment is to see how students approach a concept (rather than a problem) from different perspectives, getting students to work on new problems at each station generates a clearer picture of their thinking. ■

Station: Concrete Model
Max has 7 pencils. His sister has 15 pencils. How many more pencils does his sister have than Max?

Station: Representational Model
Max has 17 pencils. His sister has 9 pencils. How many more pencils does his sister have than Max?

Station: Abstract Model
Max has 9 pencils. His sister has 18 pencils. How many more pencils does his sister have than Max?

Station: Concrete Model
Jose wants to share 32 cookies among 7 people. How many cookies will each person get?

Station: Representational Model
Nancy has 45 candies and wants to share them with her 6 friends (7 people in all, counting Nancy). How many candies will each person get?

Station: Abstract Model
We have 38 pencils for 5 people to share. How many pencils will each person get?

In these CRA problems for grades K–2, the numbers have been changed.

In these CRA problems, small changes have been made in the context of each.

Ease the Struggle

CRA Template and Tasks

To get you started using CRAs, this resource includes a CRA assessment template as well as sample tasks at first-, third-, fifth-, and seventh-grade levels. See Reproducibles 4.1 through 4.5. ■

Ease the Struggle

An Example CRA on Additive Reasoning

Here's an example of a CRA focused on a particular aspect of additive reasoning with eight-year-olds. Review the CRA and think about the criteria explored so far in planning a CRA (both in choosing a mathematical focus and choosing problems). Does this match up to what you've learned? In what ways?

CRA: Additive Reasoning

MATHEMATICAL FOCUS: the concept of part/part/whole understanding as part of additive reasoning

Station: Concrete Model

- *Materials:* square tiles, stickers, cubes, or any similar counting objects; a mat to put work on; camera (optional—for adult to document student work)

- *Problem 1*
  When Tommy left for school in the morning he had 6 baseball cards. At school he traded and got some more cards. When he got home he had 14 baseball cards. How many cards did Tommy have when he went to school that morning?

- *Instructions:* Use the materials provided to solve the problem. When you are finished, draw a simple picture of your work or have an adult come see your work (and perhaps take a photo of it).

Station: Representational Model

- *Materials:* plain, lined, and graph paper; pencil

- *Problem 2*
  Harriet had 7 baseball cards. Her mom gave her some more cards for her birthday. Now she has 12 cards. How many cards did Harriet get from her mom?

- *Instructions:* Solve the problem using pictures or words to show your thinking

Station: Abstract Model

- *Materials:* paper and pencil

- *Problem 3*
  Ernie has 11 baseball cards. Sammy also has some cards. Together they have 24 cards. How many cards does Sammy have?

- *Instructions:* Solve the problem; write an equation to go with your work. ■

Three Ways to Administer a CRA

1. *Option 1:* Three Stations/Student-Determined Rotation: Use three separate stations (one for each type of model); students individually choose the order in which they progress through the stations.

2. *Option 2:* Three Stations/Teacher-Determined Group Rotation: Use three separate stations (one for each type of model); students progress through the stations in groups determined by the teacher.

3. *Option 3:* Whole Class: Administer the CRA as a whole class.

Step 2: Administer the CRA

There are several ways that a CRA can be administered. This section explores three primary approaches: using three separate stations (one for each type of model) in which students individually choose the order in which they progress through the stations; using three separate stations (one for each type of model) in which students progress through the stations in groups determined by the teacher; and administering the CRA as a whole class.

Option 1: Three Stations/Student-Determined Rotation

In this option, use three separate stations (one for each type of model) and have students choose the order in which they progress through the stations. Once the stations are established, students are free to choose which station to go to first. They must be sure that, over the course of about forty-five minutes, they visit all three stations.

In the years that I've worked with CRAs we've had numerous discussions about the order in which students do the stations. Some teachers believe that students should always start with the concrete station and move up the scale of complexity to the abstract station. In numerous informal trials we've concluded that the order doesn't seem to matter. The most common approach to CRA administration is to set up the three stations and allow students to move through them at their own rate and in any order they choose.

Ease the Struggle

Setting Up Stations

At each station, place appropriate quantities of the corresponding materials. The concrete station, for example, usually requires counting tiles, interlocking cubes or place-value blocks, and copies of the concrete problem. The representational station offers graph paper, colored pencils, markers, rulers, and copies of the representational problem. The abstract station generally only has paper and pencils and copies of the abstract problem. Sometimes teachers add a calculator if computation is not part of the assessment (it usually is). Also place a student work container (box, bin, or crate) at each station to facilitate the collection of student work. ∎

Option 2: Three Stations/Teacher-Determined Group Rotation

In this option, use three separate stations (one for each type of model) and have students progress through the stations in groups determined by the teacher. Students work individually (as they did during the Student-Determined Rotation). Some collaboration invariably takes place, though we don't encourage this (collaboration is usually not a problem since each student must explain his thinking at each station; the explanation is the demonstration of the learner's understanding and represents his individual point of view).

For this option, create three groups of students—one for each station. Give each group a set period of time to work at a station. When the time is up, the whole group moves on to the next station.

Some teachers prefer this approach because it allows greater control of the group during the assessment. For younger students, moving through stations as a group can alleviate anxiety about what to do and where to go. If a class has not learned to work well independently, a group rotation approach will support their focus as they work on each problem.

The group rotation approach to CRA has the benefit that the teacher can position herself at a particular station and know that she'll see each student's work as they come through that station. Many teachers who use this approach like to stay at the concrete station. This gives them the opportunity to observe their students making physical models and ask them clarifying questions to understand their thinking.

Ease the Struggle

The Importance of Movement

Why, in administering a CRA, do we have students move from one station to another? Because the short break and physical movement is helpful to learners. Young students in particular have difficulty sitting still and concentrating for extended periods of time. Having students move creates a natural break between activities and allows them the chance to reset and refocus before beginning the next problem.

Physically moving from one activity to another is also helpful to students who struggle with attention challenges because it gets them moving and helps them regulate attention. The short break that takes place when moving from one activity to another is sometimes referred to as a "brain break" and has reportedly positive effects on attention and learning (Caine and Nummela-Caine 1997; Caine, Nummela-Caine, and Crowell 1999; Hallowell and Ratey 1994; Sousa 2011). ■

Option 3: Whole Class

In this third approach, CRA assessments are administered using more traditional management techniques. The teacher gives the whole class the assessments one at a time, collecting all the samples for each model. When using the whole-class option teachers generally begin with the problem that is solved with concrete models, move on to the problem to be solved with representational models, and finish with the problem to be solved using abstract models or equations. The advantage of this approach is that the teacher has the most control over the classroom environment. If management of class processes is a concern for you, this will probably be the most comfortable approach. Whole-class administration allows the teacher to see every child work on the same model at the same time. Using this approach, administration of the CRA can be spread out over several class sessions using a different model (concrete, representational, abstract) with each session.

Ease the Struggle

Anticipating Class Administration Challenges

Administering a CRA presents challenges that are common to most classroom activities: ensuring first that there are enough materials to work with and second that students who finish at various times have something to do. For the first, students should always have tools at their disposal to work with. Most commercial curricula include enough manipulatives for all the students in a class, but if this is not the case, more commonly available materials like beans, tiles, or colored chips must be provided for a successful CRA class administration.

You will likely find that some students finish before others and need to be occupied while waiting for classmates to catch up. Others will be rushed by having to finish "on time." Having a math activity that follows the assessment—a game or exploration for example—will help occupy students who finish at different times. The activity should also be made available at some point to students who did not finish early, so they don't miss out. ■

Ease the Struggle

Recording Student Work at the Concrete Model Station

The goal of the CRA is to understand student thinking; to accomplish this, we need to document the work students do. This poses a unique challenge for the station with concrete models. Students at this station are working with manipulatives that ultimately will be cleaned up and stored away. How can you preserve what they've done and effectively record their work?

Use Drawings

Older students will readily draw pictures of what they've done. (It's important to note that while the pictures themselves can be viewed as representational, they are not really models because the student is using them to record his or her work—not to think through the problem.) For younger students (kindergarten and first grade), however, their own drawings often don't capture their thinking as well as teachers would like.

Observe Students at Work

The concrete station gives us a chance to watch students as they work. When you sit at the concrete station and take notes, what do you observe?

Take Photos

Many teachers take pictures of student constructions (piles of base ten blocks, stacks of cubes, etc.) so they can remember what the student did and/or prompt a conversation with him or her at a later time. This is an especially popular strategy with early elementary teachers, perhaps because so many of the assessments for children at this age are handled similarly. ■

Ease the Struggle

What If a Student Gets Stuck?

A CRA assessment is aimed at understanding student *thinking*, not student *proficiency*. We are much more interested in learning what's going on in a student's mind than correcting the student— at this point. For this reason, whenever a student doesn't know what to do with a problem during a CRA, ask the student to tell you whatever he can about the problem and then to move on. Emphasize to students that during a CRA, you are much more interested in understanding *how* they got their answer versus just seeing their answer.

Sometimes when we ask questions of students they feel that we are guiding them, that by simply asking them a question about their thinking we're telling them something's wrong. We can soften this by being specific. Begin an inquiry into student thinking by referencing something the student said or did. For example, you might say, "I noticed that you stopped as you were working just then. It looked like you were thinking about something. What were you thinking about?" In this way you can send the message that you're really interested in the student's thinking, not just in the correct solution.

It's a struggle for everyone to watch a student who circles around a solution without finding it. We are tempted to give the student the final piece so he or she can get the problem right. We need to resist this tendency so we can find out what's really going on in the child's thinking. One way to doing this, by practicing listening, is explored in greater detail in Chapter 6, page 105. ■

Ease the Struggle

CRAs and the RTI Tiers

From an RTI perspective, a CRA assessment identifies where we might need Tier 1 intervention. Providing support for difficulties in the regular classroom is an excellent outcome for everyone involved. CRA assessments give the teacher the kind of information about student understanding that, in many cases, allows her to accommodate specific learner needs. In some cases, for example, a student may not have had sufficient time to develop a variety of strategies for solving problems with a particular mathematical focus. The CRA assessment will often make this clear to the classroom teacher and provide the opportunity for him to support the learner with more extensive strategy development. ■

Step 3: Analyze the Results

Appropriately analyzing the results of the CRA helps inform our instruction in the regular classroom. Quite a few insights can be determined from a CRA (see the list below).

To successfully analyze CRA results, I suggest a two-step sorting process that takes about thirty minutes total. After collecting work from all three CRA stations, go through the pile of samples twice. The first time through, simply look at each work sample and see if any models, strategies, or algorithms are repeated (do this regardless of whether there is a correct answer). This takes five minutes or so. This first pass is to get a sense of the categories that exist across the work. In the second pass, sort student work into categories, creating new categories as necessary. These categories, and the work that falls into them, tell what kinds of models, strategies, and algorithms students are using.

This two-step sorting process is an efficient way to find patterns in the work and make plans for using those patterns in instruction. However, to do this successfully we need to know what to look for in each student's work and what our findings will mean for instruction. In some cases we may need to probe more deeply, especially when student thinking is unclear (often indicating a struggle). Let's take a closer look on the following pages at how to analyze student work from CRAs.

From a CRA, We Can Determine . . .

▶ the models students commonly use for our mathematical focus,

▶ particular strategies for solving problems (we can also learn which strategies are not being used, which may prove to be more important),

▶ knowledge (or lack thereof) of algorithms common to our mathematical focus,

▶ common misconceptions, and

▶ whether students demonstrate any "red flags" for content gaps or cognitive challenges.

My Story

The "Got It" Approach

When I first began working with teachers to analyze the results of CRA assessments we didn't use any particular criteria for sorting. Our approach was to look at the work and to see what we could find.

Over time, two general approaches to sorting developed: a "got it" approach and a "characteristics of the work" approach. Using the "got it" approach, we sorted student work according to whether students "got it," "almost got it," or "didn't get it." In my early work this was by far the most common approach to sorting. Over time we realized that the information we got from this type of sorting was limited. We found it hard to understand the thinking of a student who "almost got it." This category only told us that the student may have some workable models or strategies, but there was no information to guide us about which ones or how they were used. A "got it" approach to sorting student work didn't help understand student thinking.

What to Look for in CRA Student Work

In my experiences the best approach for sorting is one that I call a "characteristics of the work" approach. Using this approach we closely look at the characteristics of the work students completed during the CRA. Finding common patterns of student thinking gives us insights that are in turn helpful for instruction. When sorting student work using this approach, three categories are key: models, strategies, and misconceptions. I also create a "what the heck" category when I have no idea what thinking organized a student's work; this can more politely be referred to as the "questions" category!

Category 1: Models One of the key characteristics of student work lies in the use of each of the three types of models (concrete, representational, and abstract). Often teachers sort by models that students used successfully and models they didn't. For example, in many types of problems students are able to use representational models to solve problems but not

Key Categories When Sorting

1 Models (use of)

2 Strategies (use of)

3 Misconceptions

4 Questions

Ease the Struggle

"Multiplication Makes Things Bigger"

Sometimes model use will demonstrate a common misconception. For instance, students who use grouping strategies to model multiplicative relationships sometimes develop the idea that "multiplication makes things bigger." Five groups of six is, for example, bigger than four groups of six. When confronted with multiplication with fractions, however, the grouping model needs to be modified; the idea that multiplication is making things bigger is a misconception, sometimes called an "overgeneralization." (For more on this see Ryan and Williams 2007.) ■

concrete models. We could place these samples in a category and ask ourselves, "Why would a student be able to use a representational model, but unable to use a concrete model for this focus?"

Another common way to sort CRA work using the lens of model use is to focus on the particular kinds of concrete models students use. One teacher noticed that all her students used place-value blocks when modeling subtraction with regrouping. They were successful at correctly solving the CRA problems when using place-value blocks, but about half of the students were unable to write accurate equations and/or were unable to solve without the use of blocks. She wondered if the students were making the connections between the work they did with the model and the way this work could be represented with numbers and symbols. This became the focus of her lessons.

Using a similar CRA, a teacher found that his second-grade class had difficulty regrouping with subtraction at all three model stations. He noticed that none of his students used an open number line to solve any of the subtraction problems. This observation led him to see if focusing on this unused model might improve student understanding of subtraction.

Category 2: Strategies Strategies that students use to solve CRA problems seem to stand out the most for teachers when sorting CRA work. By *strategy* I mean the way students apply a model to solve a problem. Following is a list of the most common strategy-focused ways teachers sort CRA student work.

Common Strategy-Focused Ways to Sort CRA Student Work

▶ Students in the class use a common strategy.

▶ Understanding of a model seems evident but not how to use the model to solve a problem.

▶ There are levels of strategies for the same problem.

▶ Strategies are baffling and seem ungrounded in mathematical thinking.

Students in the Class Use a Common Strategy When a school or district has implemented a math program with high fidelity, CRA results often yield highly similar strategies across the whole group. The reason for this is probably that students have either been taught and/or have practiced the same approaches to problems like the ones in the CRA. I have observed this result also for children who have learned in multiage settings. In this case, having the same teacher may have led students to develop similar approaches.

There's nothing wrong with students' demonstrating similar strategies in a class, though more strategies for problem solving are generally desirable. We want to develop flexibility in the thinking of our students. If the tools they bring to problem solving are limited, they may have less flexibility. On the other hand, if students all have a strategy that's conceptually based on a good model, they will have a good understanding of the math they're doing. Some research on special needs children even suggests that teaching a single, robust strategy to students who struggle is advantageous (Montague 1997; Tournaki 2003).

Understanding of a Model Seems Evident but Not How to Use the Model to Solve a Problem Another common observation made when sorting student work is model development without using a strategy to solve a problem (this can be observed from the instruction frame—see Chapter 2). This occasionally happens when a student has difficulty making meaning from a model and, for a variety of reasons, the teacher repeats model-building activities to the point where the activity, rather than the use of a model in problem solving, becomes the final goal.

When students have trouble, for example, understanding grouping tens into hundreds, the instructional tendency is to give them more opportunities to practice it. For students having grouping difficulties, we might provide lots of opportunities to trade ones for tens and tens for hundreds. This kind of practice is helpful for developing the base ten blocks model. But if application with the model in a problem-solving situation doesn't accompany the practice, students sometimes ritualize the trading without seeing it as a means to solve more complex problems. The result is that students show they know what the models mean (they might do some kind of set up for the problem using blocks or tables) but don't know how to use the model to solve the problem.

There Are Levels of Strategies for the Same Problem One very common approach to sorting by strategies is to sort by the variety or sophistication of the strategies students use. Do students use the number line, for example, in efficient or procedural ways? Do they streamline the process of trading by asking for "change"? Do they draw concrete models or actually use more sophisticated mathematical representations like tables?

In solving a problem about subtraction, some students may use a decomposition strategy (this is often shown in the abstract model station), others may work with an open number line, while still others may use base ten blocks to record the regrouping they do. All three of these strategies depend on model use but represent different approaches to solving a problem. For these reasons they can make excellent categories for sorting students' work.

Strategies Are Baffling and Seem Ungrounded in Mathematical Thinking
Last but not least, sometimes strategies are just baffling. Kaley did the following work at the representational model station in response to the problem *How many legs do four horses have?*

It seemed that Kaley had some kind of strategy, since there were four shapes that could have been "horses." What I couldn't figure out (without some explanation) was how Kaley went from that drawing to figuring out that there were legs. A later interview with Kaley revealed that the inside circles were "the horses" and the outside circles were "the pens for the horses"(!). Kaley drew the representation and then counted by fours to get sixteen. Since I didn't know what Kaley was thinking, and since it was a seemingly unique strategy, I pulled this cryptic sample out and put it in the questions category. Strategies that can't be classified—but are understood—might make up their own category. Strategies that aren't understood, on the other hand, may require further investigation.

16 legs

Kaley's response to the problem *How many legs do four horses have?*

Category 3: Misconceptions The third key category when sorting CRA student work is misconceptions. Much research has been done on student misconceptions in mathematics (Bamberger, Oberdorf, and Schultz-Ferrell 2010; Cockburn and Littler 2008; Tobey and Minton 2011; Ryan and Williams 2007). The term *misconception* might not be the best way to describe these ideas students put forth since, often, the ideas are an emerging or an evolving understanding, not a *mis*understanding. When sorting by strategies, work that ends up in the misconceptions pile generally does so because students have overgeneralized a rule or model.

Category 4: Questions Sometimes student representations are difficult to decipher. Sometimes the logic that links steps in a student's problem-solving process is unclear. Still other times the student may demonstrate a series of steps that seem to have no connection to the mathematics in the CRA. If you find CRA student work difficult to understand, place it in the fourth category, "Questions." The questions category requires more investigation by the teacher. This investigation may take the form of a flexible interview—a short conference between teacher and student to see if student understanding can be made clearer (for more on flexible interviews, see page 68 later in this chapter as well as Chapter 3, page 36). The questions category is especially important because it may contain work from students who have content gaps or cognitive challenges.

Ease the Struggle

What It Means to Generalize—and to Overgeneralize

If students had to learn every concept as something brand-new, humanity would probably still be living in caves and lighting our homes with fire. What accelerates all learning is our ability to transfer what we learn from one setting to another. When students learn to skip-count by twos and fives, they quickly learn that they can skip-count by any number because they *generalize* what it means to skip-count—to *count on* by a particular number. This ability to use what we've learned and apply it in new ways is critical to learning mathematics.

Sometimes, though, students apply something they've learned to a new situation in an inappropriate way. When learning about decimals, for example, students will sometimes think that 0.28 is greater than 0.9 because, "Twenty-eight is bigger than nine." In this instance the transfer of understanding doesn't appropriately fit the new circumstances. When this happens it is referred to as *overgeneralizing*. ■

When the problems chosen for a CRA are a good match for the students taking it, there should be relatively few samples of student work that end up in the questions category. The number of pieces of student work that end up in this pile, therefore, can give important information about the class as a whole. If, for example, there are more than two or three students with work in this category, it may be that the problems in the assessment were too difficult for students *at this point*. A thick questions pile can also indicate that understanding in the group is limited for the mathematical focus.

Using CRA Results for Instruction

As previously mentioned, administrating a CRA usually takes about one class period. Analyzing the results—sorting student work into categories that give teachers information about student understanding—often takes about thirty minutes. The real work begins when the analysis is complete. Information gained from the CRA should be used for instruction in three key ways.

Three Key Ways to Use CRA Results for Instruction

1 Focus instruction to develop models, strategies, and algorithms.

2 Address misconceptions.

3 Use flexible interviews to probe for understanding.

Focus Instruction to Develop Models, Strategies, and Algorithms

The sorting analysis from the CRA gives us meaningful information about the needs of our students for developing models, strategies, and algorithms. Generally speaking, developing concrete models is most needed when a concept is being initially explored. Once these models have been internalized, strategy work should be done to make use of concrete and representational models to solve problems. Finally, as efficient and automatic strategies are developed, algorithms should be the focus of instruction.

When sorting student work based on model use, the teacher should pay close attention to which of the three models—concrete, representational, or abstract—students use most easily. Instruction can be made more learner centered by teaching to address trends in student work exhibited through model use. For example, if students demonstrate facility with concrete or representational models but not with algorithmic fluency, instruction should focus on building strong connections between concrete and representational model use in problem solving and the use of algorithms, or abstract models, as efficient strategies.

By contrast, if students solve primarily through algorithms but cannot demonstrate understanding using other models, then concrete and representational model development should be the focus of instruction to be sure students are able to make the extensive connections that must exist between those models and algorithms. The patterns that emerge in sorting student work can tell teachers where they should place instructional emphasis (models, strategies, or algorithms).

Address Misconceptions

One of the most interesting aspects of students' mathematical ideas is how resistant they are to change. Even highly educated students will find ways to doggedly cling to misconceptions, sometimes reworking them to accommodate their self-developed ideas. (The movie *A Private Universe* is an interesting exploration of this phenomenon. In this movie, students demonstrate their resistance to change their personal theories about the reason we have seasons and the phases of the moon.) When teachers, paraprofessionals, or teacher assistants discover that a student has an unworkable or incorrect mathematical idea, the most common approach is to try to explain to the student where his work is incorrect. In my observations, explaining to students how their work is wrong rarely works.

The most effective method I've found for addressing misconceptions is to create opportunities for students to doubt the incorrect solution/method they have developed. If a student questions his own solution, he seems to be open to rethinking his approach. If the student does not develop doubts

> "The most effective method I've found for addressing misconceptions is to create opportunities for students to doubt the incorrect solution/method they have developed."

about his work, he will likely try to fit any new information he gets from you into his old misconception.

A simple example can be found in the common problem students have with the standard algorithm for subtraction. When subtracting, students will often simply subtract the lesser number from the greater:

$$\begin{array}{r} 62 \\ -\ 15 \\ \hline 53 \end{array}$$

We have found that explaining the reasons why this is wrong can some-times, but not always, get students to use the algorithm correctly. Often they still don't understand how it works. This is where raising doubt is important.

Ease the Struggle

Mathematical Content Knowledge

In order to support students, teachers must understand what researchers call "mathematical content knowledge for teaching." This knowledge includes an understanding of the mathematics being taught that is broader than the mathematics being learned. A student can, for example, successfully subtract with regrouping using a model developed from place-value blocks. The student will develop the connection between the concrete model (the place-value blocks) and the number system it represents. Through problem solving with place-value blocks, the student will develop increasingly efficient strategies for making trades and computing, using the blocks less and less of the time. Finally, the student will use an efficient algorithm without relying on the blocks at all. To learn subtraction effectively, the student can learn to think mathematically using a single model that helped to develop strategies and led to algorithm use. On the other hand, to *teach* subtraction, one needs to know far more math content and the pedagogy that supports it.

To teach subtraction content a teacher needs to know the meaning of subtraction, its relationship to other operations like addition, its meaning on the number line, and the way properties of number (like the associative, commutative, and distributive properties) affect it. She needs to understand how equivalence works in a subtraction equation and the ways that quantities added or subtracted from one side will affect the other.

To teach subtraction a teacher needs to know how to build concepts using several different kinds of models (the hundreds chart, number lines, beans and cups, and money, to name a few). He needs to know a wide variety of strategies to use for each of the models. He needs to know, for example, how subtraction can be done from left to right or right to left, how decomposition of the minuend and subtrahend might affect computation, or the different ways to use an open number line for subtraction.

This is just one example of the importance content knowledge for teaching. In each grade level there are specific areas where teachers need a broad understanding of the math they teach to help their students be successful. NCTM's *Curriculum Focal Points,* and the *Common Core Standards for Mathematics,* both provide insights into specific math content at each elementary grade level. ■

Using a number line, we might ask students to count backward 15 from 62. Or we might give students sixty-two base ten blocks and have them work the trades out. In both cases a student will come up with the correct answer of 47, but when we ask with which answer she feels more confident: the 53 she got from the algorithm, or the 47 she got from the number line, she will likely trust the answer she got using the model because she understands where it came from. Answers obtained using algorithms are less understood unless the algorithm was developed directly from student-created strategies. Since the student now has doubt about her answer from the algorithm, she is open to figuring out why it doesn't work.

Another common way of raising doubt about errors and misconceptions is to engage students in mathematical arguments so that they get the chance to confront each other's ideas and come to conclusions together. The way to do this with the subtraction misconception presented here is to put the class into small groups, present them with the equation ($62 - 15 = ?$), and tell them that some people say the answer is 53 and some people say the answer is 47. Explain to students that their group must reach consensus on the right answer and present their evidence to the rest of the class. This approach to addressing misconceptions allows the students themselves to confront their own thinking. It creates the chance for everyone to do their best thinking together.

Use Flexible Interviews to Probe for Understanding

Flexible interviews were first introduced in Chapter 3, page 36, for developing theories. When sorting CRA student work, the questions pile leads, inevitably, to flexible interviews to better understand student thinking. A flexible interview is a quick way to see if you can understand what a child was thinking when he answered one of the CRA problems.

In this context, the problem you use for the flexible interview should come directly from the CRA. Sometimes teachers simply give the student a copy of the problem he did on the CRA that was difficult to understand. In this case the teacher will ask the student to explain his thinking, listen as the student explains, and then ask questions to understand the student's reasoning. Most often, the student's verbal explanation will make his work clear. Keep in mind that understanding student thinking is not the same as the student's providing a correct answer. A flexible interview may simply show you where the student's misconception lies. This is the kind of insight into student thinking that can allow for more effective instructional choices.

My Story

A Flexible Interview with Tarika

When conducting a flexible interview with a third-grade student, Tarika, I noticed that she kept looking around the room while doing her thinking out loud. This wasn't my class and I didn't know the child well. As I watched her I could see that she had a hard time focusing on the multistep problem on which we were working. The theory I developed while talking with her was that she might have attention challenges. However, since I was doing a flexible interview, I simply asked her why she kept looking around the classroom. She replied, "My mom is bringing in my birthday cupcakes today and she's late!" Tarika was distracted but (perhaps) not from attention deficit disorder!

Sometimes teachers will give students a blank copy of one of the problems from the CRA and ask them to solve the problem again while thinking out loud. When using this approach it's important to remember to ask good questions whenever the student does something that you don't understand (see the questions list on page 37 in Chapter 3).

Looking Ahead

We've learned that CRA assessments are a screening tool that teachers can use to investigate student thinking about a particular mathematical concept. The assessment looks at the students' use of three kinds of models: concrete, representational, and abstract. Using data from problem solving with these models, teachers gain insights to student thinking and plan instruction accordingly. CRA results lead to remediation with models, strategies, or algorithms; confrontation of misconceptions; and/or flexible interviews to better understand student thinking. If, after conducting an interview, you still have questions about a student's understanding, you'll want to implement one of the other assessments; see Chapter 5, "Collaborative Study," and Chapter 6, "Student Interviews."

Reflection Questions

1. Why might a CRA assessment be worth conducting in your classroom? How might you and your students benefit from this assessment?

2. What mathematical topic could you address more thoroughly if you understood student thinking about it? How would knowing student thinking about this topic inform your instruction?

3. Where might you find problems to use for a CRA assessment? What resources do you already possess that might be a resource for problems?

4. Which of the CRA administration approaches most appeals to you? Why? How might you implement your first CRA?

5. What obstacles might hinder your implementation of a CRA assessment? How might you address them?

Collaborative Study

The Big Ideas

● Collaborative Study is a "group-think" approach entailing a structured meeting between classroom teachers and other learning specialists to review data on a particular student and to explore theories and remediation.

● Any student who is struggling is a potential candidate for Collaborative Study. However, most of the time these students are unresponsive to the most obvious and/or easily implemented interventions.

● The outcome of a Collaborative Study meeting should be one in which specific theories are set to be tested by specific group members with deadline dates for results. Some groups refer to this as an "action plan."

● The ultimate goal of the Collaborative Study process is to have an intervention plan in place to further support the student.

Chapter Outline

What Is Collaborative Study?

The solitary nature of classroom teaching is well understood by anyone who's done it. Over the years teachers have had to figure out most student struggles on their own. Luckily, this trend is changing. Teachers, learning specialists, curriculum specialists, and administrators are working together more often to find ways to support students in their learning of mathematics. One of these ways is through a "group-think" approach called Collaborative Study.

> "Collaborative study is a way to make use of several minds to come up with ideas about the ways students understand math concepts."

Collaborative Study is a way to make use of several minds to come up with ideas about the ways students understand math concepts. Collaborative Study entails a structured meeting between classroom teachers and other learning specialists to review data on a particular student and to explore theories and remediation. In many schools groups like this already exist for the purpose of identifying and addressing student difficulties. These groups go by a variety of names: student study team, building and staffing team, and intervention team, to name a few. The goal of meeting in these groups is to better understand student thinking and to come up with a plan to support students to become more successful math learners.

Collaborative Study shares basic properties with Concrete–Representational–Abstract (CRA) assessments (see Chapter 4), but it is used less frequently and, often, by a different group of educators. The CRA assessment is used, primarily, by classroom teachers to get a sense of what students understand. Teachers report that Collaborative Study is used most often by math coaches, curriculum coordinators, or learning specialists. These professionals make use of Collaborative Study to support classroom teachers, help create Individual Education Plans (IEPs), and provide professional development. Teachers benefit from the conversations, conjectures, and deconstruction of student thinking that transpires in Collaborative Study meetings. By learning more about one individual student in a Collaborative Study meeting, teachers learn more about teaching all students. Reproducible 5.1 offers a helpful template for organizing and implementing a Collaborative Study meeting.

Ease the Struggle

Collaborative Study Checklist

To help you get started immediately with Collaborative Study, in addition to this chapter see Reproducible 5.1, Collaborative Study: Template. ■

Three Steps to Implementing Collaborative Study

Most of the time any difficulty with understanding student thinking can be handled through a quick flexible interview. In a flexible interview, we develop theories about student understanding and test those theories by asking students questions (for more on flexible interviews, see Chapter 3).

PART 1: Amy's CRA Assessment— a Case for Collaborative Study

Amy was a student in a rural school of approximately 120 students. She was the oldest of four children. Both her mother and father worked on a local dairy farm. She was a child who seemed to get along well with other children. She was often included in group games and ate lunch daily with a steady group of other girls. Academically, Amy did not attract much attention. She seemed to do well enough in most subjects, though she exhibited less enthusiasm when it was time for math. Her teacher noted that she was often the last student to come to the center (or classroom) rug when it was time to begin math (this was different from other times of day).

Amy's teacher, Jean, was concerned about Amy's ability to subtract with regrouping. In a beginning-of-the-year assessment of arithmetic skills, Amy had demonstrated some difficulty with regrouping. When Jean had given the third-grade class a CRA that involved solving word problems with subtraction, Amy's responses made her wonder whether she really understood place value (to familiarize yourself with the format of a CRA, see Chapter 4).

In the concrete model station, Amy had place-value blocks, place-value chips, and money available to use for solving. She was given the following problem to work with:

Marie's trip was 130 miles. Anne's trip was 210 miles. How much farther did Anne travel?

Amy was unable to create a concrete model for the problem. When Jean asked her about her thinking, Amy replied, "I think I could add them together, but I'm not sure." Jean asked Amy what she might add and Amy answered, "one hundred thirty and two hundred ten." Jean then asked Amy, "What will the answer tell you?" Amy wasn't sure.

At the representational model station, Amy was given the following problem (note that Amy's class had just visited the historic Bennington Monument; pictures of it accompanied the problem). She was given no other prompt but the problem.

continued

My Story continued

> The Bennington Monument is 293 feet tall. The Washington Monument is
>
> 555 feet tall. How much taller is the Washington Monument?

Amy's solution to this problem was to draw two figures that looked like obelisks (not to scale), one taller than the other. She wrote under the drawing, *The Washington is taller.* No other figures accompanied her work.

    Finally, at the abstract model station, Amy was given the following problem and asked to write an equation to find the answer.

> Henry wants to buy a bicycle for $250. He has saved $183. How much more
>
> does he need to buy his bike?

Amy wrote:

$$\begin{array}{r} \$250 \\ -\ 183 \\ \hline 133 \end{array}$$

Jean asked Amy to tell her about her equation. Jean remarked that Amy seemed to feel more confident about this station than the other two. She asked Amy, "How did you get one hundred thirty-three?" (Jean already had a developing theory that Amy was not clear about place value. Her question was aimed at testing this theory.) Amy responded, "You can't take three away from zero, so you have to borrow the three."

    At this point Jean got out place-value blocks and asked Amy to show her 250. Amy did this with no difficulty, pulling two hundreds flats and five tens rods out of the bin of blocks. Jean asked Amy if she could trade one of her hundreds flats for tens rods. Again, Amy was not confused. She put one of her hundred flats to one side and counted out 10 tens rods. Jean asked her if this was a fair trade. Amy told her that it was. Jean said, "Show me." Amy picked up the tens rods and piled them neatly onto the remaining hundreds flat.

    Jean was perplexed. It seemed that Amy understood the differences in the place-value model. Why was Amy having such a hard time using this information to solve the problems?

However, when our initial attempts to uncover a student's understanding are not successful, Collaborative Study may help. Following is a three-step guide to implementing Collaborative Study.

Step 1: Gather Data ("Case History")

Any student who is struggling is a potential candidate for Collaborative Study. However, most of the time these students are unresponsive to the most obvious and/or easily implemented interventions. On the Response to Intervention (RTI) scale these are students who might move from Tier 1 to Tier 2, depending on what teachers discover about student understanding. See the "My Story" section on page 73; Amy is just the type of student that a teacher might bring to a Collaborative Study. Amy is having difficulty with a concept she should have mastered at this stage in her learning. The teacher, Jean's, initial attempts to understand Amy's thinking were inconclusive. Jean needs help to understand and support Amy's learning.

Three Steps to Implementing Collaborative Study

▶ **Step 1:** Gather data ("case history")

▶ **Step 2:** Set up the Collaborative Study group

▶ **Step 3:** Conduct the meeting

Ease the Struggle

Understanding RTI and Its Tiers

Response to Intervention (RTI) is an approach to supporting struggling students and identifying students with special needs. It is built on student responses to interventions and supported with research. The RTI approach is rooted in the idea that students should be supported in the least restrictive (and least invasive) environment. There are three stages, or *tiers*, to the RTI system that provide progressively greater amounts of support for math learning.

Tier 1

In Tier 1 of RTI, all students in a class are screened to identify those students who might be at risk for failure. As a result of screening, those students identified as needing support can benefit from early intervention that is provided in the regular classroom.

Tier 2

Tier 2 intervention is for students who continue to demonstrate weak assessment results and/or do not respond well to whole-class interventions introduced in Tier 1. These students will receive more intensive small-group instruction four to five times per week, often for twenty minutes or more. Small-group instruction is targeted at specific math content and student performance is carefully monitored.

Tier 3

Students who receive Tier 3 interventions are often (but not always) eligible for special services. Tier 3 intervention generally takes place in a one-on-one setting and often outside the regular classroom. Instruction may be given by a wide variety of learning specialists outside of the regular classroom teacher. ■

Data to Consider Collecting for Collaborative Study

▶ unit assessments

▶ standardized test results

▶ report cards and/or progress reports

▶ Primary Number and Operations Assessment (PNOA)

▶ Math Recovery Assessments

▶ district assessments

▶ informal/formal observations

What data are needed for Collaborative Study? Effectively preparing for a Collaborative Study is equivalent to what some special educators call a "case review" or "case history." There should be a case manager (the classroom teacher, the math coach, or a learning specialist) in charge of collecting these data. The case manager needs to gather data that will allow the group discussing the data to have a comprehensive picture of the student under review. When the student is beyond fourth grade this is a somewhat easier task since all states must test elementary and middle school students. The data available for review on younger students varies depending on the school and district.

Ease the Struggle

What Is Math Recovery?

Math Recovery is an early intervention program for children in grades K–2. The six strands in the Primary Number and Operations Assessment (PNOA) are drawn from it. The program originated in Australia and draws on the research of Robert J. Wright, Garry Stanger, Ann K. Stafford, and James Martland. It is used in Australia, the United States, the United Kingdom, and Ireland.

Math Recovery offers a professional development (PD) program for teachers aimed at developing expertise with early intervention in mathematics. The PD program helps teachers learn to implement the Math Recovery program by administering early number assessments and using the results to help children make sense of mathematics.

An excellent resource on Math Recovery assessment is the book *Early Numeracy: Assessment for Teaching & Intervention*, by Wright, Martland, and Stafford (2006). ■

Ease the Struggle

What Is the PNOA?

The Primary Number and Operations Assessment (PNOA) is used to assess the development of number concepts in grades K–2. It was developed by two math professional development specialists, Sandi Stanhope and Loree Silvis, in collaboration with a group of primary teachers and the Vermont Department of Education.

The PNOA uses a one-on-one interview to assess student understanding. It has six components: forward counting, backward counting, symbolic notation, place value, fact fluency (only for grades 1 and 2), and properties of number. The PNOA is used by math specialists and classroom teachers to get a picture of student understanding of multiple aspects of the number system including magnitude and place value—two of the most important elements in additive reasoning. ■

When the Collaborative Study team meets, they will not have time to review all these documents. The case manager should prepare synopses of the available data and highlight areas that might be of interest. Many teachers include information about the student's reading ability along with data about math performance. Some research suggests there may be links between reading and math performance, though the greatest difficulties seem to be present when students have trouble in both areas (Fuchs, Fuchs, and Prentice 2004).

In addition to data, the case manager should include theories about the student's thinking. Preparing these theories, and the evidence that supports them, is a crucial element in the Collaborative Study process. Since the teacher is bringing the student to Collaborative Study because she is not sure why the student struggles, theories at this point tend to be general and help focus attention on particular aspects of the student's thinking. For detailed guidance on developing theories, see Chapter 3.

My Story

PART 2: Preparing Amy's Data

Jean contacted the school's math coach, Greg, and asked that Amy be put onto the next Collaborative Study agenda. Greg asked Jean to collect as much information as possible before the meeting. He told Jean that the group would want to see if Amy's difficulties were something new, or if she had a history of struggle with particular math concepts. Greg asked Jean to collect any previous report cards, math assessments, and standardized test data. He emphasized that all the names from these data must be removed to ensure Amy's privacy.

Jean left her conversation with Greg feeling positive that she was going to have support for working effectively with Amy. Jean gathered Amy's report cards from kindergarten and from first and second grade. She noted that there was no mention of difficulties with math in kindergarten or first grade. However, Amy's second-grade teacher, Mark, mentioned (in his notes for individual children) that Amy would "need more practice with her facts to be successful in third grade."

continued

My Story continued

Since Amy had not been tested for special education and was not on an IEP, Jean spoke with Mark about Amy's math work in second grade. Mark told Jean that Amy "wasn't catching on" when it came to adding and subtracting multidigit numbers. Mark indicated that he had checked on Amy's counting several times and that it seemed fine for her age. Mark also told Jean that he had worked on trading ones for tens and tens for hundreds with Amy. Mark said that Amy seemed fine with this—something Jean had also verified.

Amy had never had any district or state testing, so these data were not available. Jean's case history would have to be based on previous report cards, her conversation with Mark, and her own observations.

Jean then worked on including theories about Amy's mathematical understanding. Jean was concerned about Amy's place-value concepts and about her ability to subtract three-digit numbers with regrouping. Her theories were not specific because she had contradictory information; on the one hand, Amy seemed to understand the relationship between ones, tens, and hundreds. She had a model (place-value blocks) that she seemed able to use. On the other hand, Jean had questions about how Amy used her knowledge of place value, since she consistently seemed to ignore it when subtracting. Jean's general theories on Amy would help focus the Collaborative Study meeting without limiting the potential conclusions the group might come to.

Step 2: Set Up the Collaborative Study Group

There are often many opinions about who should be involved in a Collaborative Study meeting. Some teachers hold Collaborative Study with the whole staff (this may happen during a staff meeting or inservice day); others prefer smaller groups. While the specific composition of meeting members may vary, there are common representatives in all of them. These include a math specialist, a learning specialist, a colleague, and a school leader. Let's take a closer look at each of these roles and what they might mean in your school.

The Math Specialist

The job title of this person may vary from school to school, but the function this person serves is likely the same. Sometimes the math specialist is a coach, teacher-leader, or curriculum coordinator. Other times the specialist is another teacher with a more extensive background in math and/or math education. Groups seem to work more effectively when someone with this expertise is present. In the meeting, the math specialist provides theories about math content and pedagogy issues that might be a part of the student's difficulties. If we fit this into the context of the three frames (Learner, Math Content, and Instruction) explored in Chapter 2, the math specialist is the person who has significant insight into math content and instruction.

Common Members of a Collaborative Study Group

▶ math specialist

▶ learning specialist

▶ colleague

▶ school leader

The Learning Specialist

Though many student struggles are related to an understanding of content and instruction, others are the result of specific learning differences. The learning specialist is the member of the group who pays particular attention to theories of student understanding that are the result of cognitive challenges. These might include memory, perceptual, and attention challenges. Considering learning challenges is a critical part of the process, since sometimes learners will later be referred for special education testing. The information gathered from a Collaborative Study meeting is also often helpful when considering a student for an IEP.

A Colleague

Teachers especially like having another teacher present who has experience with the learner in question. Having another teacher who knows the student may present privacy challenges, though most teachers report that the student, while known to the two teachers, can be successfully kept anonymous to the rest of the group. When this is not possible (as is the case with students receiving special education services), the meeting may be held as an IEP meeting with parental consent and, often, parent attendance.

A School Leader

The school principal and district leaders may be the driving force behind the creation of regular Collaborative Study in a school. Sometimes they facilitate meetings. In general, though, school leaders see their role as helping to carry out decisions that are made during the meeting. In the event that more resources are requested (like additional testing), school leaders are able to

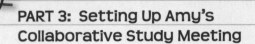

PART 3: Setting Up Amy's Collaborative Study Meeting

Greg, the school math coach, set up and facilitated the Collaborative Study on Amy. He invited Mark (Amy's second-grade teacher), the principal, and the school learning specialist. This group was typical for a Collaborative Study at Greg's school. Mark was invited because Amy's teacher, Jean, thought his perspective (as Amy's second-grade teacher) would be helpful. Since this was a small school, Mark was also invited as a colleague to help Jean feel comfortable. The learning specialist, Henry, was invited to help the group with theories that involved cognitive and/or perceptual challenges. In the event that some kind of special education testing was requested from the meeting, having Henry in the room would save time for everyone. Greg always invited the principal, Judy, so she could give input and stay informed about students at the school.

The meeting was scheduled during the school day when Jean's class was in gym. Both Greg and Judy felt that teachers would be more willing to participate in Collaborative Study if it happened during school. Scheduling meetings during the school day was not always possible, but the teachers appreciated the administration's attempts to accommodate their many responsibilities.

make this happen. Having administrators as part of the group means that the group has the legitimacy and authority they need to create and enact plans on behalf of struggling students.

Step 3: Conduct the Meeting

Refer to the five key steps on the following page for conducting a successful Collaborative Study meeting.

A successful Collaborative Study meeting will offer a structure that unites the best thinking of a group in discussing student struggles. The outcome of the meeting should be one in which specific theories are set to be tested by specific group members with deadline dates for results. Some groups refer to this as an "action plan." Having a school leader involved in the creation and maintenance of such a plan adds an additional layer of accountability that teachers find helpful.

Steps for Conducting a Collaborative Study Meeting

1 Identify a specific concern about the student.

2 Give background on the student (allow members to ask clarifying questions).

3 Share recent student work.

4 Brainstorm theories that might account for the student's struggles.

5 Create an action plan to test the group's theories.

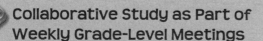

Ease the Struggle

Collaborative Study as Part of Weekly Grade-Level Meetings

In many schools teachers have regular, in some cases weekly, grade-level meetings. As part of these weekly class meetings, teachers bring in particularly interesting profiles of struggling math learners in their classes. The group then comes up with theories that they feel might explain the thinking of the struggling student and suggests ways to test these theories. Key questions to ask may be:

- Is this student's difficulty new, or has it been a problem for a while?
- Did this issue show up on any of the student's tests?
- Do we know anything about the kind of math instruction the student has received?
- Is the student's difficulty connected to any other learning strengths or challenges? ■

Ease the Struggle

Collaborative Study as Professional Development

Math coaches and/or curriculum coordinators find that using a modified version of Collaborative Study is a useful technique for professional development. When using Collaborative Study for professional development, coaches present anonymous student histories and data as a case study for faculty to consider. As a group, the faculty brainstorm theories of student understanding, ways of testing the theories, and potential interventions once follow-up data have been gathered. At such gatherings teachers often comment on the connections they make between the case they use for study in the workshop and students in their own classes. Further, they report that they feel they have new tools for helping to support struggling learners as a result of the collective thinking of the group. ■

PART 4: A Collaborative Study Meeting for Amy ("The Student")

Greg, the school math coach, facilitated the Collaborative Study meeting for Amy (who was identified as "the student" during the meeting to protect her privacy). Greg asked Jean (Amy's teacher) to present her specific concern for the student. Jean told the group about the student's difficulties and gave some background from her research. Mark filled in details from the student's performance in second grade.

When Jean was finished, Greg asked the group for clarifying questions. The learning specialist, Henry, asked Mark if he noticed any issues with the student's memory in second grade. Mark told him that the student seemed to have difficulty remembering math facts, but this wasn't unusual for second graders. Mark explained that he had spent a considerable amount of time with the student practicing trading hundreds for tens and tens for ones.

The principal, Judy, asked the group whether the student was receiving any services or had ever been referred for testing or guidance. Jean said that neither was the case.

Greg then asked Jean to share recent work with the group. Jean shared the work the student had done during the CRA assessment (see "My Story, Part 1" on page 73). Greg commented on the fact that, although these problems could all be solved using subtraction, the fact that they were comparison problems may have made them more difficult for the student. He also noticed that, although the student had successfully demonstrated regrouping out of context (trading), the student was unable to use the model to solve a problem. Greg wondered whether the student was really using the model or if the student had only learned a procedure for trading.

The learning specialist, Henry, probed Jean more about the student's memory. He wondered whether the student had learned how to regroup but had forgotten over the summer. He theorized that the student might have difficulty retrieving information from long-term memory.

Jean wondered whether the student might have difficulty with magnitude and/or counting. Perhaps the student did not really understand the counting sequence past one hundred?

Greg wondered whether the student was making meaning from the problems. He felt that the work suggested that, with the exception of the station for the representative model, the student was simply looking for a formula to apply. Greg suggested that they might want to investigate whether the student had understood the problem and knew what it was asking to find.

After more discussion, the group identified three theories to investigate and assigned a person to pursue each one:

Theory 1: The student doesn't understand the counting sequence beyond 100. This is why the student comes up with answers that don't make sense when subtracting. Investigator: Jean (the student's teacher)

This theory would be tested by asking the student to count across several different decades and centuries to see if she used the correct sequence. The student would also be asked to compare numbers with the same digits but different place values (234 and 324, for example) to see if the student knows which is bigger.

Theory 2: The student isn't making meaning from the problems. Investigator: Greg (math coach)

Using a flexible interview (see page 36 in Chapter 3), Greg would present the student with a series of problems and ask the student to explain what the problem was about and what it was asking for as a solution. As part of this investigation, Greg would use several different types of subtraction problems—take-away, missing addend, and comparison—to see if the problem type was the issue.

continued

My Story continued

Theory 3: The student has a memory challenge. Investigator: Henry (learning specialist)

Henry agreed to do an informal memory inventory task with the student to see if there were any signs that the student might have difficulty retrieving information from long-term memory.

Greg and the principal, Judy, helped the group construct a time line for completing the investigations of these theories. The group also determined the date and time for a follow-up meeting (a week later) to discuss what the results suggested.

Using Collaborative Study Results for Intervention

After group members have completed their investigations, they come together for a follow-up meeting to discuss the results. The ultimate goal of the Collaborative Study process is to have an intervention plan in place to further support the student. In most cases this plan is for instructional changes to help the student make better sense of the math he is trying to understand. Sometimes, the plan is for further testing. Whenever it makes sense, a final meeting to assess the results of the intervention plan is scheduled. This final meeting can also be used to make amendments to the intervention plan if needed.

The goal of any intervention plan is for the student to make correct mathematical meaning of the problems he solves independently. The student should understand what he's doing and why he's doing it. The process of creating an intervention plan is similar to how it's done with student interviews (see Chapter 6, "Using Student Interview Results for Intervention," page 119).

Ease the Struggle

Using Collaborative Study with RTI

There are a variety of ways schools use the process of Collaborative Study. Many states have, for example, a pre-referral requirement for special education testing. Using the RTI approach to identifying children with special needs, educators are required to try in-class interventions to see how the student *responds to intervention*. The goal with the RTI process is to accommodate learning needs in the regular classroom whenever possible. Collaborative study works well as a protocol to develop an appropriate intervention for this purpose. ■

Examples of Interventions That Come from Collaborative Study

▶ developing new models

▶ explicitly teaching strategies for using models

▶ creating organizational supports (like graphic organizers)

▶ teaching the use of specific mathematical representations to help support memory

▶ changing the interaction of the teacher and/or paraprofessional with the student

▶ using think-alouds to help students express their reasoning

▶ adjusting the complexity of problems or numbers within problems

My Story

PART 5: The Follow-Up Meeting and an Intervention Plan for Amy ("The Student")

At the follow-up meeting the next week the team reported the results of the investigations of their theories (see "My Story, Part 4," page 82).

Theory 1: The student doesn't understand the counting sequence beyond 100. This is why the student comes up with answers that don't make sense when subtracting.

The student's teacher, Jean, told the group that she had asked the student to count from 68 on, from 95 on, and so on, crossing decades and centuries. Jean reported that the student was able to use the correct sequence but was not able to create a number line to properly represent numbers beyond 100. The student told Jean, "There was no number line after one hundred."

Theory 2: The student isn't making meaning from the problems.

Greg, the math coach, reported that he and the student had worked on a series of problems where subtraction might be used. The contexts involved money and collections of items common to the student (rubber ducks, for example, since the student had a collection of these). Greg found that

continued

My Story continued

the student had no trouble identifying "take-away" kinds of problems like subtraction, but the student did not really understand the connection between comparisons and subtraction. Greg observed that "the student was really stuck when asked a comparison problem. The student seemed to have no way to approach it."

Greg also asked the student to demonstrate solving a subtraction equation with blocks. After watching, Greg believed that the student only understood trading—not how trading is used to solve subtraction problems. He believed that the student was not making the connection between the model and a necessary strategy for solving subtraction problems.

Theory 3: The student has a memory challenge.

The learning specialist, Henry, reported that he had spoken to the student's parents before administering an informal memory assessment. He had received their consent and a request to keep them informed of the results. The student's responses to the memory assessment fell within normal ranges. Henry noticed that the student showed slightly weaker memory where number sequences were concerned, and the student also appeared more stressed (fidgeting and moving away from the table). Henry pointed out that stress can have a direct impact on memory.

After a discussion, the group decided that the student was having difficulty with both the idea of subtracting and with the model the student was using for it. The student had an understanding of the order (and perhaps the magnitude) of numbers but not a clear mental approach to organize this information. They decided to try getting the student to use an open number line model. This approach would have the dual effect of helping the student organize her current understanding of numbers and develop a new model for thinking about subtraction that might help her make more sense of comparison problems.

The group decided that Greg would work with both the student and with Jean to develop this new model. Ultimately, Jean would use it for both this particular student and with other students in the class who might be struggling to understand subtraction with regrouping.

Looking Ahead

Collaborative Study is a group-think process that supports teachers to develop theories for students who are struggling with math. The process asks teachers to gather data, share the data with colleagues, and make plans based on the group's best thinking. Collaborative Study is generally aimed at supporting Tier 1 and Tier 2 interventions; that is, interventions that can be carried out with the whole class or in small groups. Students who continue to have difficulty despite interventions suggested from Collaborative Study are candidates for a student interview (see Chapter 6). Student interviews are generally targeted at students who receive, or are candidates for receiving, Tier 3 individual interventions.

Collaborative Study is one more tool to help teachers *solve for why*. It allows teachers to work together to better understand student thinking—many minds are often better than just one!

Ease the Struggle

Collaborative Study Checklist

To help you get started immediately with Collaborative Study, in addition to this chapter see Reproducible 5.1, Collaborative Study: Template. ∎

Reflection Questions

1. What student study groups already exist at your school that might provide the basis for a Collaborative Study team? Who might need to be on that team who is not already? Which colleagues are particularly knowledgeable about math learning whose expertise might be helpful?

2. Think of a student in your class who might benefit from a Collaborative Study. What difficulty is he or she struggling with? How would you focus an investigation of that student? What would you want to know about his or her thinking?

3. What assessment resources are available to you for conducting an inquiry into a student's math understanding? What other resources might support your investigation?

Student Interviews

6

The Big Ideas

- A Student Interview is based on the belief that, through conversation and a student's demonstration of his thinking, we can begin to solve for why.

- Teachers report many positive benefits from the process of conducting and analyzing a Student Interview; these include greater insight into the process of preparing materials for an individual learner, refinement of questioning strategies, a greater propensity to listen to the student without preconceptions, appreciation for the variety of ways learners understand the same concept, and a clearer notion of how particular concepts develop in students' thinking.

- The five-step protocol for facilitating Student Interviews entails gathering student data, developing theories, collecting or creating problems to use, securing the logistics (consent, materials, and setting), and conducting the interview.

Chapter Outline

What Is a Student Interview?

Defined differently by various practitioners, a Student Interview is a structured dialogue, a flexible questioning approach, and a conversation with a purpose. A Student Interview is, perhaps, the most effective way for educators to understand a student's thinking. A Student Interview is based on the belief that, through conversation and a student's demonstration of his thinking, we can begin to solve for why.

One of the best-known resources on student interviews is Herb Ginsburg's book *Entering the Child's Mind* (1997). Ginsburg challenges the idea that standardized testing is the only "scientific" approach to understanding the thinking of children. He argues for deliberate nonstandardization of interviews (which he refers to as *clinical interviews*) in order to be flexible with questions and respond to each child's individual conjectures and conclusions.

Though standardized tests can be helpful in understanding children's thinking and proficiency, a Student Interview will almost always reveal much deeper insights on a student's understanding.

Student interviews share a common purpose with both CRAs and Collaborative Study. All three are aimed primarily at understanding student

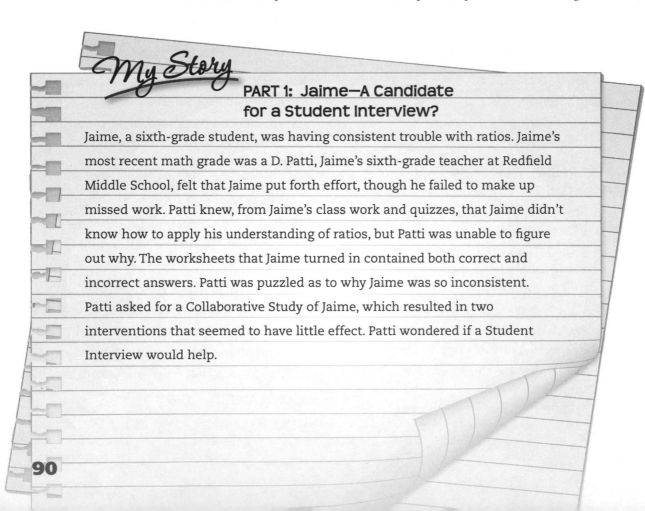

My Story

PART 1: Jaime—A Candidate for a Student Interview?

Jaime, a sixth-grade student, was having consistent trouble with ratios. Jaime's most recent math grade was a D. Patti, Jaime's sixth-grade teacher at Redfield Middle School, felt that Jaime put forth effort, though he failed to make up missed work. Patti knew, from Jaime's class work and quizzes, that Jaime didn't know how to apply his understanding of ratios, but Patti was unable to figure out why. The worksheets that Jaime turned in contained both correct and incorrect answers. Patti was puzzled as to why Jaime was so inconsistent.

Patti asked for a Collaborative Study of Jaime, which resulted in two interventions that seemed to have little effect. Patti wondered if a Student Interview would help.

Ease the Struggle

Quantitative Versus Qualitative Measures of Student Understanding

In the world of special education, assessments are standardized and normalized in an effort to give accurate and reliable results. These can be thought of as "quantitative measures" of student understanding. While there is a great deal of work being done to develop mathematical instruments for assessing understanding (Clarke, Baker, Smolkowski, and Chard 2008; Richardson 2003; Wright 1994; Wright, Martland, and Stafford 2006), few quantitative measures provide an in-depth picture of student thinking across the years of elementary and middle school.

An alternative to quantitative measures is a qualitative approach. Qualitative inquiry emphasizes probing student thinking through questioning, rather than analyzing scores on a test. The advantage to this approach is that the teacher-researcher can ask a student about his thinking as she watches him solve a problem, create a representation, or use a model. Having the ability to probe the student as he's thinking is a powerful tool in solving for why. ■

thinking (solving for why), rather than at trying to remediate first. Our goal with all these assessments is to create multiple theories for why a student might be struggling in order to find interventions that will work. Like CRAs and Collaborative Study, Student Interviews focus on using questioning to closely examine the students' mathematical reasoning and use of models, strategies, and algorithms to solve problems.

Student Interviews are also similar to the flexible interviews that often follow CRA assessments. The key differences are the levels of preparation and inquiry. Flexible interviews are based on a quick sorting of work from each of the three CRA stations and take five to ten minutes. Student Interviews require significant time to prepare and last much longer—often forty-five minutes to an hour.

Who Conducts a Student Interview?

Educators in three different roles most commonly conduct Student Interviews: learning specialists, math coaches, and classroom teachers. Learning specialists find Student Interviews a helpful tool for understanding student strengths and using these to set up Individual Education Plans (IEPs). For example, one learning specialist, Glenna, noted in a Student Interview with Candace, that she was very strong using place-value blocks but did not understand how to use a number line model. The Student Interview led Glenna to link the number line to place-value blocks to help Candace improve her understanding of magnitude (for more on this case, see page 91).

Student Interviews often reveal that the challenge a student is actually facing is conceptual, not cognitive. Special educators conducting Student Interviews have found that it's more likely, for example, that a student struggles because she misunderstands place value than because she has a memory deficit (for more on cognitive challenges, see Chapter 7).

Despite having the most contact with students, classroom teachers are *not* the most frequent users of Student Interviews. There are a number of reasons for this; the most common is that Student Interviews require a substantial amount of time: usually an hour to prepare, forty-five minutes to an hour to conduct, and an hour or more to analyze. Classroom teachers can find that the time required to prepare, conduct, and analyze a Student Interview is overwhelming. However, student interviews can be especially helpful in developing teachers' own understanding of how students think about math concepts. Teachers should be encouraged to conduct them whenever possible. A Student Interview may be one of the best professional development experiences a teacher can have at a personal level. Teachers report many positive benefits from the process of conducting and analyzing a Student Interview; these include greater insight into the process of preparing materials for an individual learner, refinement of questioning strategies, a greater propensity to listen to the student without preconceptions, appreciation for the variety of ways learners understand the same concept, and a clearer notion of how particular concepts develop in students' thinking.

> " Student interviews can be especially helpful in developing teachers' own understanding of how students think about math concepts. Teachers should be encouraged to conduct them whenever possible. A Student Interview may be one of the best professional development experiences a teacher can have at a personal level. "

Ease the Struggle

Math Reasoning Inventory (MRI) by Marilyn Burns

Math Reasoning Inventory (MRI) is a free, Web-based, formative assessment tool that focuses on students' numerical reasoning strategies and understandings; in other words, it is an online tool for conducting Student Interviews. This tool may help decrease the time typically required to set up Student Interviews. Visit www.mathreasoninginventory.com to learn more. ■

Five Steps to Conducting a Student Interview

A Student Interview requires extensive preparation. Since the format is more or less open-ended, we need to be prepared to engage the interviewee in a variety of contexts so we can probe his responses. To make the process as user-friendly as possible, I use a five-step protocol for facilitating Student Interviews. This protocol was created with the understanding that Student Interviews must be flexible and tailored to the individual needs of the interviewees. There are, however, steps that all interviews share. These steps include gathering student data, developing theories, collecting or creating problems to use, securing the logistics for the interview (consent, materials, and setting), and conducting the interview.

Five Steps to Implementing a Student Interview

▶ **Step 1:** Gather Data ("Case History")

▶ **Step 2:** Develop Preliminary Theories for Why the Student May Be Struggling

▶ **Step 3:** Collect and/or Create Problems and Questions to Use in the Student Interview

▶ **Step 4:** Secure the Interview Logistics

▶ **Step 5:** Conduct the Interview

Step 1: Gather Data ("Case History")

Sometimes a student's math thinking evades understanding. When a teacher has asked a student about his thinking, conferred with other professionals, and used assessment and diagnostic tools but hasn't been able to create an intervention that moves the student's understanding forward, a Student Interview can help.

Once you've identified the student, you'll need to gather data. This step is similar to step one for implementing Collaborative Study (see Chapter 5, page 75). When conducting a Collaborative Study we gather data on an individual student's math progress. These data include assessments, report cards, and conversations with teachers. If the student identified for an interview has been through collaborative discovery, this information will already be available. If not, it must be gathered.

My Story

PART 2: Gathering Data for Jaime's Student Interview

With Patti's (Jaime's teacher) suggestion, the Collaborative Study team decided it would be helpful to conduct a Student Interview. They asked Bob, the learning specialist on the Collaborative Study team, to do so. The team had already collected some data to conduct the Collaborative Study (for more on this assessment, see Chapter 5). These data were helpful to get started with preparation for the Student Interview. The data included the following information.

Jaime was on a 504 plan (other health impaired) as a result of difficulties with Crones disease. Per parental consent, information from the 504 plan was released to the Collaborative Study team; the team thus had insights into the way Jaime's health concerns negatively affected his learning. Symptoms related to the Crones disease had necessitated medical treatments that had caused irregular attendance.

Jaime lived with his older brother and both parents. Jaime's mother reported that there was a family history of learning disabilities. Jaime's older brother had received academic support through IEP services. Jaime's parents did not graduate from high school and reported difficulties during their school years.

Step 2: Develop Preliminary Theories for Why the Student May Be Struggling

Student Interviews that are entirely open-ended are interesting and informative. However, for practical considerations most schools require a focus on particular concepts and/or understanding. The development of theories helps focus a Student Interview. These theories also guide the interviewer in creating interview questions. Preliminary theories for a Student Interview should always carry a caution sign—if we are too enamored with these

Jaime was reported by his parents to be very active and enjoyed basketball, baseball, and swimming. Patti reported that he had a stable group of friends and presented himself as a young man who was confident with individuals and groups of any age.

Jaime had participated in state testing since the fourth grade. He consistently scored substantially below proficient on the math tests. This result was mostly supported by district test results except in the area of "skills." Jaime's district conducted formative math assessments twice each year. They reported the outcomes in categories that included "skills," "concepts," and "problem solving." While Jaime's scores were consistently below proficient in concepts and problem solving, several of his assessments showed him as proficient with skills.

During a flexible interview conducted for the Collaborative Study by Patti, Jaime subtracted whole numbers by counting backward. Jaime subvocalized, often speaking aloud to himself while he worked. Jaime skipped one of the problems Patti provided because, Jaime said, "It would take too long." Jaime did not attempt any problems involving fractions or ratios. He did use skip-counting and counting on. When conducting a quick review of math facts for Patti, Jaime demonstrated almost instant recall of all his times table facts up to 10 times 10.

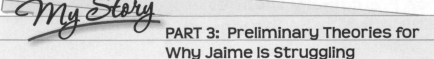

PART 3: Preliminary Theories for Why Jaime Is Struggling

Bob, the learning specialist, began his work on Jaime's Student Interview by reviewing the data and results from the Collaborative Study. He wanted to come up with initial theories for Jaime's Student Interview. Since Jaime was in the sixth grade, the Collaborative Study team decided it was important to focus on his understanding of proportional reasoning. The team felt that Jaime's access to higher math in high school would be dependent on his understanding of proportional reasoning; they wanted to begin intervention for this while he was still in middle school.

The Collaborative Study team recommended an intervention to improve Jaime's understanding of multiplication concepts. As Bob reviewed the results of that work, he noticed that Jaime had improved with facts, but his avoidance of problems with multiplication and with ratios made Bob wonder if Jaime really understood multiplicative relationships. Since this was a critical element for proportional reasoning, Bob developed his first theory:

Theory 1: Jaime doesn't understand multiplicative relationships and struggles to contrast them with additive relationships.

theories, we might miss what students tell us about their thinking. For this reason they should simply be considered a starting place. For detailed guidance on developing theories, see Chapter 3.

Step 3: Collect and/or Create Problems and Questions to Use in the Student Interview

One of the most important—and perhaps daunting—steps in preparing for a Student Interview is the collection of necessary problems that will drive the interview. The problems you choose need to test the preliminary theories you've developed (Step 2), focus on a particular mathematical concept (or concepts), and be complex enough to allow for a rich conversation with the interviewee. I usually plan on bringing at least ten problems to a Student Interview, though I may only use two or three of them.

Bob decided he would need to see if Jaime could detect the difference when comparing quantities additively and multiplicatively. Bob also wondered if Jaime's frequent absences might have created gaps in his understanding about multiplication and ratios. Bob created his second theory:

Theory 2: There are conceptual gaps in what Jaime knows about multiplication and ratios.

If this theory were true, Jaime might be hesitant or unsure when solving problems. Bob decided that he would explore this in the interview with some general questions about multiplication and ratios.

Finally, Bob wondered if Jaime might have a memory difficulty that was preventing him from putting together what he'd already learned. Nothing in the Collaborative Study had suggested that Jaime had memory challenges, but Bob made a note to be aware of signs that Jaime was having difficulty with memory:

Theory 3: Jaime has an as yet unidentified memory challenge that is making connecting new learning to old learning difficult.

The problems should connect to the student's real-life experiences—but be careful! If the problems are written down on paper and *look* like schoolwork (rather than a real-life situation) students may tend to approach them in the same disconnected way they sometimes work with other math problems (I've found that posing the problem as a verbal question before handing a copy of the problem to the interviewee can be helpful with grounding the problem in real-life experience).

The problems should also vary in complexity and contexts. In the "My Story, Part 4" example that follows, the money problems are

Ease the Struggle

Where to Find Problems for Interviews

One excellent source for both problems and protocols for interviews can be found at mathreasoninginventory.com. See Reproducible 6.1, Planning a Student Interview: Template and Reproducible 6.2, Conducting a Student Interview: Template for forms that support the collection and creation of problems for Student Interviews. ■

straightforward, though they could be answered from experience with money or use of multiplicative reasoning, or both. The *Orange Drink Problem* is a more complex approach to ratio and proportion. The interviewer won't necessarily use both these problems during the interview, but he has them ready so that his conversation with the student can go in a variety of directions.

I've found that problems for a Student Interview should range in difficulty from about two grades below the student's grade (a Student Interview for a fourth grader, for example, should include typical second-grade problems) to about one grade level above. The goal is flexibility in both contexts and difficulty. There are a number of websites that offer interesting math challenges for a variety of grade level, including The Math Forum at Drexel's Problems of the Week, AIMS Puzzle Corner, McRELS Math Mountain, NRich, and Aunty Math.

In addition to collecting problems, it's essential to prepare questions for the student as he explores the problems. I bring a list of questions with me during an interview. I print them out and keep them handy to remind me where to go when I get stuck.

The goal with all these questions is to try to make the student's thinking more explicit so you can get a better sense of what's actually going on in her mind. It's critical that we remember to listen with an open mind, rather than with our own ideas, so that we can hear and digest what the student is telling us. Preparation and practice with asking questions like these will lead to a more effective interview; the ability to be flexible comes from planning well before the interview begins.

Questions to Ask During a Student Interview

▶ What do you predict will happen?

▶ Do you see any patterns?

▶ Can you solve it a different way?

▶ What are you thinking?

▶ How did you figure it out?

▶ Why did you_____? [write that, draw that, etc.]

▶ You wrote _____. How did that help you?

▶ I noticed that you stopped what you were doing just now. What were you thinking?

▶ Why did you change your mind (answer)?

▶ I don't know what you mean by that. Will you show me?

▶ Will you draw a picture of that?

▶ Will you show me with _____? (cubes, blocks, a number line, etc.)

▶ You started with this (point) and then went to this (point). Tell me about your thinking.

▶ Can you tell me (show me) what _____ means?

▶ Are you right? How do you know?

▶ What do you notice?

▶ Is there another way to show me? What is it?

My Story

PART 4: Collecting Problems for Jaime's Interview

As we learned in "My Story, Part 3" (page 96), Bob (the learning specialist) developed three theories about Jaime's understanding:

1. Jaime doesn't understand multiplicative relationships and struggles to contrast them with additive relationships

2. There are conceptual gaps in what Jaime knows about multiplication and ratios.

3. Jaime has an as yet unidentified memory challenge that is making connecting new learning to old learning difficult.

Bob collected the following problems to explore these theories:

Comparing multiplicative and additive relationships:

Bus Problem

Mr. King's class has 10 students who walk to school and 10 students who ride the bus.

Ms. Queen's class has 8 students who walk to school and 16 who ride the bus.

Compare the classes. If all the buses broke down, which class would be affected more?

Investing Problem

Terry invested $20 in Smith-Pictures (a movie company). At the end of a year his investment paid him $40.

Alice invested $5 in Jones-Movies (another movie company). At the end of a year his investment paid $20.

Who made the better investment? Why?

continued

My Story continued

Caterpillar Problem

A monarch caterpillar was 4 cm long. A week later he was 8 cm long.

A gypsy moth caterpillar was 2 cm long. A week later he was 6 cm long.

Which caterpillar grew more?

Investigating gaps in understanding about

multiplication and ratios:

Money Problems

How many pennies would I get if I traded pennies for 9 dimes?

Every online movie costs $2.99. If I buy 6, how much do I spend?

Month Problem

If a month has 30 days, how many days are in 7 months?

Orange Drink Problem

I'm making orange drinks.

Glass 1 is full of water. I add 3 spoonfuls of orange mix to it.

Glass 2 is half full of water. I add 2 spoonfuls of orange mix to it.

Glass 3 is $\frac{1}{3}$ full of water. I add 1 spoonful of orange mix to it.

Which one has the strongest orange taste? (Is the most "orangy"?)

Field Trip Problem

Redfield School is going on a field trip. They will be taking mini-vans that can

hold 7 children and a driver. Sixty-one children are going on the field trip.

How many mini-vans will the school need?

Traveling Problem

Gina is taking a trip. She is taking 3 shirts to go with each pair of pants.

If she packs 4 pants, how many shirts is she bringing?

Pizza Problem

If you liked pizza, would you rather have 4 slices of a pizza that was cut into 6 pieces or 5 slices of a pizza that was cut into 8 pieces?

There are several things to notice about these problems. First, the problems are grounded in Jaime's reported experiences. Jaime's sister's name is Gina; Jaime attended the Redfield School. Jaime's teacher, Patti, had mentioned (in a pre-conference interview with Bob) that Jaime liked to download games and movies from iTunes. Jaime's class had just gone on a field trip to Boston with parent drivers. Bob's goal as the interviewer was to add as much meaning as he could to the problems so that Jaime would approach the problems as he did a problem in real life.

Step 4: Secure the Interview Logistics

The final step before actually conducting the Student Interview is to arrange the logistics—from requesting permissions (parental consent) to attaining the appropriate materials to establishing where the interview will take place. Let's look at each of these logistics, one by one.

Schedule the Interview

You'll need to arrange an hour of time to conduct the interview. You might not need all of this time, but you'll find it's disruptive if the student has to leave before you're finished. For this reason it's better to conduct the interview in one setting. The exception to this is when working with very young children (seven and under). For this age span, thirty minutes is usually the limit for productive work. When interviewing a younger student, you may have to set up two sessions so that the child is not overwhelmed and you get good information to work with.

It's a good idea for the classroom teacher to let the student know about the interview—and to meet the interviewer, if possible—before the interview begins. Teachers generally introduce me to students as someone who "wants to help you with math." The students seem to accept this readily. The idea is to minimize anxiety about the interview as much as possible.

I have conducted interviews at different times throughout the school day. I would recommend, though, that interviews be scheduled for mid-morning, when students seem to be at their most attentive. I strongly recommend that you *not* schedule interviews after school, or when the other students are at lunch or recess. While this is convenient (the student won't miss class) there can be a misunderstanding that the interview is a kind of punishment—something that should always be avoided. It's important to send the message that the interview is to help the student, not because he has failed in some way.

Request Consent for the Interview

Best practices from both the field of research and education suggest that parental consent should *always* be given before conducting a Student Interview. Even though a Student Interview is a less formal technique than standardized testing, it still represents research and testing. I've never had a parent refuse consent; usually parents are aware of their child's struggles and are relieved that the school is gathering more information to help them.

Parents should sign consent forms (see Reproducible 6.4) that acknowledge that their child will be involved in an interview for the purpose of better understanding his/her mathematical thinking. I think it's always wise to have a personal conversation with at least one of the parents—either in person or by phone—before having them sign the consent form.

Ease the Struggle

Parental Consent

See Reproducible 6.4 for a helpful form in getting parental consent. ■

Attain Appropriate Materials

There are two main categories of materials to prepare for Student Interviews: recording devices and math manipulatives.

Recording Devices   When I first began working with teachers to conduct Student Interviews, recording the interviews was optional. It didn't take long for us to realize that a recording of the interview was invaluable in recalling what was said (most of our insights come from listening to the recording; analyses that are not recorded almost never have the depth of those that are). In the digital age, an interviewer has a wide variety of recording equipment choices. In addition to the suggestions that follow, there are also extensive online discussions about recording equipment. (See the discussions at www.vermontfolklifecenter.org/archive/res_audioequip.htm and www.productiontranscripts.com/transcripts/tutorials/equipment-for-transcription.htm.)

   I recommend the use of a recorder that can easily upload interviews to a computer (make sure the recorder is compatible with your computer's operating system). The recorder does not need to be large, expensive, or complex—you only need to be able to hear clearly what the student is saying. Pocket recorders and iPods work well. You might also bypass a recorder altogether and simply use a computer; many computers have microphones and recording software built in. This will, of course, depend on the type of computer and the setting in which the interview will take place (laptops provide the most flexibility here).

Some interviewers prefer video recording; the advantage to this is that the recording will also capture a student's body language and expressions. Ideally, it's helpful to have a second person working the camera (in my experience I end up paying too much attention to the videoing logistics and hence my attention is detracted from the interview). There are many compact and easy-to-use video cameras on the market; attaining a tripod is recommended.

In the many Student Interviews I've done, having a second recorder on hand has saved me on a number of occasions (whether it be that the batteries died or the device got knocked over and stopped functioning—both of which have happened to me!). If you plan to use Student Interviews regularly, consider having a backup recording device.

Whatever device you use, be sure that you talk about it with the student before the interview begins. It can be intimidating to be expected to think when you have microphones and cameras pointing at you. Many teachers find it helpful to begin the interview by having students play with the recording equipment—giving students an opportunity to see how it works and record and play back their voice. Doing this can make the equipment seem less intrusive.

Math Manipulatives In addition to a recording device, make sure that math manipulatives of all kinds are readily accessible. It's important to think about the kinds of materials you *might* need and have them all on hand (be overprepared!). Consider all the materials that can be used as models for the math concept being explored, then plan accordingly. Here are some suggestions; however, any common materials that are used in your classroom should be made available for the interview. The idea is that students have whatever they need to demonstrate their thinking.

Suggested Manipulatives to Have on Hand for Student Interviews

- interlocking cubes
- base ten blocks
- tiles
- pattern blocks
- place-value chips
- money
- graph paper in various sizes (for primary children ¾-inch and ½-inch work well)
- colored pencils and markers
- rulers

Establish an Appropriate Setting

When I first started doing Student Interviews I was happy to interview students wherever a place could be found—from empty classrooms to offices to dining rooms. I quickly realized that the setting makes a significant difference, especially in student participation. The environment should be as familiar as possible and devoid of interruptions.

Anxiety is a concern for many struggling math learners. Care should be given to conduct the interview in a setting that will cause the student the least amount of anxiety. I have conducted a few interviews in the principal's office; while this environment is helpful for eliminating disruptions, some students find it stressful. Familiar environments, like the classroom or the school's resource room, tend to help students feel more at ease.

Whereas the familiarity of the setting is important, it's critical that the interview be devoid of interruptions. Many of my first Student Interviews were interrupted by other students wanting to talk with the teacher in the room, announcements over the intercom, and so forth. Interruptions disrupt a student's train of thought. When the interruption is over, the student has to backtrack to begin again. To prevent discontinuity and to support the student's best attempts at communicating her thinking, try to arrange for an environment that will be undisturbed for the duration of the interview.

Step 5: Conduct the Interview

Congratulations—if you've done Steps 1 through 4 you're now ready to conduct the interview! Student Interviews should begin by building trust with the student; hopefully you've begun to do this by selecting a familiar setting in which to conduct the interview. Being singled out, taken out of class, or brought to school at a special time can be scary for some children. I find that spending several minutes talking with the student about her interests, her school experience, and what we'll be doing helps put her at ease. Emphasize (repeatedly) that you're not very concerned with the correctness of the answers she gives, but are much more interested in her thinking. Tell the student that you want her to *think aloud*.

As you present the problems and listen to the student's reasoning, keep in mind the following list of things to look for. Know the question you'll start with and follow up with questions to improve clarity (recall the list of questions in this chapter, "Questions to Ask During a Student Interview," page 98). Reproducible 6.2 offers a template to help you conduct a successful interview.

Ease the Struggle

Your First Student Interview

Many teachers who conduct Student Interviews report that the first few are a bit chaotic. One teacher compared it to driving when you can only see about ten feet in front of your car. I feel this analogy conveys a good sense of the way student responses determine our questions. Most teachers report that having a clear focus is essential for a successful interview (it's easy to get pulled in several directions), but that flexibility is needed to adjust and adapt to the student's responses. ∎

What to Look for in a Student's Explanations During an Interview

▶ Do any responses or behaviors suggest the student might struggle with memory issues?

▶ What models (if any) does the student use to think with?

▶ What kind of logic does the student apply?

▶ In what way(s) do the student's explanations make sense?

▶ Do any responses or behaviors suggest that the student might struggle with language issues?

▶ Do any responses or behaviors suggest that the student might struggle with affective issues (anxiety and/or attention challenges)?

Ease the Struggle

Avoid the Jurassic Park Route

Conducting a Student Interview can be challenging; students often surprise us with the way they think about, and understand, concepts. I've found that one of the most difficult elements of doing a Student Interview is to suspend my own expectations (as much as possible) in order to focus on what the student is telling me. If I know what I am looking for, I will either find it or not. This does not give as much information as seeing what we might find. I like to think of an example from the movie *Jurassic Park* for giving a good analogy of how expectations can be limiting during a Student Interview.

In *Jurassic Park* visitors were given a tour of the hi-tech monitoring facility that kept track of the dinosaur population on the island. The programmer at the facility told the visitors, "There are sixty dinosaurs; the computer makes sure all sixty are accounted for at all times." A mathematician in the group of visitors asked the programmer to clarify, "What does the computer look for?" The programmer emphasized, "It looks for sixty dinosaurs." The mathematician thought for a moment, then suggested that the programmer ask the computer to count all the dinosaurs in the park. At first, the programmer resisted, believing that's what the computer has been doing all along. To accommodate the visitors, the programmer rephrased his query and, to his astonishment, found that there were many more than sixty dinosaurs.

The programmer was looking for sixty dinosaurs and always got that answer. The mathematician was interested in a more open-ended question. As a result, he got a more accurate (and interesting) answer. As we approach Student Interviews we must always be on the lookout for questions or problems that lead us to a foregone conclusion or assumption. We must try, as much as possible, to continually ask questions that allow the student to give us a clear window into her thinking. *Don't assume that what the student said is the same thing as what you heard. Check!* ∎

PART 5: A Student Interview with Jaime

Bob, the learning specialist, met Jaime in the math coach's office. The math coach, Beth, had set aside time so that we would not be disturbed. Because Bob didn't know Jaime well (the math coach did), and because Beth was interested in the Student Interview process, she stayed in the room during the interview. She asked Jaime if this would be OK and he agreed.

Bob started the interview by asking Jaime, "Why do you think we are meeting?" Jaime told Bob, "I'm not good at math and you're here to help me." Bob told him that, strictly speaking, he was only there to try to understand his thinking. Jaime's teachers would be the ones to help him. At that point (and several others during the interview) Bob made it clear that he wasn't focused on right answers; rather, he really wanted to know what was going on in Jaime's head while he was thinking about the answers.

For Jaime, the request to think out loud was easy. He was very articulate and he seemed to really like being able to share his thinking. He smiled often and watched Bob's face for clues about whether Bob had understood him. Several times he rephrased himself after checking Bob's expression.

Thinking aloud is not easy, or welcomed, for many of the students. It was a relief that Jaime was willing and able to tell Bob what he could about his reasoning. After probing Jaime's understanding of multiplication with some of the prepared problems, Bob decided to focus on Jaime's understanding of ratio and proportion. Bob asked Jaime to tell him about his thinking in solving the following Bus Problem:

Bus Problem

Mr. King's class has 10 students who walk to school and 10 students who ride the bus.

Ms. Queen's class has 8 students who walk to school and 16 who ride the bus.

Compare the classes. If all the buses broke down, which class would be affected more?

Jaime considered the problem for a moment and then pointed out that there were more kids who walk in Mr. King's class but more kids who take the bus in Ms. Queen's class. He also noticed that there were more kids in Ms. Queen's class. He paused for a minute and then wrote the equation in Figure 6.1.

$$
\begin{array}{lll}
\text{King} & 10w & 10b \\
\text{Queen} & 8w & 16b \\
\end{array}
$$

$$
\begin{array}{cc}
10 & 16 \\
-\,8 & -10 \\
\hline
2 & 6 \\
\end{array}
$$

Figure 6.1 Jaime took an additive approach in his first attempt at solving the bus problem.

Jaime pointed out that there were more students who took the bus in Ms. Queen's class, so her class would be more affected. When Bob asked him if the number of kids who took the bus was the only part of the problem that mattered, Jaime considered and said, "There might be some kids who were absent." Jaime had taken an additive, rather than proportional, approach (many middle school students apply additive approaches instead of multiplicative when solving proportional problems). Though Jaime had used an additive approach, Bob didn't assume that this was his preference. Bob considered that Jaime might just be using an additive approach in this context, or he may have interpreted this particular problem in an additive way. Bob kept this in mind while probing more deeply to understand Jaime's thinking and reasoning in relation to ratios and proportions. Bob's next question was about ratios.

Bob asked Jaime, "Can you show me the ratio of kids who walk to school to kids who ride the bus in each class?" Without any hesitation he wrote what you see in Figure 6.2.

continued

My Story continued

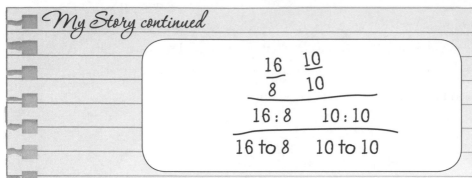

Figure 6.2   Jaime's work when asked to show the ratio of kids who walk to kids who take the bus.

Jaime's work showed that his teacher had worked with him on expressing ratios. Bob asked Jaime what his expressions meant. Jaime said, "They're ratios." He appeared to be confident that he had rendered the ratios properly as he had done it three different ways, almost automatically.

Bob asked Jaime, "What do the ratios mean?" Jaime pointed to one of the numbers and said, "This is how many bus riders are in Mr. King's class." He proceeded to do the same with all the other numbers. Bob was tempted, at this point, to conclude that Jaime knew what the ratios meant, but he pushed a little deeper by asking Jaime if the information about the ratios could be used to answer the question, "If all the buses broke down, which class would be affected more?"

Jaime smiled, nodded, and said, "Oh, I know what you want." He then wrote the equation in Figure 6.3.

$$\begin{array}{r} \overset{15}{\cancel{16}} : \overset{1}{8} \\ 10 : 10 \\ \hline 5 : 8 \end{array}$$

Figure 6.3   Jaime's second attempt at solving the bus problem.

Jaime's work was baffling. Bob asked, "Will you explain your thinking, Jaime?"

Jaime said, "I was comparing classes."

Still unclear about Jaime's thinking, Bob asked, "Will you explain your thinking out loud to me?" Jaime explained that he "didn't have enough" for the ratio on the right and so he had to borrow from the ratio on the left. This was one of those situations where the answer was quite odd; Bob was tempted to point out that you can't borrow with ratios! Instead, he chose to move on to another problem to see if he could gain more clarity about Jaime's thinking.

Bob chose to use the *Caterpillar Problem* to see if Jaime's approach would be similar.

Caterpillar Problem

A monarch caterpillar was 4 cm long. A week later he was 8 cm long.

A gypsy moth caterpillar was 2 cm long. A week later he was 6 cm long.

Which caterpillar grew more?

Bob chose *not* to ask Jaime to create a ratio but simply to compare the growth rates of the two caterpillars. Jaime told Bob, "This one is easier."

Bob asked, "Why is this one easier?"

Jaime replied, "Because they both grew the same amount. They both grew four centimeters."

To be sure he understood, Bob asked, "How do you know that?"

Jaime looked exasperated by patiently explained, "Four plus four equals eight and two plus four equals six. They each grow four. It's kind of a trick question!"

Bob probed, "Why a trick question?" Jaime answered, "Because they grew the same, but the question asks which grew more." Jaime's answer to the second question was providing evidence that Jaime was using additive reasoning. Finally, Bob asked, "Is there any other way to think about how these caterpillars grew?"

Jaime said, "What do you mean?"

Bob said, "Well, suppose they grew for two weeks instead of just one week. How big would each of them be?" By asking this question, Bob was probing to see if Jaime would change his mind and use a multiplicative approach to growth. Jaime replied, "The monarch would be twelve centimeters, because eight plus four equals twelve; and the gypsy moth would be ten centimeters, because six plus four equals ten. The monarch would still be bigger." Bob's questions added significantly to the conclusion that Jaime was using additive reasoning for proportional problems.

Sometimes you think you know how a student thinks, but a follow-up question paints a different picture. One second-grade student I interviewed, Lila, seemed capable of regrouping with addition. She had demonstrated her ability to "carry" from ones to tens and from tens to ones on three separate problems. I was about to conclude—without checking her use of models—that she understood this process when I asked her to solve the equation 17 + 17 + 17. She solved it this way:

$$
\begin{array}{r}
{}^{1} \\
17 \\
17 \\
+\,17 \\
\hline
42
\end{array}
$$

I had assumed that Lila knew why she "carried the one." Her solution gave me pause. I asked her to tell me about her solution and she replied, "I added the three sevens and I got twenty-one. I put down the two and carried the one. I added the four ones and put down the four."

Lila's answer suggested that she understood the *process* of adding, but not the underlying place-value concepts. When I asked her why she carried the one, she replied, "Because that's what you do when there's too much." By checking Lila's understanding with a follow-up question, I was able to get a clearer picture of her thinking. Her explanation showed me that she was not entirely clear what happened during regrouping.

Questions to Avoid During Student Interviews

These questions lead to teaching instead of the understanding of student thinking.

▶ What if you . . . ?

▶ You know that if you just . . .

▶ But you know that you're supposed to . . .

▶ And (what you've written) is just another way to say . . .

▶ Oh, I see what you did. You . . .

Resist the Temptation to Teach During a Student Interview

I have worked with close to two hundred teachers conducting Student Interviews with struggling students. Among the difficulties teachers have with the interview process, the one they report the most is resisting the temptation to teach students instead of understanding their thinking. Following is a list of typical "teaching" responses to students during interviews.

The temptation to make a misunderstanding clearer is second nature to us as teachers; we find ourselves teaching without even knowing we're doing it.

Karen's Interview: An Interview or a Teaching Moment?

Karen was working with her fourth-grade student, Theresa, to solve the following problem (involving functions):

The Restaurant Table Problem

A restaurant has square tables. Four people can sit at 1 table. Six people can sit at 2 tables. Eight people can sit at 3 tables. How many people can sit at 37 tables?

Theresa produced the table in Figure 6.4 after thinking about the problem for a moment or two.

Number of tables	Number of People
1	4
2	8
3	12

Figure 6.4 Theresa's chart to show her thinking about the *Restaurant Table Problem*.

Karen asked Theresa, "Will you tell me about your chart?"

Theresa responded, "Each table has four people, so you add four for every table: four, then four plus four equals eight, then eight plus four equals twelve. It's a pattern."

Karen queried further, "But what about the people in between each table?"

"What?" Theresa puzzled. Karen responded, "See, when you put two tables together you can't have people sitting in between them."

Theresa continued to seem confused and started to say, "I don't see what you . . ."

continued

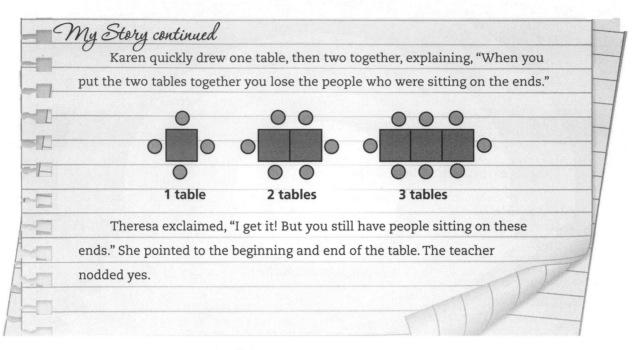

My Story continued

Karen quickly drew one table, then two together, explaining, "When you put the two tables together you lose the people who were sitting on the ends."

1 table **2 tables** **3 tables**

Theresa exclaimed, "I get it! But you still have people sitting on these ends." She pointed to the beginning and end of the table. The teacher nodded yes.

> 66 Remember, having theories before beginning a Student Interview is important. As we've learned, our preliminary theories tell us where our investigation might begin. However, once we've started the interview, we must remind ourselves that these theories are meant to inform, not to limit our inquiry. 99

Consider what transpired between Karen and Theresa in "My Story, Karen's Interview: An Interview or a Teaching Moment?" page 111. At what point does the interviewer, Karen, stop focusing on the student's thinking and proceed to insert her own expectations? Why does she do this? We can likely all relate; we want the student, Theresa, to see that the pattern she's created is wrong. We might feel that really, Theresa understands but has forgotten that part or tried to solve the problem too quickly. What happens between Karen and Theresa is an example of teaching rather than investigating during a Student Interview. The interview should remain focused on Theresa's thinking; teaching Theresa about the particular pattern, and/or noticing the elements of the problem, can come after the interview.

So what could the interviewer, Karen, have done differently? She could ask Theresa, "Will you draw a picture to go with your chart?" This gives Karen the opportunity to further explore the way Theresa is thinking about the problem. Perhaps Theresa planned to squeeze the extra people around what remained of the table. Perhaps Theresa didn't understand that the tables were contiguous. We don't know if any of these theories are correct unless we keep investigating and resist the temptation to teach. Now consider "My Story: Ginny's Interview: An Interview or a Teaching Moment?" Notice what happens. Could you see yourself doing this? As the interviewer, what could you do differently to investigate Ginny's thinking?

Remember, having theories before beginning a Student Interview is important. As we've learned, our preliminary theories tell us where our investigation might begin. However, once we've started the interview, we must remind ourselves that these theories are meant to inform, not to limit our inquiry. As interviewers it is our responsibility to put aside preconceived notions and listen fully to the student's explanation of her thinking.

Ginny's Interview: An Interview or a Teaching Moment?

During a Student Interview, Ginny, a seventh grader, seemed agitated and close to tears. She was trying to solve the equation $3\frac{1}{2} \div \frac{1}{4} = $ _____. She had written several equations and then erased them. "I can't remember," she said, "which one goes upside down."

"What do you mean?" asked Martha, the interviewer.

Ginny said, "You're supposed to flip one of them and then multiply but I can't remember which one . . . what's three and one-half flipped?"

Eventually Martha suggested restating the problem to try to make sense of it. Martha was trying to understand why fractions were so difficult for Ginny. One of her theories was that Ginny didn't understand the arithmetic operations with fractions. So far Ginny's responses were supporting that theory.

Seeing Ginny's frustration, Martha asked, "How many one-fourths are in one?"

"What?" Ginny responded.

Martha asked the same question differently, "How many quarters are in a dollar?"

Ginny replied, "Four."

"So," Martha continued, "how many one-fourths are in one whole?"

"Oh," said Ginny. "I know what you mean now. There's four one-fourths in one."

"So . . . ?" said Martha. "How many one-fourths in three and one-half?"

"I'm still not sure," said Ginny.

"How many quarters are in two?" asked Martha.

"There are eight quarters in two . . . and twelve quarters in three and two more for the half. Now I get it," said Ginny.

Three Steps to Analyzing the Results of a Student Interview

▶ **Step 1:** Listen to the recording and take notes. What patterns seem to emerge from the interview?

▶ **Step 2:** Create theories based on your notes.

▶ **Step 3:** Listen a second time to see if the theories still seem plausible; refine them as needed.

Analyzing the Results of the Student Interview

Once a Student Interview is complete and has been recorded, it's time to analyze the results. Listen to the recording; what patterns emerge from the interview? Create theories based on your observations. Listen to the recording again and revisit your theories—do they still feel plausible? Let's take a closer look at each of these steps. Reproducible 6.3 offers a template for analyzing the results of your interview.

Step 1: Listen to the Recording and Take Notes. What Patterns Seem to Emerge from the Interview?

While there are detailed ways to create notes from an interview (especially in formal qualitative research), the teachers I've worked with have found that simplicity is perhaps the best. To start, listen to the recording of the interview and take notes on the student's responses. Be sure to have copies of the student's written work in front of you while you do this. Look for patterns in the responses. Use the following three questions to guide your observations.

Three Questions to Ask Yourself as You Listen to the Student Interview Recording

▶ Does the student consistently avoid certain kinds of problems or techniques (like regrouping)?

▶ Does the student use a particular strategy (like counting on) on a wide variety of problems?

▶ Are the student's responses similar to your expectations based on a review of the student's math history? If there are differences, how are these evident in the student's responses?

Step 2: Create Theories Based on Your Notes

In step two we apply our knowledge of both math learning and child development to create theories that might give us a plan for intervention (these theories should of course be more refined than the preliminary theories we created to help structure our Student Interview). Theories can be created using the three frames: Learner, Math Content, and Instruction (see Chapter 2 for more about these three frames).

As we review data from the interview we can use the *Learner Frame* to consider theories that concern the learner's development: Is there any evidence of cognitive challenges? For example, was the student especially anxious when a problem was difficult, or did the student seem to be often distracted? Did we notice any issues with memory? Is the learner demonstrating that she has some kind of model to work from?

The *Math Content Frame* can be used with interview data to help develop theories about gaps in math—"missed" concepts: Did we notice consistent difficulty with place value, or with regrouping? Was the student applying additive reasoning (as in Jaime's case) when multiplicative reasoning was called for?

We can use the *Instruction Frame* to explore theories about inadequate development of models to think with; undeveloped computational or problem-solving strategies, or inaccurately applied algorithms fall into the Instruction Frame.

Sometimes it's difficult to tell whether a student's response is cognitive or mathematical. The three frames are a valuable tool for interpreting Student Interviews and for creating theories to help understand the struggling learner. For an in-depth look at developing theories, see Chapter 3, "Developing Theories for Why a Learner May Be Struggling."

Step 3: Listen a Second Time to See If the Theories Still Seem Plausible; Refine Them as Needed

This step originally was not part of the process; in my work with teachers I found that most listen to the recording just once. Teachers are always strapped for time and listening to a long interview twice is often unworkable. However, there are benefits from a second listen, most notably that it helps identify evidence to support or refine a developing theory.

My Story

The Importance of Listening to a Student Interview Twice

I once conducted a Student Interview with a learner, Al, who was deaf. We communicated through an interpreter who signed my questions and verbalized the student's responses. As I listened to the recording of our interview, I noted that Al had difficulty with problems involving money (this was an emerging theory that I came up with after I listened to the interview recording the first time). I noted that he took long pauses before answering questions that involved buying and selling, and he frequently asked me if he was supposed to add, subtract, multiply, or divide in these problems.

When I listened to the recording a second time, I noticed that Al had similar issues whenever subtraction was involved in solving a problem that wasn't money related. The fact that he asked about operations in the money problems may have been coincidence, because he was just as confused in other places; he just didn't phrase his confusion the same way. I believe I would have missed this if I hadn't listened to the recording a second time.

I also like to re-listen to interviews to look for evidence of cognitive challenges. During the first listen I don't always catch hints that a student's memory isn't working well or that she is showing signs of stress. While I try to pay attention to these issues during the interview itself (it's hard to notice attention issues unless you've videoed the interview), a second close listen helps me to be sure I've gotten all the information I can from the conversation.

PART 6: Analyzing the Results of Jaime's Interview

When Bob listened to the recording of Jaime's interview, he found out more about the logic Jaime was using to make the comparison. Listening to the conversation again, and even a third time, Bob noticed a pattern in Jaime's reasoning. Whenever Jaime was asked to compare quantities, he subtracted. This confirmed for Bob that Jaime was thinking of comparisons additively, rather than multiplicatively. It seemed to Bob that, for Jaime, comparisons were always a matter of subtracting the smaller quantity from the larger. He had applied this thinking to the *Bus Problem* (see "My Story, Part 5," page 106) while including some of what he had learned in class about ratios: how to write them. He wrote the ratios as if they were whole numbers and then went to work with subtraction.

$$\begin{array}{r} \overset{15}{\cancel{16}}\,\overset{1}{:}\,8 \\ 10:10 \\ \hline 5:8 \end{array}$$

Jaime's second attempt at solving the bus problem.

Bob's theory was that Jaime had a clear idea about comparing quantities additively, but he was muddled about how to do that multiplicatively. He seemed to know how to write ratios, but not what they represented. As a result, he wrote the ratios and then applied his subtracting strategy in his own way, using the colon as a marker for place value.

Jaime obviously had some serious confusion about ratios (and possibly place value) but he hadn't responded randomly. He was using a

continued

My Story continued

kind of personal logic that needed to be considered if he was going to progress from where he was to a clearer understanding of proportion. To ignore Jaime's thinking would be to lose the chance to build on his own thinking to a clearer understanding.

Bob's analysis of Jaime's interview led to a refinement of his earlier theories:

Theory 1: Jaime did not understand what ratios are and so was unable to use them for comparisons.

This was a theory that came from considering the Math Content Frame. Bob knew that Jaime would not be able to move forward with proportional reasoning until he had "filled the gap" around ratios.

Theory 2: Jaime has not developed the ability to think multiplicatively—and this is why he doesn't recognize these relationships in ratios.

Bob considered this theory, and the intervention that would follow, from the Instruction Frame. Bob believed that Jaime had not fully developed models that allowed him to understand the ways in which multiplicative reasoning was different from additive reasoning. Creating instructional opportunities for this could help to address the gap that was identified in the first theory.

Through the use of the Student Interview Bob had gained valuable information about Jaime's thinking that could lead directly to an intervention.

Using Student Interview Results for Intervention

The theories developed from listening to the interview recording and ana-lyzing the results lead to interventions aimed at supporting the student. The process of creating and implementing interventions based on theories from Student Interviews—like all teaching—is more art than science. Empirical studies that connect specific student difficulties with associated remedia-tion are few, though growing (see Gersten, National Center for Education Evaluation and Regional Assistance, and What Works Clearinghouse 2009). For now, we must rely on expertise from the field, existing remediation work, and conclusions that come from the Student Interviews themselves. The process is similar to how it's done with Collaborative Study (see Chap-ter 5, "Using Collaborative Discovery Results for Intervention," page 84). Focus on the central idea in the theories, then look for models, strategies, or algorithms that will support the learner (if the theories are correct). These three concepts are also addressed in Chapter 2, "Frame 3: The Instruction," page 19).

> "The process of creating and implementing interventions based on theories from Student Interviews—like all teaching—is more art than science."

Interventions That Focus on Models

By far the most common interventions revolve around connecting students to more personally meaningful models. Struggles seem to occur when stu-dents have learned a formula or procedure without understanding the mathematics that underlies it. Models help students make connections from their own knowledge to new mathematical ideas. They give students "something to think with" (see Chapter 2, "The Use of Models in Instruc-tion (Stage 1)," page 19).

After Jaime's interview, Bob's theory was that he did not understand the multiplicative relationships in ratios. Bob believed that Jaime had learned something about the formulas and facts for multiplication, but he did not have a strong model to connect them to the multiplicative relation-ships in ratios.

Bob suggested that Jaime's teacher, Patti, use ratios from the context of everyday life to give him a model to refer to and use when thinking about ratios; a more familiar context might help him make similar real-world con-nections to ratios when he was solving problems. Bob suggested that Patti ask Jaime to articulate both the additive and multiplicative differences in the real-world examples to be able to distinguish the difference. By doing so, Bob hoped that Jaime would be able to articulate multiplicative relation-ships need to work with proportions.

Patti was able to use a ratio that had meaning to Jaime (hot lunch: bag lunch) to create a model he could generalize to other, similar situations.

Patti aided his generalization by helping make explicit connections with comments like, "How is this (new) situation like matching hot lunches and bag lunches?" and, "What is the adding difference between hot lunches and bag lunches? What is the multiplying difference between hot lunches and bag lunches?"

Applying a model in a variety of new situations helps students create strategies they can use consistently. The model, in Jaime's case, was the lunch list. He was able to use the strategy of multiplicatively matching one group to another in other situations (see "My Story, Part 7").

My Story

PART 7: Jaime's Intervention Plan Focused on the Use of Models

Jaime's teacher, Patti, and Bob decided, based on the theories they'd created (see "My Story, Part 6," page 117), to spend some time with Jaime on ratios in meaningful contexts. They gave Jaime almost daily opportunities to create ratios and use them for comparison. This was similar to the instruction he'd been given previously, except that the context for these problems was always familiar to him and he was asked to articulate differences between the additive approach he had been using and the multiplicative approach that was required for ratios. The classroom paraprofessional also spent time with Jaime, asking him, "What does that ratio mean? What is the difference if you add? What is the difference if you multiply?" Patti worked with the paraprofessional to help her curb her natural instinct to explain each ratio to Jaime, as this would not allow him to make the connections he needed.

For example, Jaime was put in charge of the lunch list for his grade level (three sixth-grade classes). Patti would ask him, "How many kids are getting lunch today? How many kids are not getting lunch? How would you compare them?" Jaime was consistent in using a subtraction approach to tell Patti how many more students were getting lunch. His answers seemed to confirm that we were on the right track about his additive approach to comparisons.

Interventions That Focus on Strategies

Strategies come from the application of models. As learned in Chapter 2 (see "The Use of Strategies in Instruction (Stage 2)," page 21), a strategy is more complex than a model; a strategy uses models in a specific context to solve a problem. Problem-solving strategies are familiar to most math teachers: *Make the problem simpler, work backward, draw a picture*, and so on. When strategies are well-connected to context and make meaningful use of models, they help students develop a repertoire of generalizable approaches to mathematical problems. When a Student Interview reveals that a student has a workable model, but is unable to apply it to new situations, a focus on strategies may be called for.

To help Jaime progress to articulating multiplicative relationships, Patti manipulated the daily numbers in the list so that they were exact multiples. Early on in the process, she posed the problem, "Jaime, what if there were forty kids getting lunch and only twenty who didn't?"

Jaime responded, "There are twenty more kids getting lunch."

Patti asked, "How many times more is forty than twenty?" This question was confusing to Jaime, so Patti tried a different approach. "How many students getting lunch would match up with students not getting lunch?"

Jaime answered, "You mean if they sat together? There'd be two hot lunch kids with every bag lunch kid."

Patti asked, "How do you know?"

"Because," Jaime said, "there are twice as many hot lunch kids as bag lunch kids."

Patti reported this statement as a breakthrough *for her*. She said she began to think that Jaime actually did know about reasoning multiplicatively, but that he just hadn't made the connection to ratios. For the remainder of her remediation work on ratios with Jaime, she and the paraprofessional with whom Jaime worked continued to ask him what each ratio meant. They asked him to compare the groups by adding and then by multiplying. Patti also used the lunchroom problem as a model for other ratio problems by referring Jaime to it when he got stuck: "Which part is like the hot lunch group and which part is like the bag lunch group? How can you compare the groups by matching?"

My Story

Candace's Intervention Plan
Focused on the Use of Strategies

I worked with a fourth-grade student, Candace, in a small, rural school. Candace used place-value blocks well. Candace was able to accurately represent numbers up to 1,000, and to regroup (though inconsistently) for addition and subtraction. The place-value blocks model had meaning to her, though she was not always able to use it in problem-solving situations. She also was perplexed by the number line. In my experience children generally understand the number line immediately. Her inability to work with the number line made us concerned about her sense of magnitude because she was unable to accurately order numbers on the number line.

The learning specialist, the classroom teacher, and I all worked with Candace. Our work involved helping her develop a strategy to connect her knowledge of the place-value blocks with the number line. We did this by having her represent numbers on the number line with place-value blocks (see Figure 6.5).

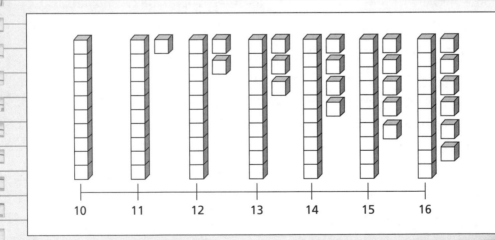

Figure 6.5 Candace connected her knowledge of place-value blocks with the number line.

Candace used this strategy to effectively negotiate values on the number line and connect the order and magnitude with her knowledge of place-value blocks.

We also had Candace use a number line that she could walk on to develop a strategy for moving along the number line and to connect these movements to addition and subtraction. We focused on having her find a "starting place" (the first number in the equation) and then move based on the operation. With this approach she was also learning "counting-on" and "counting-back" strategies. She learned that addition—at this point in her learning—meant she was walking from lower numbers to higher numbers and that subtraction meant she was moving from higher numbers toward lower numbers. While these understandings can present difficulties down the road (for example, when adding negative numbers), we chose to focus on the simplest explanation

at this point. We showed her simple equations like 16 – 4 and asked her four questions:

1. Where will you start?
2. How many steps will you take?
3. In which direction will you move?
4. Where will you end up?

These questions helped Candace build a strategy for adding and subtracting using the number line model. They also helped Candace develop deeper ideas about magnitude of numbers; she noticed their position on the number line.

Interventions That Focus on Algorithms

As learned in Chapter 2 (see "The Use of Algorithms in Instruction," page 22), algorithms are the shortcuts—the procedures—we use to do something efficiently over and over. Rarely will the result of a Student Interview suggest that a student's difficulty is that she is not using an algorithm properly.

My Story

Angela's Intervention Plan
Focused on the Use of Algorithms

Occasionally when a student first learns the standard algorithm for multiplication (after having developed strong models and strategies for applying them) her knowledge will "leak" into her work in addition.

For example:

$$\overset{1\ 1^1}{368}$$
$$+\ \ \ 25$$
$$\overline{923}$$
$$\underline{390}$$
$$4823$$

In this case Angela used the order of steps from the multiplication algorithm to approach addition, even when she has been successful with addition previously. This particular example came from Angela's thinking aloud as she solved the problem. Angela said that she added the 8 and 5 and got 13. She carried the 1. (So far, so good.) Next she added the 6 and 5 to make 11 and then added in the 1 (as she would have done if she were multiplying). Finally, she added 5 and 3 and added in the 1 she carried. This gave her 923.

This is because difficulties with algorithms are usually noticed early in the solving-for-why process and are (generally) easily remediated. The general strategy for focusing on algorithms is to ask students questions about the reasonableness of their solutions and/or ask them to solve using a different strategy than the algorithm. Confusing the addition and multiplication algorithm provides a good example.

Angela's teacher knew that Angela understood place value and had good models for multiplication. Following the Student Interview, the teacher created a plan to help Angela focus on the reasonableness of her solution. The teacher resisted the temptation to simply tell Angela what to do. He was convinced that, if Angela understood the error herself, she would not continue making it.

Angela's teacher gave her the same problem he had given her during the interview. He asked her to estimate her solution before solving. Angela estimated that it would be about 400. When her teacher asked her, "How do you know this?" She replied that 375 and 25 was 400, and the problem was close. Next the teacher asked her to solve with the algorithm. She repeated her solution and looked satisfied. The teacher asked, "Is your answer close to your estimate?" At first Angela responded, "Yes!" The teacher paused to let Angela reconsider her initial reaction. Angela thought about it; then the light dawned. Angela corrected herself, saying, "No, wait . . . that's four *thousand*, it should be four *hundred*."

The teacher had Angela show him how to solve the problem using a number line strategy. When Angela was convinced that her algorithm was incorrect (she had convinced herself—this is very important!) she was able to work on correcting her misconception.

Looking Ahead

Though Student Interviews can take more time than other assessments, they are one of the most effective tools currently available to inquire deeply into students' conceptual understanding of mathematics. The result of these interviews, like Collaborative Study (see Chapter 5), is an intervention plan based on the theories that emerge. In the next section, we look at accommodating some of the particular cognitive challenges that learners face. We examine ways to support learners with memory difficulties, attention challenges, and math anxiety.

Reflection Questions

1. What makes Student Interviews different from standardized testing? How are the results from these two kinds of assessments different?

2. Think of a student you teach whose thinking is difficult to understand. If you were to interview him or her, what mathematical area would you focus on? What questions might you want to ask?

3. What aspects of the Student Interview process seem most interesting to you? What might you be able to learn from it? What seems daunting about the process?

4. When does questioning go from "probing thinking" to "teaching through questioning?" How do you know when you've crossed from inquiry to instruction?

5. What about Jaime's story is familiar to you? Can you recognize yourself or one of your students in the way it unfolds? How is Jaime's story like or unlike your experiences?

Part Three

Supporting Students Who Struggle

Supporting Learners Who Struggle with Memory Challenges, Attention Deficit Disorder, and Affective Difficulties (Math Anxiety)

The Big Ideas

- Memory challenges, attention deficit disorder, and affective difficulties (specifically, math anxiety), are the most common cognitive struggles that affect math learning and can often be addressed with common instructional approaches.

- One of the main ways to support students with cognitive challenges is to make sure the information they are learning is connected to something they already know or find useful.

Chapter Outline

What Is a Cognitive Challenge?

Cognitive challenges, as described here, are neurologically based differences that can make learning mathematics more difficult. Students in this group are those who struggle with math disability (Fuchs, Fuchs, and Prentice 2004), memory issues, attention deficits, sequential and spatial organization difficulties (Levine 2002), and physical challenges (like blindness). These students require specialized instruction matched to their particular learning needs.

A thorough examination of the myriad ways cognitive differences might affect mathematics understanding is well beyond the scope of this resource. This chapter focuses on the most common struggles that affect math learning and can often be addressed with common instructional approaches. In the English-speaking world, reading challenges are the most common disability. While some research (see Fuchs and Fuchs 2002) indicates that a reading difficulty can negatively affect mathematics learning, in general a child must have difficulties in both areas at the same time for such an impact to be significant. The following pages take a closer look at each of these struggles and the instructional strategies that can be implemented to support them.

Memory Challenges

The study of memory is an area of psychology that is constantly evolving. There are several models for the way memory works (see Cowen 2008; Levine 2002). For the purpose of supporting learners of mathematics, we address memory challenges through three interrelated components: short-term memory, working memory, and long-term memory.

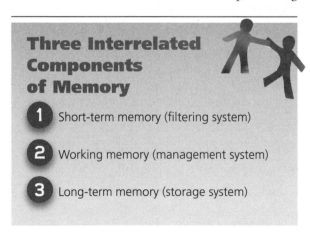

Three Interrelated Components of Memory

1. Short-term memory (filtering system)

2. Working memory (management system)

3. Long-term memory (storage system)

Creating interventions for students with memory challenges depends on knowing which kind of memory is adversely affected. Short-term memory is a kind of filter system that decides which of the thousands of bits of information coming into a person's mind every second gets attention. Working memory is a kind of management system, organizing information that helps a person focus attention on immediate needs and retrieve resources from long-term memory. Long-term memory is a kind of storage system, filing away images, facts, models, strategies, and algorithms for potential later use.

Supporting Students with
Short-Term Memory Challenges

Some psychologists believe that information exists in short-term memory for about thirty seconds. Then it moves into working memory, is stored in long-term memory, or is forgotten. To move incoming data into working or long-term memory, the information needs to be connected to something you already know or find useful. A good example of this is when you meet someone for the first time, briefly. You learn the person's name, but unless you make some kind of connection between the person and your own knowledge, you will likely quickly forget it. (For example, if you briefly met someone named George who looks like your favorite celebrity, George Clooney, you're more likely to remember the person's name.)

When a student has difficulty with short-term memory it generally manifests as the inability to identify the most important information in a problem or equation and move it into working memory. Perhaps the most common indication of this struggle is when a student raises his hand after immediately reading a problem and exclaims, "I don't know what to do!" (Of course, this is not the only possible explanation. Learned helplessness is another, more common cause.)

To support students with short-term memory challenges it's necessary to help them improve their ability to identify and quickly chunk or connect important information.

Focus on the Key Question in a Problem

The simplest thing we can do to support students with short-term memory challenges (and all students for that matter) is to take time to focus students on the key question in each problem. Always begin a problem by querying, "What is this problem asking us to figure out?" Once a student has determined this, encourage him to quietly repeat the important ideas and write them down. These actions help students move the information into working memory. Consider the following bus problem:

> **Bus Problem**
> *Thirty-four children are going on the field trip from grade 4. If mini-vans can hold 6 students each, how many mini-vans do we need?*

First ask the student, "What is this problem asking us to figure out?" There are several numbers in this problem so it may take a moment for the student to work out that we want to know the number of mini-vans needed. Once the student has determined this, ask him to quietly repeat "How many mini-vans?" several times, then have him write it down on his paper. In this way the student transfers the important information from his short-term memory into working memory. This technique is sometimes called *rehearsal.*

> "To move incoming data into working or long-term memory, the information needs to be connected to something you already know or find useful."

Chunk Information

Chunking is another technique that can be used to help students' short-term memory. Chunking is the process of connecting incoming information by relating it to prior knowledge. If I were to ask you to memorize the sequence *1821314123*, you would likely have difficulty doing so through strict rote memorization. On the other hand, if you broke the sequence into numbers and connected each to something you already knew, you are more likely to remember the entire sequence. I did so by "chunking" the sequence into the following related bits of information:

> *18—age that someone graduates high school*
>
> *21— drinking age*
>
> *314—pi*
>
> *123—counting*

By "chunking the information" together, I only have four things to remember instead of ten. To remember the sequence I think: *high school, drinking age, pi, counting.*

We can encourage chunking by asking students questions like the following:

Questions to Encourage "Chunking" When Solving Problems

▶ "How is this problem like other problems you've done?"

▶ "What seems familiar in this problem?"

▶ "What do you notice?"

Supporting Students with Working Memory Challenges

Working memory is the manager of information. As new information arrives, our minds have to do something with it—in the context of mathematics this usually means using the information to solve a problem, add to the understanding of an existing concept, or store in long term-memory for future retrieval.

Students who struggle with working memory challenges often get lost in the middle of a problem. They don't have enough "brain space" to handle all the elements they need to be successful. As a result, they get stuck. When a person is stressed, her working memory is especially vulnerable. The experience of giving an important presentation and feeling as if your mind has gone blank is a common example. Similarly, when stress is part of problem solving, the mental resources we need to complete the task at hand diminish. Some students struggle with this type of challenge all the time—what can we do?

Move Some of the Mental Resources out of Working Memory

Moving some of the mental resources out of working memory can be very helpful for students with working memory challenges. To do this, encourage students to write down the problem's key information on paper, rather than keep it in their heads. Let's revisit the *Bus Problem* introduced in the short-term memory section:

Bus Problem
Thirty-four children are going on the field trip from grade 4. If mini-vans can hold 6 students each, how many mini-vans do we need?

A student immediately might see that division is needed to solve this problem; if this is the case her dependence on working memory resources is minimal. Most students, however, will approach the problem by drawing something to represent buses and something to represent children (in fact, children will likely do this until they are guided toward the more efficient strategy of using symbolic notation) (see Figure 7.1). A child with working memory challenges might get lost in the process of drawing a picture like this and forget what she was drawing, or how many groups she needed.

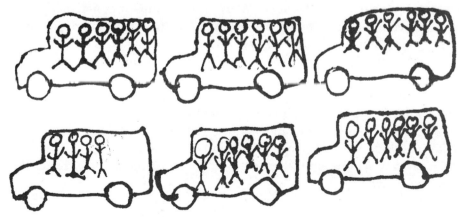

Figure 7.1 A child's drawing to represent the bus problem.

> **"**The experience of giving an important presentation and feeling as if your mind has gone blank is a common example. Similarly, when stress is part of problem solving, the mental resources we need to complete the task at hand diminish.**"**

34 students: 6 in each bus.
How many buses?

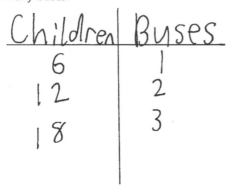

Figure 7.2 A child's notes and table to represent the bus problem.

To help students with working memory challenges, we try to get as much information as we can onto paper. The idea is to store as much relevant information as possible outside the mind, so that the working memory doesn't have to juggle quite as much information. Storing information on paper can be done in many ways—through pictures, organized lists, notes, or a mathematical representation (like a table) and some notes (see Figure 7.2).

A child needs far less working memory if she can find a way to move some of the information out of working memory and onto paper. Teachers should provide explicit directions when students are first learning to use representations to help store information. When a student is thinking aloud I often remind him to "put that down so you'll remember." Over time, students learn to use representations (drawings, lists, tables, graphs, notes) on their own.

Supporting Students with Long-Term Memory Challenges

Long-term memory is the storage system of the brain. When we need information, our working memory retrieves it from our long-term memory if possible. For example, if a student encounters an addition equation that needs to be solved, his working memory will retrieve the algorithm from his long-term memory. According to some psychologists (most notably, Vygotsky; see Vygotsky and Kozulin 1987), information is stored in long-term memory in two different ways: (1) isolated from other knowledge and (2) connected to other knowledge. I find it helpful to use the metaphor of a garden in thinking about these ways (see the Ease the Struggle feature).

When we think of memory challenges, we generally think of students who have difficulty retrieving information from long-term memory. These are the students who don't remember their math facts, even though they've written down the facts over and over. There are a number of general strategies that can support math students who struggle with long-term memory challenges; the following pages focus on two main strategies: (1) building stronger connections and (2) moving some of the mental resources out of long-term memory.

Ease the Struggle

Thinking of Long-Term Memory as a Garden

Think of long-term memory as a vegetable garden—the vegetables represent all the information planted there (math facts, algorithms, formulas, and more). Think of the gardener, on the other hand, as working memory. When information is required to solve a problem, the gardener (working memory) goes to her garden (long-term memory) and pulls a vegetable (the information) for examination and replacement.

There are two types of information "planted" in the garden: information isolated or disconnected from other knowledge and information connected to other knowledge. The isolated information grows by itself; I like to think of this information as carrots in the garden. A single carrot grows from a single seed and, while carrots can grow near each other, they are separate from one another. Carrots in this garden analogy are information learned solely by repetition—for example, learning math facts through flash cards. Some psychologists refer to concepts learned this way as "pseudo-concepts" (Confrey 1995; Vinner 1997). It is important that this information be repeatedly retrieved (practiced) or it will be forgotten.

We all have the experience of what happens when we learn something through rote memorization and then don't practice it. When we learn a foreign language in school without context (simply memorizing vocabulary words through repetition), we are planting a carrot—an isolated bit of information—in our long-term memory. When we stop using those words, we often quickly forget them. In a sense the working memory "forgets" where this information is located—where this "carrot" is growing.

The other type of information that we plant in our garden is information that is connected to prior knowledge. This type of information can be represented by potatoes in the garden. Potatoes are planted from a piece of a potato, which then grows to give rise to several potatoes that are connected. If you could view potatoes growing underground you would see a network of spuds all connected by white rhizomes, one potato growing from another. This is a helpful analogy for the development of concepts: They grow from previous concepts and are connected to one another.

When information is connected, we don't need to remember every piece of it because we know we can work our way through the connections in our memory. When, for example, I ask graduate students, "What is a standard deviation?" They draw pictures in the air of bell curves and share descriptions like "distance from the mean." They haven't memorized a definition; rather they are using concepts that are connected to standard deviation to help describe it.

It's easier to retrieve concepts that are planted as potatoes (connected) than concepts that are planted as carrots (isolated). This is why helping students make connections between prior knowledge and new learning is so important. ∎

Build Stronger Connections

Perhaps the best way to support students who have long-term memory challenges is to make sure that important information they learn is *always* connected to other key concepts. When students compare concepts, sort or organize ideas, or reflect on new thinking, they are making strong connections that will allow them to retrieve new information from long-term memory. We can help students build connections when they follow the models-strategies-algorithms sequence. We can get a sense of this by looking at the connections students develop when they learn to subtract.

> "We can help students build connections when they follow the models-strategies-algorithms sequence."

First we can help students create a mental model for the numbers they use when they subtract. For this illustration, consider the use of base ten blocks as a model. The potato piece (prior knowledge) that we plant here is knowledge about cardinality (the quantity of a number), number recognition, and place value. By having students represent numbers using base ten blocks, we build connections between what they know about numbers and the model that will serve them to develop the concept of subtraction. As students work to represent numbers the base ten blocks begin to "stand in" for them. For example, when a student compares twelve blocks and eight blocks, the blocks themselves—and the relationships that can be observed when they are stacked next to each other—take the place of the numbers 12 and 8. This is an excellent example of how a model works to help develop concepts. Instead of the abstract idea of the number 12, the student now has a concrete notion of twelve blocks.

When students begin to solve problems using the blocks, they've begun to expand their understanding and are developing strategies. This happens, for example when a student compares twelve blocks and eight blocks, realizes that *both* piles have eight blocks and sees that there are four left over. As students work on regrouping with base ten blocks (see Chapter 3, page 31) they will develop ways to make trades (trading 10 ones for 1 tens, for example) that are directly connected to what they've been learning about subtracting (taking away, comparing) with the blocks. The idea of what subtraction is and how it works grows out of cumulative experiences with the model. Each new concept becomes the catalyst for another: regrouping tens to ones leads to regrouping hundreds to tens and, finally, to regrouping any place value based on the rules of base ten. All the concepts are connected.

When strategies have become developed and efficient students no longer need a concrete or representational model to work from, they internalize the ways that the base ten blocks work. The models they use to think with at this point are abstract, represented by equations. These abstract models serve as understanding that can be built on for further learning. This is the point in concept development where students are using algorithms. When concepts are built this way they are robust (aren't forgotten easily) and serve as knowledge that can be used to develop more complex concepts in future learning.

Ease the Struggle

Practice and Conceptual Understanding

Practicing math skills is common in American classrooms. The value of that practice, though, varies. By far the most common approach for helping students to remember ideas in mathematics is drilling. Drilling facts for retrieval is similar in its limitations to memorizing algorithms before doing the necessary work with models and strategies. Flash-card repetition is an example of this type of drill. Van De Walle, Karp, and Williams (2009) offer an excellent discussion of how to learn math facts through the development of number sense in Chapter 10 of their book *Elementary and Middle School Mathematics.* Games that include math practice, on the other hand, usually allow students more opportunity to connect concepts and have benefits for learners. Video games may hold a promising route for mathematical practice in the future (Mayo 2009), while board games can be helpful in examining magnitude (Ramani and Siegler 2008).

Alternatively, the researcher Arthur Baroody (2006) articulates a pathway for memorization of facts that resembles the models-strategies-algorithms pathway discussed in this book. Baroody suggests that, in the memorization of math facts, students begin with counting, move toward a system of reasoning (number sense development—seeing the connections and the patterns), and end with automatic retrieval of information. The early stages of counting and reasoning are key to the eventual retrieval of information. This is because when students develop conceptual understanding of mathematical concepts— rather than just the ability to retrieve isolated facts—information is stored in long-term memory as connected to other information. ∎

Move Some of the Mental Resources out of Long-Term Memory

In addition to building strong connections between concepts, it's helpful to do what is also suggested for dealing with working memory challenges: move some of the mental resources out of long-term memory to an external source.

Since students have practiced math facts from first grade, a student's inability to master these facts in high school may suggest she has a long-term memory challenge that is making the task difficult or even impossible. Support her by offering the use of external resources such as fact cards, special dictionaries that include important math vocabulary, pocket-sized times

Ease the Struggle

Mastering Math Facts?

There is a common (though not unanimous) belief that unless students master math facts, they will be unable to do higher-level mathematics. This belief can penalize students who suffer from memory retrieval challenges, never allowing them to work with more challenging (and interesting) mathematics because they have such difficulty mastering basic facts. I have seen students in ninth and tenth grades who are still being drilled on this content. ∎

tables, and notebooks for "thinking on paper" with math representations to free up some of the dependency on mental resources. Retrieving facts then becomes a task of visually scanning rather than dependency on long-term memory.

What students need to understand are underlying mathematics concepts. Multiplicative and proportional reasoning are, for example, critical to moving on from elementary mathematics. Fact retrieval certainly facilitates learning in these areas, but the inability to retrieve facts will not prevent students from reasoning at higher levels. Knowing math facts is important, but fact retrieval is to mathematics what spelling is to literacy: we want students to be proficient at the skill, but the skill is a small part of the overall picture. If a student is able to spell but cannot write a coherent essay, the spelling does them little good. The same is true with math facts.

> "Knowing math facts is important, but fact retrieval is to mathematics what spelling is to literacy: we want students to be proficient at the skill, but the skill is a small part of the overall picture."

Attention Deficit Disorder (ADD)

Attention deficit disorder (ADD) is another cognitive challenge that can affect a student's learning of mathematics in three main ways: the student with ADD has difficulty concentrating, is easily distracted, and has difficulty regulating effort or attention (these apply with or without hyperactivity). ADD makes learning mathematics particularly difficult because math concepts often require significant focus and attention. Though the best classrooms for learning math are those that offer a great deal of math activity, this active learning can sometimes be challenging for children who are easily distracted—especially those with ADD.

There are a variety of specialized techniques for supporting students with ADD. These include special seats and weighted vests. Let's take a closer look at three more common techniques: self-regulation, the use of a menu lesson plan, and the use of items to manipulate.

Supporting Students with ADD Through Self-Regulation

One approach to working with students who have attention challenges while learning math is to focus on self-regulation (Reid, Trout, and Schartz 2008). Self-regulation is the ability to be aware of one's own thinking and to use both the thinking and the awareness to accomplish tasks (Zimmerman

Ease the Struggle

Accommodations for ADD and ADHD

Following is a list of common accommodations for students with attention challenges.

Medication

A physician may prescribe medication after gathering data on the student's behavior at home and at school. Teachers should never make the assumption that we know beforehand whether a student will need medication. Statements to parents like, "Your child might need Ritalin to control his behavior," are unwise.

Behavior Modification

Behavior modification can be helpful in supporting students to self-regulate. The rewards that students receive for demonstrating self-regulating behavior (choosing to move away from an area of distraction, completing an item on an assignment checklist, taking a break to refocus, etc.) don't need to be stickers and should not be food. Rather, the reward for self-regulating behavior—making "good" choices—might be participation in a favorite activity, or the chance to work on something personally interesting to the student (with a classmate or adult). Being rewarded with the chance to do something preferred not only re-enforces self-regulating behavior, but it gives the student a feeling of autonomy and agency.

Sensory Intervention

Sometimes children with ADHD or autism benefit from sensory interventions like deep pressure or strenuous exercise. Deep pressure appears to sooth students and helps with sensory integration, a condition that sometimes accompanies attention challenges. Deep-pressure interventions can take the form of specially created weighted vests that children wear during the school day. Or, in some cases, teachers allow students with attention challenges to wear their backpacks or coats to try to achieve the same effects.

Some learning specialists make use of special seats that provide additional sensory input. These include "bubble seats" that are circular pads with a little air in them. The student can rock and move around on the seat without causing disruption. Some bubble seats have bumps on the surface—more sensory input to help with sensory integration. A few classrooms even allow students to sit on exercise balls (large rubber balls common at the gym). These provide lots of "in-seat movement," but if students get bouncy, they can be distracting, and the balls tend to roll around the classroom unless the floor is level (not so in most older schools). Unattached seats/desks seem to serve these children well, since they are less restrictive.

Classroom Changes

In the classroom, students with attention challenges are best accommodated by supporting their need to have a less distracting environment. This is trickier than it sounds. On one hand, you don't want a Spartan environment for learners. On the other, it's easy for an elementary classroom to be overstimulating. What's needed is a way for attention-challenged learners to have control over the amount of stimulation they receive. Common recommendations include seating students at the edges of the group (there is usually more going on in the center), providing them space to spread out, and not seating them near a window (windows are a constant source of distraction).

Some teachers allow students with attention challenges to listen to music while working independently. The idea is that the music will block out other distractions. There is a small amount of research to suggest that this can be helpful. ■

2001). Self-regulation means that students are aware of their level of attention and know when they are having difficulty with focus. It also means that a student can identify an impulse and make a judgment about whether to follow it or not. It addresses the most common difficulties associated with attention deficit. Self-regulation can also help students with the impulsivity that sometimes accompanies ADD by helping them become aware of the impulse to act—rather than simply acting.

Encouraging self-regulation means helping students create shorter periods of time in which to focus and pace themselves to get tasks done. Encourage students to "make a deal with themselves" by deciding to work for a set period of time (ten minutes, for example) and then change the activity to help maintain focus. Create a checklist of what the student with ADD wants to accomplish during a particular period of time. This checklist in turn helps students keep track of their goals and progress during math. Like the supports discussed for memory challenges, the checklist externalizes a process that other students might be able to depend on internally.

> "Encouraging self-regulation means helping students create shorter periods of time in which to focus and pace themselves to get tasks done."

Supporting Students with ADD Through the Use of a Menu Lesson Plan

Another way that teachers can help students with ADD is to use the lesson plan format introduced in the last part of this resource—Chapter 8, "A Main Lesson—Menu Lesson Plan Structure to Support All Students." This lesson plan format breaks a math lesson into smaller parts and includes a long portion during which students can be working independently or in small groups. The part of the lesson, called "the menu," creates opportunities for students with ADD to take frequent breaks. These breaks—and the change in activity that follow—are helpful for self-regulation.

Supporting Students with ADD Through the Use of Items to Manipulate

In addition to checklists for self-regulation and the use of a menu lesson plan, give students pliable items (putty, beeswax, Velcro, etc.) to manipulate while they are working. A neurologist working with one of my students told me that having ADD is like having someone tap you on the shoulder all day, every day. He suggested giving students small pieces of beeswax or modeling clay to play with when I want them to listen. Indeed, I've found that, though these students often need to keep their fingers *very* busy, they pay better attention to whole-class activities when allowed to do so.

Affective Difficulties (Math Anxiety)

One of the most devastating challenges for math students is the development of anxiety associated with mathematics. This condition is relatively uncommon in very young children, but by the time students are in the fourth grade some students develop the belief that they are not good at mathematics. This single belief can lead to anxiety that is debilitating when working with new concepts or solving difficult problems. When anxiety is high, working memory resources diminish and students close down. At that point they are incapable of learning, whatever their abilities might be.

What causes math anxiety? There are a variety of reasons why people develop an aversion to mathematics. Most of these are the same reasons people get anxious about anything: they have a strong negative experience, they feel that others are judging them on their success or failure, or they are unsure and afraid to admit it. It's important to know, though, that no one is born with this anxiety. This unfortunate challenge is something that lies somewhere between cognitive challenges and conceptual struggles (see Chapter 1 for an explanation of these).

Usually an affective aversion to math comes from either persistent negative experiences with math or a few highly charged incidents. The result is that students develop internal self-talk about their inability to understand mathematics. This point of view is sometimes supported by parents who have had similar experiences. I've more than once heard a parent at parent conferences say, "I'm not surprised that my child isn't good at math. I've told her that I was never good at it either." With negative experiences and the reinforcement to support the conclusions that come from these experiences, students develop an expectation of failure. In observing students who struggle, I've found that those who believe they are not good at math often convince their teachers to share in this view as well. When this happens, the expectation for both the student and the teacher is the same: the student will learn little and it will be a difficult process.

> "I've more than once heard a parent at parent conferences say, 'I'm not surprised that my child isn't good at math. I've told her that I was never good at it either.' With negative experiences and the reinforcement to support the conclusions that come from these experiences, students develop an expectation of failure."

How can we support students who struggle as a result of anxiety? Following are three main suggestions: emphasizing that everyone can learn math, understanding that math is a process, and changing a child's internal notions (self-talk) about math.

Supporting Students with Math Anxiety: Everyone Can Learn Math!

Perhaps the most critical support we can provide is to emphasize that almost everyone can learn math. As educators we need to transfer the expectation for success that we have for reading to mathematics. The belief that everyone can learn math—and the actions that flow from it, both conscious and unconscious—helps to send the message to students that whatever their difficulties, they have the capability to learn.

Supporting Students with Math Anxiety: Math Is a Process!

> "In math, there are no extra points for understanding quickly. The real goal is to understand *thoroughly*."

Beyond creating positive learning expectations for students, emphasize that understanding math is a *process*. The process can be short or long—sometimes it depends on the math we're doing and sometimes it depends on us. In either case, there are no extra points for understanding quickly. The real goal is to understand *thoroughly*. I tell students about the journey of doctoral students who might work two years on a problem before coming to a solution. I tell them that "getting stuck" and figuring a way out is what makes math interesting.

Supporting Students with Math Anxiety: Changing Internal Notions (Self-Talk) About Math

A great deal of anxiety about math comes from students' self-talk about their relationship to math:

> *"People who do math are smart. I can't do math, so I'm not smart."*
>
> *"I've never been good at math, so why should I be any better now?"*
>
> *"I can get by without math. Don't lots of people?"*

The internal dialogue of math-anxious students can be debilitating. It casts the experience of learning math in the worst light, creates expectations for failure, and sets up resistance to the potential for interventions to be successful. Math-anxious learners must consciously develop more positive self-talk in order to change their relationship with math.

The creation of individual identity is complex. Where math is concerned, it has to do with the way a learner sees herself in relation to the subject of math. If she believes that she is capable and skillful, her relationship to math will be positive and her internal dialogue will reflect the expectation of success. Students with positive attitudes toward math tend to persevere longer when they're stuck and tend to perform at high levels (Bryan and Bryan 1991). Some evidence suggests that improving students' attitudes toward mathematics will help them achieve similar success (Yasutake and Bryan 1995).

How do we improve the internal dialogue of math-anxious students? First, students need to become aware of their negative self-talk. I ask students to write statements that show how they feel about math:

Math is *my* worst subject.

I've never been smart at math.

I feel like everybody is better at it than *me*.

When I can't find an answer I feel like I want to disappear.

This step always seems easy for both children and adult learners. They know why they don't like math: it makes them feel lousy about themselves. We talk about how unhelpful these attitudes are both for them as math students and for their own well-being. Our next step is to reframe this self-talk in more positive terms. The trick here is that the more positive reframing needs to be believable to students. If a student writes, "I will be the best math student in my class," he doesn't necessarily believe it. It's important to reframe negative beliefs in believable terms; for example:

Math doesn't have to be *my* worst subject. I can do better. I've had other experiences where I've improved and math could be like one of those.

Maybe I've never felt smart at math because I've never found a way to like it. If I can find things I like about it, I might do better.

I'm sure almost everybody has difficulty with some subject. I'm also pretty sure there are people who have more trouble with math than I have.

I don't need to let how I do at math be so important. If I relax about it, maybe I can improve.

By reframing self-talk in this manner, we are moving in the direction of lowering math anxiety and promoting more positive expectations.

Ultimately students reduce anxiety by changing the notions and conversations they have internally as they approach mathematical tasks. Using the tools that are available to us—remembering that everyone can learn math, remembering that math is a process in which we don't have to learn everything immediately, and improving our self-talk about math—we can help students be less critical of their difficulties with math, recognize that these struggles are a normal part of learning math, and create expectations of success.

Reflection Questions

1. What surprised you most about the information in this chapter? How did it go with, or challenge, an existing idea?

2. How do the three kinds of memory work together for math learning? What does each do?

3. What are new techniques you've found for supporting learners with memory difficulties? Attention challenges? Math anxiety?

4. Why is it so important to build connections between math concepts?

5. How might the information in this chapter change what you do in your classroom?

A Main Lesson—Menu Lesson Plan Structure to Support All Students

8

The Big Ideas

● A main lesson—menu lesson plan is especially effective for supporting struggling learners because it deliberately connects new concepts to prior knowledge, offers opportunities for students to work together in an inclusive environment, provides a large block of time for differentiated instruction to meet individual needs, and allows time for students to share their work and reflect on their learning.

● There are four main parts to a main lesson—menu lesson plan: the launch, the main lesson, the menu lesson, and closure.

Chapter Outline

Introducing a Main Lesson— Menu Lesson Plan

Supporting struggling learners in the regular classroom can be challenging. There is often a conflict between teaching math lessons that encourage communication among a wide range of learners and differentiating instruction for learners who struggle. This chapter comes to the rescue with a lesson plan I call the *main lesson—menu lesson plan*. This is a tool that accommodates both approaches to planning and instruction—inclusion and differentiation—and creates opportunities for students to make meaningful connections to the math they learn. Using this lesson plan answers the question teachers frequently ask: "How can I meet the diverse needs of my students without tracking them into ability groups?"

The lesson plan is especially effective for supporting struggling learners because it deliberately connects new concepts to prior knowledge, offers opportunities for students to work together in an inclusive environment,

Ease the Struggle

The Disadvantages of Ability Grouping in Mathematics

In general, schools in the United States tend to use ability grouping more for math instruction than for any other subject (Linchevski and Kutscher 1998). There is a common belief among educators that math learning occurs on a linear path and students should be grouped with others who move along the sequence at a similar pace. While there is some truth to the idea that math concepts build on one another, the way students learn to understand mathematics is rarely a predictable, linear process. If math learning is a path that students travel, they do much more wandering than walking in a straight line! The benefits of putting students into similar groups to wander together are dubious at best. Indeed, Linchevski and Kutscher (1998) warn of the pitfalls of homogeneous grouping for math. The intention with ability grouping is to differentiate instruction so each student can get what he or she needs. This goal comes from a genuine effort to support student learning, but it hurts struggling learners in several ways. In ability grouping,

struggling students don't get the benefits of hearing the thinking of more skillful classroom peers and communicating with them. Also, the expectations for struggling learners' achievement are lower from the outset, creating a self-fulfilling prophesy. Expectation of achievement has important effects on learning (Good 1981). In some sense, what teachers expect students to achieve, they achieve. In addition to the difficulty that lower expectations create, the message to students in lower-tracked math groups is clear: *You're not very good at math.* This message can be the cause of learned helplessness for some students. When students have the curriculum slowed down and approached in small, easily digestible pieces, they don't learn how to "get stuck" and figure their way out. The teachers I work with consistently report that students in low-ability groups hardly finish reading a problem before putting their hands up and saying, "I don't get it!" ■

provides a large block of time for differentiated instruction to meet individual needs, and allows time for students to share their work and reflect on their learning.

This lesson plan is an alternative to traditional lesson plans that often emphasize whole-group instruction. The structure usually takes about an hour to an hour and a half to implement. While this is similar to the recommendations for math instruction with any lesson plan, the variety of settings for instruction gives greater attention to individual learning. This type of lesson plan, like all instructional techniques, can be and should be modified for the needs of the teachers who use it. I use this approach to math lessons even when teaching college students because I believe it offers the greatest opportunity for students to be engaged in meaningful mathematics and conversations with peers.

Ease the Struggle

The Importance of Classroom Conversation in Mathematics

The benefits of mathematics-focused classroom conversation are numerous (Cobb and Bauersfeld 1995; Hiebert and Wearne 1993; Steinbring, Bartolini, and Sierpinska 1998). There is even evidence that this conversation is more important than teacher-student interaction. When students explain their thinking to each other, question each other's strategies and conjectures, and work together to find solutions, their learning of math is much richer. Structuring lessons to create inclusion—chances for students of different abilities to work together—can make the most of classroom communication and provide important support for struggling learners.

In addition to the difficulty that lower expectation creates, the message to students in lower-tracked math groups is clear: You're not very good at math. This not-so-subtle message can be the cause of "learned helplessness" for some students. When students have the curriculum slowed down and approached in small easily digestible pieces they don't learn how to "get stuck" and figure their way out. Teachers of remedial classes in our Math for Struggling Learners (MSL) groups reported consistently that students would hardly finish reading a problem before putting their hands up and saying, "I don't get it."

In remedial classes, the teacher's or paraprofessional's response to "I don't get it" is frequently to further explain the problem and/or the strategy that leads to the solution. In a class where this is the expectation, students never learn to struggle with a problem and try multiple approaches. They never learn problem solving, or how to develop math concepts. Usually in these environments they don't even know that multiple approaches to a problem is an option; students end up believing that the way the teacher showed them is the way they have to do it or they will be wrong.

By contrast, when students are involved in conversations with peers, they not only get support to think about math problems, they get to see good math thinking modeled by other students. Struggling learners in heterogeneous math groups can see that *everyone* gets stuck in difficult problems. They can also see the variety of ways that skillful problem solvers work their ways to solutions. This student-student exchange of mathematical thinking is more beneficial than the exchange that often takes place when the teacher explains content that hasn't been understood. ∎

The Origin of the Main Lesson— Menu Lesson Plan

> The elements of the main lesson—menu lesson plan—*the launch, the main lesson, the menu, the closure*—are rooted in Waldorf education, work from Marilyn Burns (1992), and my practice as a teacher.

Structuring a math lesson to meet the needs of individual learners *and* provide opportunities for heterogeneous math work is challenging. The elements of the main lesson—menu lesson plan—*the launch, the main lesson, the menu, the closure*—are rooted in Waldorf education, work from Marilyn Burns (1992), and my practice as a teacher.

Waldorf curriculum, based on the theosophical principles of Rudolph Steiner (Steiner 2003; Easton 1997), includes the idea of a main lesson, or central organizing idea, that may run for days or even weeks. In the Waldorf approach to planning, the main lesson occupies students for an hour or two every day and focuses their attention on a topic that falls into the flow of the larger curriculum. (For more information on Waldorf education, see www .whywaldorfworks.org/02_W_Education/index.asp.)

The main lesson—menu lesson plan borrows the idea that each day's math lesson should be focused on a central mathematical concept situated within the context of a larger study. The larger study might be, for example, developing algebraic reasoning. In this case each day's lesson is a refinement of the bigger idea of developing algebraic reasoning.

I saw this kind of instruction in several of my visits to elementary math classrooms in Japan. Each day the teacher offered students a specific problem that was connected to a larger mathematical concept. Math class consisted of teachers posing problems, having students work on them in small heterogeneous groups, and then allowing students to share their work with each other. I have integrated these instructional practices in the implementation of main lessons in the main lesson—menu lesson plan.

Many years ago I attended a Math Solutions summer workshop and was introduced to the idea of "menu." At the time I'd been an elementary school teacher for about ten years and had used "stations" to allow students to participate in a variety of activities simultaneously. However, I had never thought of the possibilities that the independent work modeled by Math Solutions held for differentiating instruction. At the time I was teaching in a multiage school for six- to ten-year-old children. The menu activities I brought back from the summer workshop were a perfect way to differentiate learning for students who had similar needs during math lessons. The menu approach also reminded me that the activities I oversaw as a teacher (specifically those in the main lesson) were not the only way children could learn. Subsequently, students in my class made great gains due to their engagement in the independent menu activities.

The Parts of a Main Lesson—Menu Lesson Plan

The main lesson—menu lesson plan has four parts. Each of these parts creates opportunities for meeting the needs of a diverse class of learners, including struggling students. The remainder of this chapter takes a careful look at each of these parts, featuring examples of the parts in action. Reproducibles 8-1 through 8-5 offer help in implementing a menu lesson plan with a blank template and sample templates from grades 1, 3, 5, and 7. You'll notice that the main lesson—menu lesson plan shares much with Marilyn Burns's (1992) approach to lesson planning and the planning done as part of the *Connected Math* program (http://connectedmath.msu.edu/z). Both of these programs describe a workshop-style approach to planning lessons that includes a *launch—explore—summarize* sequence. The main lesson—menu lesson is quite similar, but splits the "explore" part of the lesson into a section for inclusion and a section for differentiation. This segmenting of the "explore" portion of the lesson is extremely helpful for struggling learners, for it provides them with the chance to work with more skillful peers *and* to work on "just right" material to help them progress.

Four Parts of a Main Lesson— Menu Lesson Plan

▶ Part 1: The Launch

▶ Part 2: The Main Lesson

▶ Part 3: The Menu Lesson

▶ Part 4: Closure

Part 1: The Launch

The *launch*—sometimes called the *initiation* or *introduction*—has two main purposes: activating prior knowledge (Hartman 2001) so students can bring what they already know to new content, and introducing the concept in the main lesson. These two elements work together to help prepare students for the important work in the main lesson.

Two Main Purposes of the Launch

▶ Activate (activate prior knowledge)

▶ Introduce (introduce material for the main lesson)

Activating Prior Knowledge

Most introductions to lessons include the teacher's reminding students what material was covered the previous day. This might be done by having students put their homework solutions on the board and/or having the teacher

> "In the main lesson—menu lesson plan, the launch begins with a problem that connects prior learning with the new concept in that day's main lesson. The problem gives *every* student a chance to use what she already knows and, in doing so, activates prior knowledge."

review correct answers. The limitation of this approach is that, while it is useful for review purposes, a simple review is not sufficient for activating prior knowledge. Demonstrations of prior content, or watching others perform calculations, is passive and has only minimal effects for connecting to previous knowledge and experience. Some, especially those who struggle, may not be engaged at all. Activating prior knowledge requires the engagement of *every* student in thinking about, and working with, a specific math concept.

In the main lesson—menu lesson plan, the launch begins with a problem that connects prior learning with the new concept in that day's main lesson. The problem gives *every* student a chance to use what she already knows and, in doing so, activates prior knowledge. The launch concludes by having students share their thinking and solutions. The sequence of posing the problem, allowing time to work on it, and sharing work creates the ideal launch into the main lesson for *every* student.

Introducing the Concept for the Main Lesson

In addition to activating relevant knowledge, the launch serves as a bridge to the main lesson. This means that the topic in the launch should not only stimulate what students might already know about a topic, but it should lead them into the investigation in the main lesson. Ideally, the launch will lead students to a question that is answered in the main lesson.

A good example can be found in a lesson that focuses on division through sharing. The launch might pose a relatively simple problem:

How would 6 friends share 24 cookies?

With this as an initiation problem, students could show a variety of simple solutions that demonstrate sharing cookies. The launch could end, though, with the teacher's posing the question:

What if there were 26 cookies? What problem would the friends have?

If the main lesson were focused on division with remainders, the launch would have introduced a practical and important consideration to focus on the more complex mathematical concept.

My Story

PART 1: The Launch

Following is a dialogue that transpired between a teacher, Erin, and her students during the launch of a third-grade lesson focused on moving toward multidigit multiplication.

Erin: Yesterday we were beginning work on how to multiply numbers larger than ten. You had some interesting approaches to that. Today I want you to think about what a particular problem *means*. What does the equation sixteen times five *mean*? Take a minute and write down your thinking. (*After a minute or two the teacher begins calling on students to share their answers.*)

Noah: It means sixteen times five.

Erin: Well, that's a good way to *read* the problem; however, I'm looking for what it *means*.

Ben: If you counted the fingers on sixteen hands.

Ian: Who has sixteen hands? (*The class laughs*)

Ben: You need more than one person!

Ian: Oh. OK. Like . . . (*counting*) eight people.

Erin: How did you know it was eight people?

Ian: Each person has two hands, so eight times two is sixteen.

Erin: Great. Who has another idea about the meaning of sixteen times five?

Ashley: Sixteen bags with five cookies.

Erin: Are the five cookies spread out over the sixteen bags?

Ashley: No, *each* bag has five cookies.

Erin: Let's keep these ideas in mind—the fingers on sixteen hands and five cookies in each of sixteen bags—as we work on our main lesson today.

What makes this a "good" launch? It meets the two criteria that are most important: there is activation of prior knowledge and a strong setup for

continued

My Story continued

the material coming in the main lesson. Erin makes the connection to prior knowledge by asking for the meaning of the equation. What she is really asking is for students to go back to models they could use to think multiplicatively. Ben shows he thinks about groups of five using hands. Ashley shows that it can be done with bags of cookies.

The link to the main lesson is built into the launch, since the class will now begin to explore multiplication with groups greater than ten. Erin has gotten her class to think about what they know about multiplication (using groups) and extended it to working with a number greater than 10 (16). As they work in the main lesson, she'll help students continue this connection by asking, "What does it mean when you multiply . . . ?" In doing this, she is building a strong connection between the models that students think with and the application of these models in new ways.

Sometimes teachers launch a lesson with an attempt to activate prior knowledge that relies on telling students what to remember. Here is another (fairly typical) example of a launch that attempts to activate prior knowledge but, because it doesn't engage students individually, falls short. Fred, the teacher, has the idea of activating prior knowledge but believes that his telling students will engage them.

Fred: Today we're going to see how to multiply with numbers that are bigger than ten. Can anyone tell me a number bigger than ten?

Chris: Sixteen.

Fred: Good. Sixteen is a number bigger than ten. Let's think about what might happen if we multiplied sixteen by five. (*Writes* 16 × 5 *on the board.*) Remember that multiplication means "groups." In this case we have five groups (*draws five circles on the board*) and each group has sixteen in it (*writes 16 in each circle*). If we add all these together . . . why don't you do that at your seats. What is sixteen added together five times? (*Waits for students.*)

Sean: Ninety.

Fred: Yes. Now let's see if we can apply this to the main lesson today with other numbers.

In this second example Fred is making the attempt to activate prior knowledge by reminding students that multiplication is about grouping. He also has them do some work. But there are qualitative differences between his launch and Erin's that are especially important for students who struggle. In Erin's lesson the students do the thinking *before* there's any sharing. This is an opportunity for everyone to wrestle with the key ideas and for questions to be formulated. Everyone in Erin's class is *doing the work*. In Fred's class, he is doing the thinking and his students are passive observers. Erin asks students to share in order to develop the idea in the launch. Fred asks students to share results of computation after he has highlighted the important ideas. Erin asks students questions about meaning. Fred asks questions to help confirm what's he's just said.

Part 2: The Main Lesson

Main lessons are the mathematical threads that tie instruction together. The topics from one main lesson lead into the next so that, over time, students have the chance to experience a topic many times by solving problems related to it and sharing their understanding with each other.

The main lesson is, as its name suggests, the heart of the lesson plan for daily math instruction. The main lesson contains the core learning for the day and is *inclusive*, meaning that students with a variety of understandings and challenges work together. The main lesson follows a similar structure to the launch in that it usually focuses on a problem, allows students time to work on it individually or in small groups, and then provides time for sharing. Where the launch might last five to ten minutes, the main lesson is usually twenty to thirty minutes.

Ease the Struggle

The Main Lesson and RTI

The main lesson can function as RTI Tier 1 intervention because students with difficulties are not singled out for specialized instruction at this time. In Tier 1 of RTI, all students in a class are screened to identify those students who might be at risk for failure. As a result of screening, those students identified as needing support can benefit from early intervention that is provided in the regular classroom. ■

Two Main Purposes of the Main Lesson

▶ Exploration (focus on a particular concept, often a problem)

▶ Discussion (facilitate student conversations about mathematical understanding)

Main lessons are *not* a series of progressive explanations from teachers. They are a chance for both those who struggle, and those who don't, to build their mathematical understanding by interacting with both math content and each other.

The chief features of the main lesson are focusing on a particular concept (often a problem) and facilitating student conversations about mathematical understanding.

Exploration: Focusing on a Particular Concept

The concept development in a main lesson follows the models-strategies-algorithms sequence suggested throughout this resource (see specifically "Frame 3: The Instruction," page 19 in Chapter 2). The first set of main lessons is aimed at establishing and developing concrete or representational models to support thinking with the new concept. When working with additive reasoning in the early grades, for example, main lessons may begin with the use of base ten blocks, ten-frames, or the number line. When developing multiplication concepts (something that typically takes place in third grade), a main lesson may begin with the use of models for creating groups, like beans and cups (see the following problem), circles and stars (two stars in each circle, five circles is ten stars), or models that make use of area, like array models.

If there were 4 beans in each cup, and we had 6 cups, how many beans would there be?

Fill in the table:

Beans in a cup	Cups	Total
6	1	6
6	2	12
6	3	18

What patterns do you notice in the table? What predictions can you make for 6 × 4? For 6 × 6? Why?

These first lessons will focus on developing a strong conceptual connection between the model and the concept itself (the ability to use a model "to think with" is one of the characteristics that distinguish those who struggle from those who don't).

When students have a reliable model, the next set of main lessons focuses on developing strategies. These are probably the most important lessons for struggling learners. Our goal with strategy development is to thoroughly explore the concept in as many problem-solving contexts as possible. We want students to develop a deep understanding of the concept through exploring and applying it. When developing strategies through solving problems, students make connections, develop their understanding, and apply it to new situations. Strategies also support the *generalization of concepts*—another difficulty many struggling learners have. In the end, students develop strategies that increase in efficiency and accuracy and lead to understanding of algorithms.

Problems at the strategies stage of main lessons may look like the following problems for third graders. The focus concept is the development of multiplication, specifically, using a model in a variety of ways to solve problems.

Ease the Struggle

What Does It Mean to Generalize?

Generalization, it can be argued, is the goal of all learning. It means that students can use what they learn in class in a variety of new, unfamiliar circumstances. It is proof that students have incorporated new concepts and can use them—rather than learning them for the purpose of producing them for the teacher.

The process for instructionally supporting struggling students (model–strategy–algorithm) is aimed at helping students build generalizations. The model (what students think with—a number line is an example) is used in a variety of problem-solving situations. Using a number line to solve problems helps students *generalize* its use. Without the model, students may have no entry point to solve a problem. The model is the mental tool that gets stretched (generalized) to new situations through problem solving.

If a student learns to make "jumps" on the number line to add, for example, they develop a mental picture/process of what happens during adding. Just knowing how to move along a number line, though, isn't very sophisticated mathematics. If the student has to solve the problem:

> Jim went 4 miles and rested. Then he went 4 more miles. How far did he go?

she has the opportunity to make use of the number line in a problem-solving context. Struggling students benefit from *explicit* strategy development when helping them generalize a model to use in a problem-solving context. To encourage this generalization we might ask questions like:

> How could you use a number line to solve this? Where (on what number) would Jim start? Where would he end up?

With numerous opportunities to apply the number line model in a wide variety of situations, students will develop strategies for using it that eventually lead to efficient algorithms that work automatically (McKeough, Lupart, and Marini 1995). ∎

Notice the deliberate connection to a specific model.

How many feet might you see in a barnyard with 4 goats and 6 chickens? In this problem, what are the cups? What are the beans?

We want to take 8 vans with 6 people in each to the field trip? In this problem, what are the cups and what are the beans?

Sara has 5 nickels. How many pennies is that? In this problem, what could you think of as the cups? What are the beans?

> "The rush to teach algorithms shortchanges the students who have not fully developed a concept. I believe that many of the content-gap struggles that develop in students are a result of not enough time using models to solve problems and develop appropriate strategies."

The use of a model does not always lead to algorithms. Work with beans and cups, for example, is hard to connect directly to the standard algorithm for multidigit multiplication. Using the beans and cups model in a variety of problem-solving situations helps develop the strategies that bridge the development of concepts with the use of algorithms. My work with students over the years has led me to believe that strategy development is the most important aspect of concept development for supporting struggling learners. The rush to teach algorithms shortchanges the students who have not fully developed a concept. I believe that many of the content-gap struggles that develop in students are a result of not enough time using models to solve problems and develop appropriate strategies.

The last set of main lessons in the development of any concept should be the teaching of algorithms. When properly developed, algorithms provide students with access to efficient computation and abstract models. An algorithm works because (in the best cases) it compacts the mathematical concept into an abstract form. Rather than using skip-counting or grouping strategies (examples of multiplicative strategies), students learn methods for computing and learn the properties of numbers that make those methods work.

One of the most common struggles for both children and adults is using an algorithm or procedure without understanding. Sometimes this particular struggle began because no model was ever developed. Students might have, for example, learned the algorithm for adding fractions with unlike denominators without ever working with a fraction model. Alternatively, a student might apply procedures without understanding because she has had some experience with a model but never used the model for developing strategies (the teacher likely went directly from experiences with models to teaching the algorithm). Without an extended period of time to develop their own strategies, students often don't make the important connections necessary between the developing concept, their own previous understanding, and the procedures that are used in the algorithm (Campbell et al. 1998).

See the example presented in "My Story, Part 2: The Main Lesson." This example has all the elements that make the main lesson so important for struggling learners (and for *all* learners). The lesson is focused on a problem, allowing students to push their current understanding further using what they already know. The lesson encourages students to support their thinking with evidence. The format creates opportunities for conversation between students about their thinking. A wide variety of strategies are available to use and share, and students support each other by working together.

My Story

PART 2: The Main Lesson

This dialogue picks up where we left off with "My Story, Part 1: The Launch" on page 151. Now we see the main lesson in action in a third-grade classroom with Erin, the teacher.

Erin: The big idea for today is multiplying with numbers larger than ten. We're going to work today with a dozen. Who knows how many that is?

Ashley: There are twelve eggs in a dozen eggs.

Erin: Good, twelve are a dozen. Let's read today's problem together. (*Reading the problem chorally is always a good idea. It supports students who might have difficulty with the reading and allows everyone to hear the problem before beginning.*)

Students: (*reading the problem as a class*) A <u>gross</u> is a dozen dozens. How many is that?

Erin: What is this problem asking us to figure out? (*This is also a great question to follow the reading of every problem. Some teachers ask students to write answers to this question on their papers before they begin.*)

Noah: How much twelve twelves is?

Erin: OK. Anyone see it differently?

Ben: How many things are there in twelve groups of twelve?

Ian: Like eggs—how many eggs are in a dozen eggs?

Erin: Work on this in your table groups to find an answer. We'll share in ten minutes.

Students work in heterogeneous groups where struggling learners are supported by those who are more proficient. They use the materials available in the classroom to solve the problem. Sometimes students get interlocking cubes or other manipulatives. Sometimes the conversations in a group will make use of models that can be drawn on paper. For this reason many teachers make large newsprint or chart paper available to groups to do their work. When each group has created solutions, the groups share their work with the whole class.

continued

My Story continued

Group 1:   We did tallies to count up twelve twelves [see Figure 8.1]. We counted one hundred forty-four. We noticed that the twelve groups are like the circles and stars game we played. You could also write 3 × 4 about just the groups.

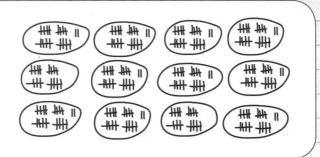

Figure 8.1   Group 1's representation of a gross (a dozen dozens).

Group 2:   We did the egg idea. We made boxes and colored in the eggs [see Figure 8.2]. It took too long! So we only did half of them. Half of them is seventy-two, so we said seventy-two plus seventy-two is one hundred forty-four. We agree with one hundred forty-four.

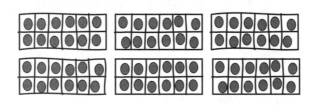

Figure 8.2   Group 2's representation of a gross (a dozen dozens).

Group 3:   We tried to do ours all with numbers. We started by finding out what four dozens was because we know there are twelve dozens all together [see Figure 8.3].

$$12 + 12 + 12 + 12 = 48$$
$$4 \times 3 = 12$$
$$50 \times 3 = 150$$

Figure 8.3   Group 3's work in determining a gross (a dozen dozens).

Group 3:   We got forty-eight so we rounded it to fifty. Three fiftys is easy. But then we couldn't figure out how much to subtract. We thought we might have to subtract two for every dozen but that would give us much less than one hundred forty-four.

Erin: Why does it matter if you're less than one hundred forty-four?

Danny from Group 3:   Because the other groups all got one hundred forty-four.

Erin: Why do the rest of you think Group 3 got a different answer?

The lesson continued with students offering their ideas about how Group 3's strategy could work and what they might have to subtract. The teacher followed up the first problem by asking students how many eggs there might be in 24 dozens. Students followed a similar routine of working in groups and then sharing/checking/questioning each other's solutions. Erin wanted students to make strong connections between the approaches for both problems. She was also hoping that students would notice that twice the number of groups would yield an answer that was twice as big.

Discussion: Facilitating Student Conversations About Mathematical Understanding

Mathematical conversations are not simply a way for students to show their understanding. Classroom discourse is the avenue for developing understanding for many children, and it is a key support for struggling learners. When learners have the chance to share their thinking, question the thinking of others, and probe new ideas with a peer they are engaged in the work of mathematics (Cobb and Bauersfeld 1995; Choppin 2007; Littleton and Howe 2010; Barlow and McCrory 2011).

> "Classroom discourse is the avenue for developing understanding for many children, and it is a key support for struggling learners."

Allow Students to Do the Work   Several classroom practices facilitate student conversations. The most important is that the teacher allows the students to do the work. In other words, the role of the teacher when supporting rich student conversations is to help students to clarify and extend their conjectures. This is often hard to do because most teachers find it easier to ask leading or rhetorical questions in order to get to the answer more efficiently. When teachers think of their primary roles in a mathematical discussion as facilitator (creating a smooth flow of conversation by helping students take turns), recorder (putting key ideas on the board), and clarifier (asking, "What do you mean by that?"), they are supporting students in doing important math thinking together.

Encourage Students to Think to Themselves   Another classroom technique that helps is to always get students to think to themselves or in small groups *before* having a larger class discussion. Students need a chance to think about something before they begin to share publically. One way to do this is to have students write down connections they can make to a problem for a minute before starting to discuss it. Students might write down other problems they think are like the one they are about to work on, ideas for solving, drawings that represent the problem, and so on.

Encourage Pair–Share Conversations   Another way to "pre-process" before a larger discussion is a pair-share conversation with a partner. Sometimes teachers call this "turn-and-talk." This simply asks students to tell the person sitting next to them what they think. Pair-share conversations almost always make the larger group conversations richer, because students have had a chance to see how their ideas sound to another and to themselves.

Encourage Small-Group Conversations   Finally, a small-group conversation before talking together as a class is almost always a good idea. In small groups students have the opportunity to share their thinking without the stress or worry of being "wrong" in front of a large group. While writing before talking is the most private and least anxiety-producing method for pre-processing a problem, it offers the least amount of feedback. Small-group discussions provide a way for students to get feedback from others to help refine their thinking.

Part 3: The Menu Lesson

The menu portion of the lesson follows the main lesson. It lasts for twenty-five to thirty minutes. During this time students work on a variety of math activities selected from a "menu." Most of these are done independently, and the teacher has the opportunity to interact with students individually and in small groups (instruction for Tiers 2 and 3). This part of the lesson plan is dedicated to differentiating instruction, its strengths residing in meeting the specific individual needs of students in the class.

Menu time is often students' favorite part of the math lesson. This is in part because students make choices about which activities to work on and, in many cases, with whom to work. Some teachers describe menu time as "controlled chaos." I prefer to think of this time as helping students to become independent learners. We all want students to be able to learn on their own—to apply whatever they've learned in school to the world around them. We cannot expect them to do this if they never get the practice.

During menu time students choose from a variety of activities. The activities are primarily tied to the main lesson but might also include review from past lessons or explorations that would lead into future lessons. The big idea during menu time is that students are challenged on an instructional level—the activities are difficult enough to be challenging but appropriate enough to be able to be done independently.

Some teachers post the menu on the board or on chart paper for students to follow. If a particular student requires different activities than the

> "Menu time is often students' favorite part of the math lesson. This is in part because students make choices about which activities to work on and, in many cases, with whom to work."

Ease the Struggle

The Menu Lesson and RTI

Tier 2 RTI instruction takes place in small, focused groups. The menu setting during the main lesson—menu lesson plan is ideal for this type of instruction. During the menu portion of the lesson, students are working independently or in small groups on a variety of mathematical tasks. This is a time when teachers are involved in a wide variety of activities including meeting for focused mini-lessons with small groups. In some schools a math coach or learning specialist will join the class during menu to meet with a small group of students who are having some difficulty (identified by assessment with a concept).

In Tier 3 RTI instruction students must receive individual, focused instruction. Often this instruction takes place outside the classroom and is tied to a student's IEP. The menu part of the lesson provides a time for students to be served *in class* by a learning specialist (in most cases since instruction is highly individualized at this time). The advantage of serving Tier 3 students during menu time is that they don't miss class and are not subjected to being pulled out of class—something that makes some students self-conscious. ■

Five Required Activities in a Menu Lesson

1 Main lesson work (if necessary)

2 Similar problems at different levels of challenge

3 Practice with number and operations

4 Math journaling

5 Games

ones posted (for individual reasons) the teacher will meet this student to create an individual list of required assignments. Some teachers issue checklists with the menu for each student on them. This system allows for a high level of both differentiation and accountability, but takes a great deal of preparation from the teacher.

In my classroom I create a menu for the week that includes activities that students are required to complete, as well as optional activities. There are almost always five required activities, listed as follows. Teachers differ in the amount of independence they give students for finishing work on the list. In general, I allow students to choose what they wish to work on, provided they complete the work by an agreed-upon deadline.

Main Lesson Work

Students often have work from the main lesson that needs to be completed. This work has to be done first, since the next day's lesson depends on its results. Students who complete their work during main lesson can move directly into menu activities while those who need or want more time with the main lesson material begin menu time by working on this.

Ease the Struggle

The Teacher's Role During the Menu Lesson

For the menu lesson to start, the teacher reminds students of the work they must complete. Sometimes this involves reading a menu that has been posted on the board, and sometimes it involves reminders for individual students. Students then begin working. The teacher often has a hand in the first choices students make. She might remind some students that they need to finish work from the main lesson. She might direct another few students to go back to the problem they started the previous day. In general, menu lessons begin with the teacher's checking in to be sure that all the students have made good choices for working independently.

During the rest of the menu time the teacher is involved in a variety of activities, many of which are aimed at supporting or scaffolding work for students who may have difficulty. The teacher

might, for example, meet briefly with students who have attention challenges to help them create a plan for the menu period. What work will they try to accomplish? How will they give themselves breaks?

Similarly, this is a time when the teacher can pull small groups together to focus on specific needs. She may gather a group of students who struggle with problem solving and have them read a menu problem together and discuss possible strategies for solving it before they work on it individually. The teacher may have noticed, from an assessment (see Chapters 4–6) or from math journaling (see page 168), that some students really don't understand a key concept or have a particular misconception. The menu lesson is a perfect time for the teacher to address these issues with students individually (conducting flexible interviews) or in small groups. ■

Similar Problems at Different Levels of Challenge

At the heart of the menu part of the lesson are problems for students to solve. Problems are different from equations in that they include a context and can be solved using more than one model or strategy. Since the menu lesson is the time for differentiation, teachers include similar problems at different levels of challenge to accommodate the variety of levels in class. A common system is to put circles or dots on the upper corner of the paper to indicate the difficulty of a problem. A "one-dot" problem is easier and a "two-dot" problem is more challenging. Some teachers even create a "three-dot" level to indicate an increased level of challenge.

Ease the Struggle

Finishing the Work of the Main Lesson

One of the most vexing logistical issues that occurs in teaching with a menu is what to do when students finish their work at different times. We don't want the early finishers to do busy work, waiting for others to catch up. But we also want those who work more deliberately to have time to finish. Following the main lesson with time during the menu lesson to finish allows students additional time. ■

My Story

Finishing the Work of the Main Lesson During Menu Time

In Erin's main lesson she and her students were investigating how multiplication works when the numbers are bigger than 10. Students used a variety of models to show their thinking—groups within circles, tally marks, and so forth. Just before ending the lesson, Erin held up a package of lifesavers and told the students that there were fourteen candies in each roll. She asked them, during menu, to figure out how many rolls of lifesavers would be needed for everyone in the class to get one. After posing this problem, the students began working on menu activities. They knew that they needed to finish this problem before starting any other menu work, as they would begin with it the next day.

Work from the main lesson is not always a part of the menu, though most teachers find that it frequently fits there. When work from the main lesson spills into the menu portion of the lesson students can work on it in the setting that is most comfortable for them. Some students choose to work on their own. More often they will work with friends. Erin likes to let main lesson work spill into the menu for just this reason. She usually assigns the groups in which students work during the main lesson. She likes the children to have the chance to work with partners of their choosing for at least part of the menu.

How do students decide which level of problem is just right for them? Often the teacher will help with this decision by letting students know at the beginning of menu which level they should choose. In my experience sometimes students who are required to solve a more difficult problem will start with an easier one. Sometimes this is to warm-up for the harder problem and sometimes it's because the student enjoys solving problems. Menus above second grade often last for several days. This allows students to work on a problem and come back to it if they have difficulty or want to refine their answers.

There are a variety of ways that teachers assign, collect, and assess these problems. The least "teacher-intensive" approach is to post the menu and provide bins (crates or boxes) for finished assignments. One might be labeled *problems*, another *practice with number sense*, and so on. When the menu is finished (at the end of the week, or on the agreed-upon deadline) the teacher can assess the work.

Many teachers provide individual folders or portfolios for students to store their work. Some of these teachers put a paper copy of the menu inside the portfolio for students to use. A colleague of mine who worked with first and second graders used this approach. She found that, for younger children, having a checklist helped keep them on task. I find that collecting problems in portfolios is especially useful. Many teachers (myself included) send number-sense work home, but save problems (or representative problems) throughout the year as an archive of student work. I especially appreciate having portfolios of student problem solving when doing parent conferences because the portfolios contain lots of information about students' math development that interests parents.

There are a variety of ways to assess student problems. Some states, such as Kentucky and Vermont (you can find the Vermont Math Portfolio rubric at education.vermont.gov), have created analytic rubrics for assessing student problem solving. As a teacher, I appreciated having this resource. However, applying an extensive rubric to a classroom's worth of problems is not always feasible. Problems can be assessed quickly for student understanding by asking three questions of each piece:

1. Was the answer correct or partly correct? (If wrong, where did it look like the student went astray?)

2. What models, strategies, or algorithms did the student use?

3. Are there any areas of concern? (If so, what are they?)

Answering these three questions gives enough insight into student thinking to be useful without being overwhelming to implement. If students have the correct answer, the information the teacher gets from the questions is about student use of models, strategies, and algorithms. If a student has an error, these questions help the teacher have some insight into where the problem might be. The teacher should follow up with students whose work raises questions. A flexible interview (See Chapter 3, page 36) is a good way to do this.

My Story

Menu Problems

Erin used two area problems for her menu following the main lesson on multiplying with numbers over 10. Her goal was to get students to work on multiplication and make connections to their work on area. The one-dot problem she used was:

> Rugs are $10 a square foot. If I want to buy a rug that is 6 feet by 4 feet, how much will it cost?

The two-dot problem for the same menu was:

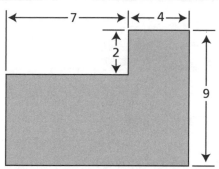

> Rugs are $117 a square foot. How much would it cost to put a rug in this room?

Both problems have a context to help generalize the idea from the main lesson. Both problems can be solved with a variety of strategies.

When Erin began the menu she had listed the required assignments on the board. When she told the class that they would be working on an area problem, she had put two piles of the problems on a table at the front of the room. One pile contained the one-dot problems, the other the two-dot problems. Brian, a student who demonstrated good understanding of multiplication, had walked to the front of the room to select a problem just as Erin was settling down with a group of students for small group instruction. She noticed that he had selected the easier problem.

Erin: You know you'll have to do the two-dot problem, too, right?

Brian: Yeah, I know. I want to do this one first.

Erin: Will you have enough time to finish the rest of the menu by tomorrow?

Brian: I think so. Everything else is done but the problem.

Erin: (*turning to sit with her small group*) OK. Go ahead.

Practice with Number and Operations

Practice with number and operations is an important part of the menu lesson. It helps students continue to deepen their skill and improve recall of facts and procedures. When observing this type of practice in Japan, I was struck by how few equations students solved each day to maintain their skill. I never saw students work on more than five or six arithmetic equations in a day. The goal is not to have students learn by drilling procedures with dozens of equations, but to keep students' skills fresh by coming back to the equations regularly.

The NCTM's *Curriculum Focal Points for Prekindergarten Through Grade 8 Mathematics* (2006) provides excellent guidelines for creating practice for number sense. In third grade (the example in this chapter), the Number and Operations and Algebra strands suggest that students should work at:

My Story

PART 3: Practice with Number and Operations as Part of the Menu Lesson

As Erin moved throughout the classroom to check in with students while they worked on menu items she felt a soft tap on her shoulder. Turning, she was confronted by two girls (Cora and Melissa) holding papers and calculators with a worried look on their faces. Cora and Melissa had been working on their number and operations practice and had run into difficulty when they checked their answers.

Erin: What's wrong, girls?

Melissa: I think we did something wrong on the subtraction problems. We both got the same answer but the calculator says that both our answers are wrong.

Erin: OK. Show me what you did.

Cora: The problem was 350 – 137. Here's my work:

$$\begin{array}{r} \overset{2}{\cancel{3}}\overset{4}{\cancel{5}}10 \\ -\ 1\,3\,7 \\ \hline 1\,1\,3 \end{array}$$

Erin: Tell me about it.

Cora: I didn't have enough ones so I borrowed a hundred . . .

"Developing understandings of multiplication and division and strategies for basic multiplication facts and related division facts."

Number and operations practice for the menu, then, would consist of students' solving equations related to this focal point, such as: "$7 \times 6 = ?$, $6 \times 7 = ?$, $42 \div 6 = ?$, $42 \div 7 = ?$" and so on. Many teachers also add an equation or two for review. In third grade, addition and subtraction with regrouping would be reviewed, so the teacher might add an equation or two that asked students to add or subtract with regrouping. Writing equations is substantially easier than creating problems with rich context. In most cases, the *Curriculum Focal Points* will provide the necessary guidance on which operations are appropriate at a given grade level; however, if state standards do not match these standards, your best bet is to follow the state guidelines, since that is what children will be tested on.

Melissa: No, we borrowed a ten, didn't we?

Erin: What do you mean by "borrowed"?

Melissa: My brother was showing us about this last night. You have to borrow when you don't have enough.

Erin: Were you thinking about this as trading or on the number line?

Melissa: We were thinking about borrowing.

Erin: Let's see if we can get an estimate and go from there. What is one hundred thirty-seven close to?

Cora: One hundred forty.

Erin: If you took one hundred forty away from three hundred fifty, what would you get?

Cora: (*after a pause to think*) About two hundred.

Melissa: We were way off!

Erin: Let's see if we can think our way through this and figure out what borrowing really means.

Erin proceeded to work with the girls using place value blocks. They had a good conversation that helped Melissa and Cora make connections between the trading strategies they understood, and the algorithm that Melissa's brother showed them.

As with the problems part of a menu lesson, practice should be differentiated. To do this, teachers simply create two or three different sets of equations and have students work on the most appropriate set. The "easier" set will generally have lower numbers than the "harder" set (for example, 54 + 17 as opposed to 347 + 488). Sometimes the textbook used in the classroom provides extensive practice for number and operations. In these cases teachers sometimes assign certain exercises as the "easier" practice and others as the "harder" practice. Generally students will spend about ten minutes on these number and operations equations during a menu.

I always have students check their answers *immediately* after working on their number and operations practice. If a student gets more than one answer incorrect, they ask for a conference with me right away. This way I can find out what went wrong in the student's thinking. This simple procedure allows me to address student difficulties as they occur rather than have students pass in their work and try to talk with them about it after the fact.

Math Journaling

Aside from the three assessments discussed in Part 2 of this book (Concrete–Representational–Abstract, Collaborative Study, and Student Interviews), I have found math journals to be a simple and effective way to gain insight into student thinking. During each menu lesson I pose a prompt to help students reflect on their math learning. The prompts focus students' thinking on what they've just learned and ask for metacognitive reflection on it. In the "My Story" sections throughout this chapter, appropriate journaling prompts are: "What is the same or different when multiplying with numbers less than ten and numbers greater than ten?" Or "How does using numbers bigger than ten work with area problems?"

I review students' math journals frequently to get a sense of what they understand and which students might need extra support during the menu lesson. Math journals are also interesting samples to share with parents during parent-teacher conferences as part of helping parents understand their child's progress with math.

Three Ways to Get Students Started Thinking in Their Math Journals

▶ Start with a Picture

▶ Group Writes

▶ I Notice, But I Wonder . . .

Unless your school has created math journal experiences for students in previous years, you'll have help them get started with "thinking" in their journals. There are several ways to do this. I use "start with a picture," group writes, and "I notice, but I wonder" as methods to get children started writing about their mathematical thinking. The big idea for all of these techniques is for students to reflect on their math thinking by putting it on paper.

Start with a Picture "Start with a picture" is a math-writing technique that works well with children as young as first grade, though I've used it with high school students, too. The idea is that students make a drawing in their journals from something that the class has worked on and use this as the basis for comments in their math journal. Sometimes teachers scaffold this approach by giving students a drawing to paste into their journals to use as the basis for writing. A first-grade teacher might, for example, give students a picture of a ten-frame with six dots in it and ask them to write about how many dots there are *and how they know.*

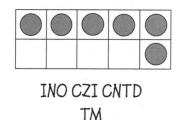

INO CZI CNTD
TM

This first grader writes how he knew that there are six dots on the ten-frame. He says, "I know 'cause I counted them."

There are a variety of ways students could know that there were six dots. The ten-frame allows them to see five and one more, for example, or four less than ten. In this case, the student is telling the teacher that she counted them individually. This is good information and reflects the child's current use of the ten-frame model. At this point, she is not using it for decomposing numbers, preferring instead to "count all."

For Erin's lesson on multiplying with numbers greater than ten (see "My Story," page 163) students might start with a picture of twelve dozen and use this to answer the question: How do you know it's twelve dozen? Why did you choose to represent it this way?"

Group Writes Another technique for getting students started with writing in math journals is to write together. This approach to writing derives a great deal from writer's workshop techniques commonly used in elementary schools. The teacher gives the students a prompt and has them write continuously for three or four minutes. At the end of this time, students share their writing and the teacher highlights work that explains student thinking. The teacher's job during this kind of activity is to facilitate student sharing and to be sure to call the class's attention to writing that focuses on mathematical thinking:

> *Erin:*   Let's write for three minutes on this topic: How is multiplying by numbers greater than ten the same as or different from multiplying by numbers less than ten? I want you to write whatever you think of. Just keep your pencil moving for the next three minutes. (*Students write for three minutes.*) Put your pencils down. I notice that almost all of you were able to write for all three minutes. Great! Now who would like to share something they wrote?
>
> *Amy:*   (*reading*) "Multiplying by bigger numbers is basically the same except the answers are bigger because all the numbers are bigger. I noticed that I didn't know the times tables for bigger numbers like sixteen . . ."
>
> *Erin:*   Thank you. Amy used the phrase, "I noticed . . . " in her writing. Did you catch that? This is a good way to get focused on things you want to mention in your writing.

66 Highlighting the effective elements of mathematical thinking when sharing in the group is an excellent way to bring attention to effective writing and to reinforce its use. 99

Notice that, in this dialogue, Erin focused attention on an element of the shared writing that will help students write good mathematical reflections. Highlighting the effective elements of mathematical thinking when sharing in the group is an excellent way to bring attention to effective writing and to reinforce its use. When students hear and understand what the teacher sees as "quality writing," they are more likely to produce it for him.

I Notice, But I Wonder . . .   Another process for helping students make good use of reflection in math journals is called, "I notice, but I wonder." In the vignette, Amy noticed that she didn't have immediate recall of numbers above ten (few third graders do). Adding, "I wonder" statements after her "I noticed" statement helps to extend the reflection and creates expectations for further insights.

> *Erin:*   Amy said that she noticed she didn't know about times tables bigger than ten. Does anyone have any thoughts about that? What might we "wonder" about what Amy noticed?
>
> *Ben:*   If we have to learn every times table?
>
> *Ian:*   You can't do that.
>
> *Erin:*   Why not, Ian?

Ian: Because there's too many, like, an infinity.

Ashley: There was to be another way to do it without memorizing all the times tables.

Erin: Ashley, can you say that with the words, "I wonder"?

Ashley: I wonder if there's a way to do it without memorizing all the times tables.

"I wonder" statements (often used in science education, too) help tie what students have observed (noticed) with the deeper thinking of inquiry and conjecture (wonder). Combining the two with a journal prompt scaffolds mathematical writing and helps students reflect more deeply on their understanding.

Games

Games are wonderful opportunities for students to work on math and have fun doing it. Some curricula (*Everyday Math* is one example) actually build the practice from games in a part of their design. Students benefit from games in the menu lesson for purposes of practice and to change the routine. The latter is especially important for students with attention challenges (who may need frequent breaks to help regulate their effort—see Chapter 7). Taking a break from problem solving to play a menu game offers students just the change of pace they need while keeping them engaged in math learning.

A game for the lesson on multiplication (described in the "My Story" sections throughout this chapter) could be *Double Dice*. *Double Dice* is a simple multiplication game that requires each player to have two dice and a piece of graph paper. Both players roll their dice at the same time. When the dice hit the table, each player multiplies her dice together. Whoever has the higher total wins. Graph paper is used to verify solutions when there is a dispute. For example, if one player rolls a 6 and a 4 and the other player rolls two 5s, the players may have to draw rectangles (something they learned in the main lesson) to determine which roll (6 times 4 or 5 times 5) is higher. Players play until one player has won ten rolls.

Part 4: Closure

At the end of the menu lesson, students put away materials and come together for the final part—closure. This is a short session (about five to ten minutes) dedicated to helping students bring together the experiences they've had during the math lesson. Closure involves students' sharing their work, their thinking, and their new learning. It is often focused on a question, such as, "When working with rectangles, what did you find out that might help you with multiplication?"

Ease the Struggle

A System for Storing Student Work

Work that students have done during the lesson will need a home. Many teachers organize student work into individual math folders. This system simply requires that students place their work in a single folder after every math lesson. Other teachers have separate storage systems depending on the type of math work (each student may have a separate folder for problems, number-sense work, and math journaling, for example). The type of system that works best depends on the preference of the teacher. The only requirement is that students have a routine for storing their work from one day to the next. ∎

The question gives students the chance to make conjectures about their new learning and to use evidence from their work to support them. In the lesson on rectangles, for example (see the "My Story" sections throughout this chapter), a student might have noticed that the rows and columns in the rectangles are like the beans and cups model: The rows are like the beans and the number of rows are like the cups. If he made this conjecture, he could support it with work from the main lesson. Another student might have observed from the dice game that whenever one of your dice was a 2, all you had to do was double the other number. Other students might verify this if they've played the game, too.

Bringing new learning together is important for wrapping up a busy math lesson. Effective closure helps struggling learners to reflect on the work they've just done and to benefit from the insights that other students have had during the lesson. Closure can also be helpful for clarifying ongoing questions that have not been answered yet by students in the class. Hearing that other students still have questions, and that there is always more to understand and investigate, helps students who struggle to know that math is a process for everyone.

Reflection Questions

1. How do you accommodate exceptional learners in your classroom? In what ways do you include students of different abilities or differentiate work for them? How might the ideas in this chapter help with that?

2. What advantages can you see to using the main lesson—menu format for a lesson? Challenges?

3. How do you promote student-student communication about important mathematical ideas in your classroom? What ideas in this chapter might help you do more of this?

4. How might you manage students in your class to work productively during menu time? What classroom management practices could help you help students stay focused on math?

Resources for Supporting Students Who Struggle

The Big Ideas

● A thorough narrative on interventions to support learners struggling with math content would fill another book. However, this chapter highlights some of the resources most useful in helping with struggles in content and instruction.

Chapter Outline

What Will You Find in This Chapter?

Solving for Why provides numerous suggestions for assessing and understanding student thinking. When these techniques are applied carefully, an educator will have refined insight into a struggling learner's challenges. In Chapter 7, we examined ways to support learners with some of the more common cognitive challenges: attention, memory, and anxiety. Struggles with math content are even more common. Students often struggle with mathematics as a result of difficulties with the math itself, or with the instruction they've received.

A thorough narrative on interventions to support learners struggling with math content would fill another book. However, this chapter highlights some of the resources I've found most useful in helping with struggles in content and instruction. The chapter is structured around four main areas related to number and operations: additive reasoning, multiplicative reasoning, fractions, and proportional reasoning. Students certainly struggle with other domains in mathematics (algebra, geometry, data, probability, measurement, etc.), but number sense is key to success in elementary school and builds the foundations for these domains in high school. For this reason I've chosen to focus attention on resources related to number.

Additive Reasoning

What Is Additive Reasoning?

Early number work focuses on counting, understanding order, and understanding quantity. With additive reasoning students begin to see some of the interesting possibilities for joining, separating, and comparing numbers.

Four Important Elements in Additive Relationships

▶ joining

▶ separating

▶ part/part/whole (partitioning)

▶ comparing (directly)

Additive reasoning encompasses the operations of addition and subtraction, but conceptually includes more. Researchers studying the mathematical content in addition and subtraction, and the way young learners interact with it, have articulated four important elements in additive relationships: joining, separating, part/part/whole (partitioning), and comparing (directly) (Carpenter, Carey, and Kouba 1990; Carpenter 1999).

Joining

As the name suggests, joining is the act of putting quantities together to achieve a larger sum. Problems that involve joining always have one missing piece. Either one of the quantities to be joined is missing, or the result is missing.

Separating

Mathematically, separating problems are quite similar to joining problems. In a sense both of them can be characterized by the part/part/whole (or partitioning) relationship. Separation, however, is closer to the idea of "pulling apart" or "taking away." This kind of thinking is conceptually related to the operation of subtraction. Here, as with joining, there are some common misconceptions that develop, often as a result of the limited opportunities that students have to explore subtraction in conceptually meaningful ways.

Separating (and subtraction) is often conceptualized (by students and teachers) as "take-away." This is a very useful analogy for subtraction, but it has the limitations that all analogies have. The concept of *separating* has advantages over the concept of *taking away* because it covers a much broader

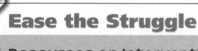

Ease the Struggle

Resources on Interventions and RTI

Assisting Students Struggling with Mathematics: Response to Intervention (RTI) for Elementary and Middle Schools by Russell Gersten et al.

This resource is simply the best review of research on math intervention available—and it's free! The Practice Guide provides extensive information about research on interventions and RTI gleaned from dozens of research studies the authors reviewed. It also ranks the level of evidence provided for each of its recommendations. Every learning specialist who works with math students should have this guide on hand.

Gersten, R., S. Beckmann, B. Clarke, A. Foegen, L. Marsh, J. R. Star, and B. Witzel, B. 2009. *Assisting Students Struggling with Mathematics: Response to Intervention (RtI) for elementary and middle schools.* (NCEE 2009-4060). Washington, DC: National Center for Education Evaluation and Regional Assistance, Institute of Education Sciences, U.S. Department of Education. Retrieved from http://ies. ed.gov/ncee/wwc/publications/practiceguides/. ∎

range of possibilities. Putting a quantity into two (or more) groups is a way of separating without removing anything. The idea of separating leads naturally into the part/part/whole relationship which brings together joining and separating as well as addition and subtraction.

Part/Part/Whole (Partitioning)

Part/part/whole thinking in additive reasoning represents a conception that is inclusive of both joining and separating approaches to computation. It is the idea that a larger sum is made up of two smaller quantities:

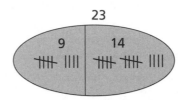

The part/part/whole understanding allows for recognition that partitioning a quantity into groups creates mathematical relationships:

$$9 + 14 = 23$$
$$14 + 9 = 23$$
$$23 - 9 = 14$$
$$23 - 14 = 9$$

The relationships can be seen as joining in some instances, as separating in others.

Part/part/whole expresses the connectedness of joining and separating. It is a more complete way of viewing additive reasoning. Unfortunately, students rarely get enough experience viewing addition and subtraction from this dual perspective. When the numbers get large enough students have difficulty seeing the relationship at all. A first-grade student, for example, who understands that 16 can be broken into parts containing 9 and 7, will often flounder in third or fourth grade when confronted with breaking 245 into parts. As a result, many struggling learners see addition and subtraction as mechanical operations rather than the expression of numerical relationships.

Comparing (Directly)

Comparison is an aspect of additive reasoning that differs slightly from the others in that it asks student to judge in absolute terms between two quantities. Comparing quantities additively provides students with a way to assess the relative magnitude of two groups. Later, during proportional reasoning, they will learn more mathematically sophisticated ways to do this.

Young children don't often have difficulty telling which quantity has more (or less). Where they often get stumped is on the question: How *many* more?

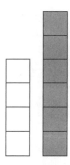

As adults, we can see that this could be answered from either an "adding on" or a "subtracting off" approach. For a young learner, though, the idea that the gray stack includes the quantity in the white stack *and some more* is a new idea. To develop this idea conceptually requires significant experience with both models and problem solving. Often learners struggle because they are rushed to use a subtraction algorithm when comparing, without understanding why that works.

Resources to Help with Additive Reasoning Struggles

Several resources can be helpful for supporting children who struggle with additive reasoning. These books are full of activities that use models and strategies to build strong conceptual understanding of additive reasoning.

- ● *Children's Mathematics* **by Thomas Carpenter**

An excellent resource for elementary teachers is *Children's Mathematics*, which is a commercial version of the University of Wisconsin materials on cognitively guided instruction. *Children's Mathematics* has lots of information on the variety of ways students can solve addition and subtraction problems, as well as helpful video vignettes of students working their way through these types of problems.

> Carpenter, T. P. 1999. *Children's Mathematics: Cognitively Guided Instruction*. Portsmouth, NH: Heinemann.

- ● *Why Can't I Have Everything? Teaching Today's Children to Be Financially and Mathematically Savvy* **by Jane Crawford**

This title is a particularly helpful resource that includes information for parents. Using a variety of engaging activities young students develop a money model for numbers and engage in a wide variety of strategy-building problem solving. In my work with struggling learners in New York City I found money to be an especially useful number model, even for young children. I used the activities in Jane's book to help students learn to think additively.

Crawford, J. 2011. *Why Can't I Have Everything? Teaching Today's Children to Be Financially and Mathematically Savvy*. Sausalito, CA: Math Solutions.

● *Teaching Arithmetic: Lessons for First Grade* **by Stephanie Sheffield**

This resource is one book in a series from Math Solutions, the Teaching Arithmetic series. I like the way Stephanie helps students connect math with everyday life—a great way to initiate first graders to mathematics. When preservice teachers ask for a resource to use to integrate math into morning meeting, this is the resource I recommend.

Sheffield, S. 2001. *Teaching Arithmetic: Lessons for First Grade*. Sausalito, CA: Math Solutions.

● *Teaching Arithmetic: Lessons for Addition and Subtraction: Grades 2–3* **by Bonnie Tank and Lynne Zolli**

This is also part of the Teaching Arithmetic series. I especially appreciate that Bonnie and Lynne provide great activities to examine subtraction as "take-away" (this is fairly common) and as comparison (this is not). Comparison is particularly tricky for young children; the activities in this book help alleviate this difficulty by using familiar counts (like letters in a child's name) for comparison.

Tank, B., and L. Zolli. 2001. *Lessons for Addition and Subtraction: Grades 2–3*. Sausalito, CA: Math Solutions.

● *Teaching Number in the Classroom with 4–8 Year-Olds* **by Robert Wright, Garry Stanger, Ann Stafford, and Jim Martland**

This is a book that is closely associated with Math Recovery. The activities and insights are from work (both classroom and research) done in Australia. This is an excellent resource for additive reasoning because it provides good development of robust models for young children. The work here on the number line is especially helpful for children who struggle as it connects movement of their bodies with movement on the number line.

Wright, R. J., G. Stanger, A. K. Stafford, and J. Martland. 2006. *Teaching Number in the Classroom with 4–8 Year-Olds*. London: Sage.

Ease the Struggle

Math Recovery

Math Recovery also provides some wonderful resources to assess early number sense in the primary grades (see Chapter 5, "Ease the Struggle: What Is Math Recovery?" page 76 for more information on Math Recovery and the PNOA assessment derived from it). ∎

- *Developing Number Concepts: Book 2*
  by Kathy Richardson

  Kathy is the person who made interlocking cubes such a common fixture in elementary classrooms. Her Developing Number Concepts series is excellent. There are lots of useful activities. One of the highlights of Kathy's work is her practical approach to formative assessment. You will find this in the book's section "Analyzing and Assessing Children's Needs."

  Richardson, K. 1999. *Developing Number Concepts: Book 2*. White Plains, NY: Dale Seymour.

- *Young Mathematicians at Work: Constructing Number Sense, Addition, and Subtraction* **by Cathy Fosnot and Maarten Ludovicus Antonius Marie Dolk**

  One of the most helpful professional development resources in New York City is the Math in the City program. Cathy Fosnot, the founder of the program, draws heavily on her work with teachers and the Realistic Math Education (RME) to create the Young Mathematicians at Work series. The series is content rich and focuses on student development of rich mathematical ideas.

  Fosnot, C. T., and M. L. A. M. Dolk. 2001. *Young Mathematicians at Work: Constructing Number Sense, Addition, and Subtraction*. Portsmouth, NH: Heinemann.

Multiplicative Reasoning

What Is Multiplicative Reasoning?

According to the National Council of Teachers of Mathematics (NCTM) (2000), multiplicative reasoning is a key focus on math instruction in grades 3–5. It is found in the arithmetic operations of multiplication and division. As an approach to quantitative thinking, multiplicative reasoning is a recognition and use of grouping in the underlying pattern and structure of our number system. Multiplicative reasoning is the basis for understanding place value and makes it possible for students to see a different kind of relationship between numbers than the sum or difference. The use of multiplicative reasoning to address concepts of growth and shrinkage is the bridge to proportional reasoning and algebra. Multiplicative relationships are qualitatively different from additive relationships. Students' inability to adequately conceptualize this difference can lead to difficulties in middle school mathematics (Misailidou and Williams 2003).

Three Ways Students Think in Groups

1 Skip-Counting

2 Splitting or Doubling

3 Computing the Composite Number

Research has contributed to understanding the ways that multiplicative reasoning develops in children (Clark and Kamii 1996; Harel and Confrey 1994; Tzur et al. 2010; Vergnaud 1988). This work suggests that students develop more complex ways of thinking about numbers as they develop this kind of reasoning. The fundamental element in mathematical thinking that characterizes multiplicative reasoning is children's ability to think in groups. This is often done in three ways.

Skip-Counting

The instructional practice of having students count groups—skip-counting—is an essential transition between additive and multiplicative reasoning. It emphasizes the structures and efficiency that grouping gives to counting. For example, counting tens rods (in base ten blocks) as: 10, 20, 30, 40, and so on, emphasizes the grouping. Likewise counting by fives (using your fingers as a model, or stacks of interlocking cubes), or twos (using eyes or stacks of cubes as models), places emphasis on the sequence and nature of group counting. Of course, if the sequence is learned without the models to support the grouping activity, the order can be learned by rote without significant meaning.

Ease the Struggle

To Add or Not to Add: Is Multiplication Repeated Addition?

Many textbooks teach the operation of multiplication as repeated addition. Conceptually this isn't wrong, but it's a limiting perspective (ironically, they usually *don't* teach division as repeated subtraction—which *would* be helpful). If I always think of 5 times 3 as 5 plus 5 plus 5, how do I deal with 256 times 123? What does it mean that something is four times bigger than something else? From the perspective of supporting struggling learners, some models will generalize more easily than others. So while beginning the multiplicative process with a focus on grouping and (to a limited degree) the connections between addition and multiplication, and subtraction and division, there is more to building a strong understanding of multiplicative reasoning than repeated addition. Susanne Prediger (2008) has an interesting discussion of the connections between multiplicative models and how they support (or don't) students' work with fractions. Resources that make use of area or array models, in addition to grouping models, can be especially helpful for students who struggle with fractions. ■

Splitting and Doubling

A more sophisticated grouping strategy is the idea of splitting (and its counterpart, doubling). Most young children are able to split and double numbers and do it almost intuitively. Splitting 12 into two groups of 6 (or doubling 6 to make 12) expands the understanding of grouping in multiplicative reasoning; it makes students reflect on the fact that *the groups are equal*. Splitting 12 unequally would be easy for students to notice because it's "unfair"—a concept most elementary students understand well. While skip-counting helps students understand the idea of repeated groups, splitting and doubling focuses attention on the groups being equal.

Ease the Struggle

Creating Meaning in Math Learning

Another valuable resource is *Teaching Mathematics Meaningfully* by David Allsopp, Maggie Kyger, and Louann Lovin. I use *Teaching Mathematics Meaningfully* as a resource for all my Math for Struggling Learners courses. The CRA assessment (see Chapter 4) is a classroom-tested refinement of an assessment in this book.

Allsopp, D., M. M. Kyger, and L. A. H. Lovin. 2007. *Teaching Mathematics Meaningfully: Solutions for Reaching Struggling Learners*. Baltimore, MD: Paul H. Brookes. ■

Computing the Composite Number

Through work with a variety of models students can develop the idea that multiplication is the way to compute the total number when a fixed number is in a particular number of groups. Twelve, for example, can be made up of four equal groups of three. This idea is strongly realized when students work with organizing objects in arrays so that the total can be easily understood as being formed as a composite of similar-sized groups.

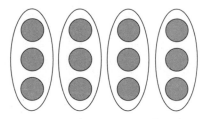

Using groups to create composite representations is an important stage in the development of multiplicative reasoning.

Resources to Help with Multiplicative Reasoning Struggles

Multiplication is an area where memorizing often seems to take the place of true understanding. The Internet is filled with sites and books with suggestions for how to learn (*memorize*) times tables. Understanding those tables seems to be less important. For struggling learners this is a particular problem.

There are, however, several resources that provide excellent activities for students to develop understanding of multiplication and division. All of these resources emphasize the development of multiplication as a grouping or area concept and provide work with models and problems to help students develop this way of reasoning. This makes them excellent resources when working with students who struggle with multiplication and division. These are listed as follows.

● *Teaching Arithmetic: Lessons for Introducing Multiplication: Grade 3* by Marilyn Burns

Teaching Arithmetic: Lessons for Extending Multiplication: Grades 4–5 by Maryann Wickett and Marilyn Burns

Teaching Arithmetic: Lessons for Extending Division: Grades 4–5 by Maryann Wickett and Marilyn Burns

These three Math Solutions books contain helpful activities for building models and strategies for multiplicative reasoning. The circles and stars activity from *Lessons for Introducing Multiplication* is one I have used for years and continue to use. It's an excellent model for grouping, and can be learned by playing a game and drawing stars. In *Lessons for Extending Division*, Wickett and Burns explore both partitive and quotative forms of division and examine some of the number theory around divisibility rules using student inquiry.

Burns, M. 2001. *Lessons for Introducing Multiplication: Grade 3*. Sausalito, CA: Math Solutions.

Wickett, M., and M. Burns. 2001. *Lessons for Extending Multiplication: Grades 4-5*. Sausalito, CA: Math Solutions.

Wickett, M., and M. Burns. 2003. *Lessons for Extending Division: Grades 4–5*. Sausalito, CA: Math Solutions.

● *Young Mathematicians at Work: Constructing Multiplication and Division* by Cathy Twomey Fosnot and Maarten Dolk

Another in Fosnot and Dolk's popular Young Mathematicians series, *Constructing Multiplication and Division* is a useful resource for understanding the way children make mathematical sense of multiplicative reasoning. Of particular interest is the way these authors use a variety of activities to help students generalize their understanding from one context to another.

Fosnot, C. T., and M. L. A. M. Dolk. 2001. *Young Mathematicians at Work: Constructing Multiplication and Division*. Portsmouth, NH: Heinemann.

● *Developing Essential Understanding of Multiplication and Division for Teaching Mathematics in Grades 3–5* **by Albert Otto et al.**

This NCTM book is a rather comprehensive, and somewhat unusual, approach to multiplicative reasoning. The book situates the idea of numbers of similar groups (circles and stars) as scalars and the quantities they describe. The idea is to lay the groundwork for higher mathematics. What's interesting in this book is the discussion of strategies (here identified as "student invented algorithms") and algorithms as well as the ways they are connected.

> Otto, A. D., and National Council of Teachers of Mathematics. 2011. *Developing Essential Understanding of Multiplication and Division for Teaching Mathematics in Grades 3–5*. Reston, VA: National Council of Teachers of Mathematics.

Fractions

More than any other concept in elementary mathematics, fractions are often taught exclusively with step-by-step procedures and little real understanding. When students are asked to work with fractions outside the school context, however, they tend to use their commonsense perceptions to guide their thinking rather than a procedure they learned in school (Kamii and Clark 1995). Evidence of struggles with fractions is not hard to find. Many learners (children and adults) avoid fractions whenever they can. People convert fractions to decimals (so they can use a calculator) or ignore them completely in most everyday situations.

While teachers sometimes use materials like fraction bars or pattern blocks to model fractions as "parts of a whole," student understanding about fractions as numbers is often not fully developed. One of the many difficulties that students experience with fractions is an undeveloped sense of their magnitude and the ability to compare the value of fractions with unlike denominators.

Student difficulties with magnitude of fractions lead to numerous struggles. Consider the following birthday cake problem.

Birthday Cake Problem

At a recent birthday party, Big Al and Tiny Tina both ate a ridiculous amount of cake.

Al claimed that he ate ²/₃ of the cake, while Tina said she ate ⁹/₁₆.

Are they telling the truth?

Who ate more?

Solving this problem does not require computation. A student who understands fractions as numbers that can be placed on the number line would recognize that both fractions are over ½ and, therefore, both Al and Tina could not be telling the truth. If a student has a sense of the magnitude of fractions, she would know that ⁹⁄₁₆ is closer to ½ than ⅔ and so it must be smaller.

The ability to know how to compare fractions and to understand both intuitively and explicitly the value of a fraction is critical to students' success (Bright et al. 1988). This ability can be developed in much the same way knowledge of whole numbers is developed, using a variety of concrete and representational models.

Ease the Struggle

Theory and Struggling Math Learners

There are three books that I frequently recommend for teachers of struggling math learners though they are written for higher education, more than for work in the classroom. While teachers tell me these books are dense, they also appreciate the wealth of information in them.

Children's Mathematics by Julie Ryan and Julian Williams

Children's Mathematics contains a great deal of information on how children construct and use (and misuse) models, as well as other ways kids struggle. The work is based on research conducted in Great Britain.

> Ryan, J., and J. Williams. 2007. *Children's Mathematics 4–15: Learning from Errors and Misconceptions*. Maidenhead, England: McGraw-Hill/Open University Press.

Why Is Math So Hard for Some Children? by Daniel Berch and Michele M. Mazzocco

This resource is a collection of writings that, in 2007, represented some of the best thinking about why students struggle with math and what we might do about it.

> Berch, D. B., and Mazzocco, M. M. M. 2007. *Why Is Math So Hard for Some Children? The Nature and Origins of Mathematical Learning Difficulties and Disabilities*. Baltimore, MD: Paul H. Brookes.

How the Brain Learns Mathematics by David Sousa

In this publication Sousa explores insights into the connections between neuroscience and mathematical thought. Many teachers and parents have found these insights helpful for understanding how their children think about mathematics.

> Sousa, D. 2007. *How the Brain Learns Mathematics*. Thousand Oaks, CA: Corwin Press. ■

Resources to Help with Fractions Struggles

Two resources provide classroom teachers with excellent insight into student learning of fractions and provide teachers with a variety of activities to support learners who are having difficulty.

● *A Focus on Fractions: Bringing Research to the Classroom* **by Marge Petit, Bob Laird, and Ted Marsden**

This is one of the most comprehensive resources I've used for understanding the variety of ways children approach fractions and how we might help them to better understand this area of mathematics. It examines a wide range of data from the Ongoing Assessment Project (OGAP) and presents numerous examples of students' work as they try to make sense of fractions.

Petit, M. M., R. E. Laird, and E. L. Marsden. 2010. *A Focus on Fractions: Bringing Research to the Classroom.* New York: Routledge.

● *Beyond Pizzas & Pies: 10 Essential Strategies for Supporting Fraction Sense, Grades 3–5* **by Julie McNamara**

This is a classroom resource that provides teachers with a menu of activities for developing real understanding through model and strategy development. It has good information on where students are likely to struggle with fractions and what teachers might do about it. It's a must-have resource to help struggling learners develop more than just a procedural understanding of fractions.

McNamara, J. 2010. *Beyond Pizzas & Pies: 10 Essential Strategies for Supporting Fraction Sense, Grades 3–5.* Sausalito, CA: Math Solutions.

Proportional Reasoning

What Is Proportional Reasoning?

Proportional reasoning is a critical (some would say watershed) way of thinking mathematically that connects many of the concepts of arithmetic with higher mathematics. It is considered by some educators to be the culminating mathematical concept in elementary and middle school. It is directly connected to algebra and to algebraic thinking, and forms the foundations for conceptual understanding in topics in geometry, measurement, and probability. The ability to reason proportionally has implications for science, mathematics, economics, and geography.

Proportional reasoning is the ability to compare quantities (or amounts, or measures) in such a way that one can be expressed *in terms of* the other. It is built on the idea of comparing ratios.

$$a/b = c/d$$

Mathematically, proportions are expressed with the equation: $y = kx$. This is a useful way to conceptualize proportions *abstractly* and creates strong connections to linear functions. However, I find that struggling learners benefit most from the notion that proportions are about multiplicative *relationships*. Without this understanding, students can have difficulty working with proportions.

We write ratios the same way we write fractions (⅓) or odds (1:3), but when we think of proportions we think about the relationship between the

Ease the Struggle

Additive Versus Multiplicative Relationships

The most common difficulties that children have with proportional reasoning lie in the differences between comparing two quantities *additively* and *multiplicatively*. A number of researchers have investigated this difficulty (Cramer and Post 1993). We can investigate the difference between additive and multiplicative relationships by considering a problem where both kinds of comparison are possible:

Bert's and Ernie's Investments
Bert and Ernie invested money in movie companies.
Bert invested $10 in YoDog Films.
Ernie invested $5 in Rainbow-Unicorn movies.
After a year, Bert received $20 and Ernie received $15.
Who made the better investment?

If we compare the investments *additively*, we find that Bert and Ernie each made ten dollars. From this perspective the profits are the same. However, over time, these investments would be very different. The *multiplicative* comparison of the investments shows that Ernie made three times his investment, while Bert only made twice what he put in. Getting students to discuss and conceptualize the differences between these two perspectives is at the heart of remediation of proportional reasoning. This process is not easy, but getting students to articulate key differences in concepts is an excellent way to help them understand. ∎

two numbers rather than the numbers themselves. The number 3 is three times as big as the number 1. If we focus on the multiplicative relationship (one number is three times bigger than the other), all numbers that have the same relationship will be equal to this ratio.

Resources to Help with Proportional Reasoning Struggles

Articles

Research has helped to identify the variety of problem types that students encounter in proportional problems. The article "Proportional Reasoning" (Lesh, Post, and Behr 1988) is especially helpful in getting an overview of the instructional issues that accompany proportional reasoning. Carol Lawton's (1993) article on the ways problem situations can throw students is also helpful for understanding the many ways students can have difficulty with proportion. These articles also discuss key elements in proportional problems that cause difficulties, and how students might approach proportionality more successfully.

Books

As with other areas of number and operations in elementary and middle school, activities that support the creation of useful models and strategies are key to developing proportional reasoning concepts. Two resources stand out as good sources for these types of investigations.

● ***Developing Essential Understanding of Ratios, Proportions, and Proportional Reasoning for Teaching Mathematics: Grades 6–8* by Joanne Lobato, Amy Ellis, Randall Charles, and Rose Mary Zbiek**

As with the earlier volume, *Developing Essential Understanding*, on multiplicative reasoning, this volume is a thorough exploration of proportional reasoning. Chapter 3 is particularly helpful for teachers of struggling learners as it identifies some key links between practices in multiplication and proportional reasoning. These transitions are essential for any student who struggles with proportions.

Lobato, J., A. B. Ellis, R. I. Charles, and R. M. Zbiek. 2010. *Developing Essential Understanding of Ratios, Proportions, and Proportional Reasoning for Teaching Mathematics: Grades 6–8*. Reston, VA: National Council of Teachers of Mathematics.

● *It's All Connected: The Power of Proportional Reasoning to Understand Mathematics Concepts, Grades 6–8* by Carmen Whitman

There are great activities in this resource for developing proportional thinking in middle school students. The activities are closely tied to the Common Core State Standards, and classroom teachers will find them helpful. The lessons are aimed at an alternative to having students set up the cross-products algorithm and solve. Of particular interest is how carefully lessons are articulated. There are specific questions included to help struggling learners dig a bit deeper without taking the learning away from them.

> Whitman, C. 2011. *It's All Connected: The Power of Proportional Reasoning to Understand Mathematics Concepts: Grades 6–8*. Sausalito, CA: Math Solutions.

● *Classroom Discussions: Using Math Talk to Help Students Learn, Grades 1–6* by Suzanne Chapin, Nancy Canavan Anderson, and Mary Catherine O'Conner

This is an excellent resource for supporting in-depth student-student discussions in the math classroom. The authors provide helpful suggestions for supporting discussions in a variety of formats. I especially appreciate the way the authors approach using classroom discussions to uncover misconceptions and support struggling learners. The tools this work provides will help children be more thoughtful and reflective about their math thinking. There is also a set of DVD examples that can be used along with the book, *Classroom Discussions: Seeing Math Discourse in Action, Grades K–6*, to help explore classroom conversations and how they can support math learning.

> Chapin, S. H., N. C. Anderson, and M. C. O'Connor. 2003. *Classroom Discussions: Using Math Talk to Help Students Learn, Grades 1–6*. Sausalito, CA: Math Solutions.

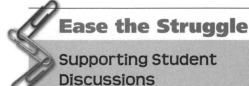

Ease the Struggle

Supporting Student Discussions

A few resources provide good templates for supporting student-student discussions about key content that can be helpful in distinguishing between additive and multiplicative thinking. Mathematical discussions of the ways additive growth and multiplicative growth differ are critical to helping students move toward a more complete understanding of proportion. The resources in this chapter offer helpful information on how to manage discussions that will be mathematically productive for struggling learners—and everyone else in class. ■

● *5 Practices for Orchestrating Productive Mathematics Discussions* **by Mary Kay Stein and Margaret Smith**

This resource makes use of student work as the springboard for classroom discussions. The instructional approach called *constructionism*, articulated by Papert and Harel, makes similar use of "artifacts" (student work) in a collaborative setting to further everyone's understanding. The tools this book provides will be helpful for engaging students in whole-class discussions.

Smith, M. S., and M. K. Stein. 2011. *5 Practices for Orchestrating Productive Mathematics Discussions*. Reston, VA: National Council of Teachers of Mathematics.

Ease the Struggle

Work by Marilyn Burns and John Van De Walle

Any in-depth consideration of math instruction to support *all* learners must include work by Marilyn Burns and John Van De Walle. Perhaps more than any other educators in professional development and higher education, they have promoted instruction that supports students to really learn what math means and how it works. These two works should be on the bookshelf of every serious elementary math teacher:

Burns, M. 2007 *About Teaching Mathematics: A K–8 Resource*. 3rd ed. Sausalito, CA: Marilyn Burns Education Associates.

Van De Walle, J. A., K. S. Karp, and J. M. Bay-Williams. 2009. *Elementary and Middle School Mathematics: Teaching Developmentally*. Boston: Allyn & Bacon. ■

Reproducibles and Additional Reference Tools

All Reproducibles are also available as downloadable, printable versions at www.mathsolutions.com/solvingforwhyreproducibles.

Developing Theories: Template

I want to know more about _____ math thinking, because
[student's name]

he/she _____
[Specific performance/behavior that caused concern]

on _____.
[assignment or assessment]

1. **Theory from the Learner Frame**

   What conceptual tools (models) does the student use (if any) to understand this concept?

   What evidence exists (if any) that a learner struggles with memory, attention, or anxiety challenges?

2. **Theory from the Content Frame**

   Which gaps in math understanding might account for this learner's difficulty? What would he or she need to understand mathematically not to struggle with this concept?

3. **Theory from the Instructional Frame**

   How might this learner have been taught this concept? In what ways might this approach have led to misunderstandings? What other approach might better serve the student?

What the student might think is . . .

1. _____,

   because_____.

2. _____,

   because_____.

3. _____,

   because_____.

CRA Assessment: Template

CRA Assessment Template

BIG IDEA/FOCUS

PLANNING

Standards

What standards will the assessment address?	

Expectations

What do you think students already know about this topic?	
What kinds of models would you expect students to use?	
Where might they have difficulty?	

(continued)

ADMINISTERING THE ASSESSMENT

How will you administer the assessment? (Student choice or teacher choice for starting station? Moving individually? Rotating groups? Whole class?)

Concrete Station

Problem	
Materials	
How will you record student work?	

Representational Station

Problem	
Materials	
How will you record student work?	

Abstract Station

Problem	
Materials	
How will you record student work?	

ANALYZING THE ASSESSMENT	
Sorting categories	
When sorting the student work by models, strategies, or algorithms, what patterns did you find?	
Models	
Strategies	
Algorithms	
Questions Pile	
What questions did you have about samples that were difficult to understand?	
What (if any) common misconceptions appeared in the work?	
Did students show any indicators of cognitive difficulties, such as memory difficulties, attention challenges, or anxiety? If so, who and what were the indicators?	
Anything else discovered with this assessment?	

CRA Assessment Example: First Grade

CRA Assessment Template
BIG IDEA/FOCUS regrouping with addition to 30
PLANNING
Standards

What standards will the assessment address? Common Core, Grade 1	(1) Students develop strategies for adding and subtracting whole numbers based on their prior work with small numbers. They use a variety of models, including discrete objects and length-based models (e.g., cubes connected to form lengths), to model add-to, take-from, put-together, take-apart, and compare situations to develop meaning for the operations of addition and subtraction, and to develop strategies to solve arithmetic problems with these operations.

Expectations	
What do you think students already know about this topic?	We've practiced trading tens for 10 ones. They also (most of them) know how to count to 30.
What kinds of models would you expect students to use?	We've been using interlocking cubes and base ten blocks, so I expect them to use these.
Where might they have difficulty?	I think about half the class will have no trouble solving the problem, but I expect them to count on, rather than regroup.

ADMINISTERING THE ASSESSMENT

How will you administer the assessment? (Student choice or teacher choice for where to start? Moving individually? Rotating groups? Whole class?)

I've put them into three groups (mixed ability). They'll move from one station to the next every ten minutes. I'll stay at the concrete station and the learning specialist will be at the abstract station.

Concrete Station

Problem	Sam has 12 books. Edie has 9 books. How many books do they have together? Show me, then draw a picture.
Materials	interlocking cubes, base ten blocks, pennies and dimes, tiles, and books
How will you record student work?	I'll ask the children to draw their solutions. I'll ask the students to draw their solutions and explain their answers in their own words.

Representational Station

Problem	Jason has 7 cents. He gets 14 more cents. How much money does he have now? Draw a picture and use numbers.
Materials	pencils, erasers, paper (plain, lined, graph), markers
How will you record student work?	I'll ask the children to draw their solutions, once they have built them with one of the manipulatives. I'll also have a clipboard and 5-by-7-inch sticky notes on which I'll make notes.

Abstract Station

Problem	Alissa has 18 stickers. Her mom gives her 7 more. How many does she have now? Write a number sentence to answer.
Materials	pencils, paper, the chart where we wrote our daily equations during meeting (to remind students what a number sentence is)
How will you record student work?	Students will write their number sentence and add their names.

ANALYZING THE ASSESSMENT

Sorting categories

When sorting the student work by models, strategies, or algorithms, what patterns did you find?

Models	The most common model was tally marks at the representational station (twelve students). I think this was because we just worked on tallies in our unit on counting. The rest of the students (who finished) drew some kind of circle. Many (eight) children used books at the concrete station. This isn't surprising since the problem was about books.
Strategies	Students used counting all frequently at both C and R stations. A few students counted on. I marked on the papers when I noticed this. (CA = counting all, CO = counting on.) Only three students made groups of ten at either the concrete or representational stations. Even when they used groups of five for tallies they still counted by fives, rather than putting two together to make ten.
Algorithms	Four students (Gina, Amy, Joel, Milo) wrote a number sentence to solve. It's unclear from their work whether they are regrouping. Kay (learning specialist) says that they were all counting on from 18 except for Milo, who started at 1.

Questions Pile

What questions did you have about samples that were difficult to understand?	Abby: I want to check in with her on her counting. She showed she could use both cubes and drawing (drew circles for pennies) but her counts were wrong in both cases. Is there a counting problem or is she rushing? Inattentive? Ben: At the concrete station he piled up books. He did make two piles but he didn't seem to connect this to the numbers in the problem. He was unable to complete the other problems. At the representational station he drew what I think is a dollar bill.
What (if any) common misconceptions appeared in the work?	All of the students except Abby and Ben seemed to have the sense of "having some" and "getting more." Abby seemed to have difficulty counting and Ben just seemed stuck. (See above)
Did students show any indicators of cognitive difficulties, such as memory difficulties, attention challenges, or anxiety? If so, who and what were the indicators?	Ben might have been anxious or distracted. He looked a little sad and lost and didn't do much with these problems, even when I offered to scribe for him.
Anything else discovered with this assessment?	Next time I give it, I should remember to have an activity for students who finish early. Several students were sitting around waiting for us to change stations. Waiting is not a good use of their time.

CRA Assessment Example: Third Grade

CRA Assessment Template

BIG IDEA/FOCUS

Can students use a multiplicative model to solve division problems with remainders?

PLANNING

Standards

What standards will the assessment address? Common Core, Grade 3	3. Use multiplication and division within 100 to solve word problems in situations involving equal groups, arrays, and measurement quantities, e.g., by using drawings and equations with a symbol for the unknown number to represent the problem.

Expectations

What do you think students already know about this topic?	I know that students have used circles and stars, beans and cups, and area as models for multiplication. What I don't know is how they can apply this to sharing among groups.
What kinds of models would you expect students to use?	I think they will use circles and stars most often, though several students seem to get the connection between that model and the area model. I would expect these students to draw rectangles because this is faster (and easier) than drawing lots of stars.
Where might they have difficulty?	I think some students might get stuck on the remainder piece. I expect most of them to have little trouble putting a total into groups.

(continued)

ADMINISTERING THE ASSESSMENT

How will you administer the assessment? (Student choice or teacher choice for where to start? Moving individually? Rotating groups? Whole class?)

I'm going to set up three stations and have students move from station to station as they finish. I'll let them choose where they start this time.

I'll have trays at each station for finished student work. I'll stay at the concrete station and Stella (classroom para) will stay at the representational station.

Concrete Station

Problem	Our class is going on a field trip. There are 24 students in our class. If each car can hold 5 students, how many cars will we need to go on our trip? Show your thinking with one of the materials.
Materials	cubes, tiles, beans, chips
How will you record student work?	I'm going to take a picture of each student's work, print it (immediately) and have the student write about it for me. I'll have them do the writing at a second table.

Representational Station

Problem	There are 48 children in third grade. All of third grade is going on a field trip. If mini-buses hold 10 kids each, how many buses will we need? Draw a picture to show your thinking.
Materials	colored pencils, markers, paper, graph paper
How will you record student work?	Students will use representations and record their solutions. Stella will ask questions and take notes as necessary.

Abstract Station

Problem	There are 39 children in second grade. They are all going on a field trip. If parent cars hold 6 children each, how many cars are needed for the field trip? Show your thinking only with numbers. (Write an equation or number sentence.)
Materials	Pencils and paper
How will you record student work?	Students will record equations to show their solutions.

ANALYZING THE ASSESSMENT

Sorting categories

When sorting the student work by models, strategies, or algorithms, what patterns did you find?

Models	Students seemed to have the easiest time at the representational station. Ten kids drew some kind of circle with something like tallies in it (not stars). No one used a rectangle. At the concrete station students used piles of beans (eleven) or stacks of cubes (eight). One student, Sam, didn't seem to understand that the groups all needed to be equal—except for the remainder. He put different numbers of kids into cars (concrete) but explained it by saying that cars have different numbers of seats.
Strategies	Mostly students used counting out individual groups until reaching a total. A few students (two) started with a guess at the number of groups and then tried giving tallies to them one at a time.
Algorithms	This was a surprise. Only one student (Evan) used multiplication. All others who had answers used repeated addition.

Questions Pile

What questions did you have about samples that were difficult to understand?	Jessica's drawing (representations) doesn't make sense to me. The boxes she made look like cubes but there are too few and she doesn't indicate an answer. Did she stop? Give up? Taylor's abstract page just has numbers on it (6 and 39). I don't know if he intended to do something with them or if this is as far as he got.
What (if any) common misconceptions appeared in the work?	The remainders were a problem for most students (twelve). This isn't so much a misconception as something that we haven't done yet.
Did students show any indicators of cognitive difficulties, such as memory difficulties, attention challenges, or anxiety? If so, who and what were the indicators?	Erika seemed frustrated when she couldn't think of an equation. She asked several times, "What's an equation?" When we gave her examples she still seemed puzzled. I don't think she was confused about equations, I think she was frustrated because she couldn't come up with any.
Anything else discovered with this assessment?	I expected the kids to make connections with the work we've done on grouping. While they used the groups that the problem asked for, most just counted on. They don't seem to have a sense of how to use the models for problems yet.

CRA Assessment Example: Fifth Grade

CRA Assessment Template	
BIG IDEA/FOCUS	
finding quotients with double-digit divisors	
PLANNING	
Standards	
What standards will the assessment address? Common Core, Grade 5	6. Find whole-number quotients of whole numbers with up to four-digit dividends and two-digit divisors, using strategies based on place value, the properties of operations, and/or the relationship between multiplication and division. Illustrate and explain the calculation by using equations, rectangular arrays, and/or area models.
Expectations	
What do you think students already know about this topic?	Students have already demonstrated the ability to compute quotients with single digit divisors using a variety of strategies as well as both standard and partial quotients algorithms.
What kinds of models would you expect students to use?	We've done quite a lot of work with the area model and the area strategy for decomposing numbers during multiplication. I hope they will apply this to division. Also, the fundamental idea that division is about making equal groups should help students. In a sense this is a test of their multiplicative reasoning.
Where might they have difficulty?	There are a couple of students who only use algorithms. I wonder if they will be able to create models for the problems. They might know how algorithms are informed by number sense but this will test their understanding.

ADMINISTERING THE ASSESSMENT

How will you administer the assessment? (Student choice or teacher choice for where to start? Moving individually? Rotating groups? Whole class?)

The assessment will be conducted as a whole class. We'll start with the concrete models and work our way to the abstract. Students will work at their tables in order to share materials but they must work independently. I think this can happen in one class period.

Concrete Station

Problem	Suzanne has $5.00. She wants to buy cupcakes that cost $.35 each. How many cupcakes can she buy?
Materials	classroom money, base ten blocks, chips for trading
How will you record student work?	Students must first create a model using materials and then draw a picture to show how they solved.

Representational Station

Problem	There are 14 candies in every roll. How many rolls can you make with 800 candies?
Materials	graph paper, unlined paper, pencils, markers
How will you record student work?	Students will record their representations and their explanations. I will remind students of the representations we've worked with already (graphs, T-charts, tables, organized lists, diagrams) with a chart of these at the front of the room that includes examples. I think this will help students whose first language is not English with the idea of "representations."

Abstract Station

Problem	196 students signed up for soccer. If the soccer league puts 16 students on a team, how many teams will the league have?
Materials	pencils and paper
How will you record student work?	Students will record an equation <u>and their calculations</u> so I get a sense of how they computed their answers.

From *Solving for Why: Understanding, Assessing, and Teaching Students Who Struggle with Math, Grades K–8* by John Tapper. © 2012 Houghton Mifflin Harcourt Publishing Company. Permission granted to photocopy for nonprofit use in a classroom or similar place dedicated to face-to-face educational instruction.

ANALYZING THE ASSESSMENT	
Sorting categories	
When sorting the student work by models, strategies, or algorithms, what patterns did you find?	
Models	Not a surprise Everyone went for the money. I thought this would happen but I wasn't prepared for how many didn't really know how much the coins were worth or how to add coins up to a dollar. There was a good deal of whispering at tables as students reminded each other of how to make 35 cents. Two students began by using pennies (!). A T-chart was the most common representation. Students put candies one side and rolls on the other.
Strategies	Except at the abstract station, virtually everyone used some form of "adding up." They would start with one cupcake or roll of candies and then work from there. About half the class figured out that they could save time by using multiples.
Algorithms	Nine of the twenty-five students in the class used some form of algorithm to solve the problem. The rest really used another counting up strategy, similar to what they did at the other stations. They don't seem to have generalized the idea of the algorithm to larger numbers.
Questions Pile	
What questions did you have about samples that were difficult to understand?	Anog seemed confused at all parts of the assessment. This is not surprising since his English is still fairly rudimentary. During the abstract part of the assessment he wrote an equation (I think) that might be the Thai version of division. This needs more investigation with the teacher supporting him in learning English. Samantha and Tyler had difficulty with the money. The drawings on their papers looked like the others at their table but when I watched them they seemed lost. I should check on their understanding of money.
What (if any) common misconceptions appeared in the work?	The value of coins was not really a misconception—just something a few students don't know. I was surprised at how the students continued to "add up" rather than use multiplication. Why?
Did students show any indicators of cognitive difficulties, such as memory difficulties, attention challenges, or anxiety? If so, who and what were the indicators?	Anog seemed anxious, but it's hard to know how much of that is simply that he is in a new country. Gerald was fidgety throughout all parts of the assessment. He was bouncing his foot and waving his pencil constantly. It didn't seem to bother his tablemates but I'm concerned it was distracting. The difficulty with money makes me wonder whether these students were taught about money and might have forgotten? Could this be a memory issue or something I should speak with the fourth-grade teacher about?
Anything else discovered with this assessment?	Using a money problem for the concrete portion was useful in the sense that we had plenty of manipulatives and it revealed a weakness some students have there. I wonder, though, as students were working on the problem if it might not really fit the focus of the assessment since it added the aspect of decimals.

CRA Assessment Example: Seventh Grade

CRA Assessment Template

BIG IDEA/FOCUS

solving a distance/rate problem with an initial position—moving from $d = r*t$ (a proportion, to $d = r*t + s$ (starting position)

PLANNING

Standards

What standards will the assessment address? Common Core, Grade 7	Use variables to represent quantities in a real-world or mathematical problem, and construct simple equations and inequalities to solve problems by reasoning about the quantities. a. Solve word problems leading to equations of the form $px + q = r$ and $p(x + q) = r$, where p, q, and r are specific rational numbers. Solve equations of these forms fluently. Compare an algebraic solution to an arithmetic solution, identifying the sequence of the operations used in each approach. For example, the perimeter of a rectangle is 54 cm. Its length is 6 cm. What is its width?

Expectations

What do you think students already know about this topic?	Students have spent a considerable amount of time over the last two years working on a variety of models for proportions. They have not written these in the $y = kx$ form, however. Earlier in the year we wrote proportions as an equivalence of ratios. They have some experience with rate problems from sixth grade. I'm not sure what students really understand about equivalence.
What kinds of models would you expect students to use?	I don't think physical materials would be useful for this CRA. I'm substituting a SimCalc simulation of distance/time graphing for a concrete manipulative. While virtual, it still allows students to use a graphing simulation to find an answer.
Where might they have difficulty?	I don't know if the problems will be so difficult, but I'm not sure if the students will see the connections with the equation for a linear function. I also think they might have some trouble separating the starting position (constant) from the rate.

(continued)

ADMINISTERING THE ASSESSMENT

How will you administer the assessment? (Student choice or teacher choice for where to start? Moving individually? Rotating groups? Whole class?)

Students will work at individual stations for each of the problems. They can choose where to start. The four computers that have SimCalc on them are connected to printers so students can print out screenshots. There may be a little backlog at the computers but all the students will eventually work their way through.

Concrete Station

Problem	Use the SimCalc simulation on the classroom computers to show a solution to the problem below.
	An elevator moves upward at a steady rate of 1 floor every 3 seconds. If the elevator starts on the third floor, how long will it take to reach the 11th floor?
	Print the screen shot of your solution and write about it.
Materials	computers, SimCalc software
	(SimCalc MathWords® can be retrieved at: www.kaputcenter.umassd.edu/products/software/)
How will you record student work?	printed screenshot and explanation

Representational Station

Problem	Tom and Mary are having a race. Mary runs 1 meter every 1.2 seconds. Tom runs 1 meter every 1.5 seconds. If Mary gives Tom a 4 meter head start, who will win the race? Show your work with a representation (chart, graph, or table).
Materials	graph paper, paper, colored pencils, pencils
How will you record student work?	Students will submit their representations and explanations along with their solutions.

Abstract Station

Problem	Lola runs the 100-yard dash. When she runs the whole distance her time is usually 12 seconds. If she starts at the 40-yard line (gets a 40-yard head start) how long will it take her to run 100 yards?
Materials	pencils and paper
How will you record student work?	Students will record answers (figured with equations) and explanations for their work. All computations will be included.

ANALYZING THE ASSESSMENT

Sorting categories

When sorting the student work by models, strategies, or algorithms, what patterns did you find?

Models	The elevator simulation produced a variety of interesting results. All the students (but one) were able to create the simulation adequately. They all were not, though, able to interpret the graph for the elevator's motion. There were several comments on the screenshots about the fact that the graph was a "slanted line" (rather than a vertical line like the motion of an elevator). Some students seemed also to be confused with the difference between the 11th floor and going up 11 floors.
	The representational problem was meant to elicit mathematical representations but several students attempted to solve the problem using a drawing of the situation and trying to reason their way through it. Most were unsuccessful. It would seem that this problem needs attention to help students visualize what's actually taking place.
Strategies	The most common strategies came up at the representational station and the abstract station. Students made charts that showed Mary and Tom's position ("How far," "distance," "distance gone") with relative times.
	Four students also made a graph of this. I think this represents sophisticated thinking to see the table as a graph with Tom and Mary's progress as separate lines. I wonder if the SimCalc program helped with this. (Did these students do that first?)
	When working at the abstract station, students solved the equation in two parts.
Algorithms	No one created a $d = r*t + s$ equation. Many students put drawings in at the abstract station, even though they were supposed to use only equations. For students who solved the problem, the approach was to use one equation to find Lola's rate and then to apply it to 60 yards instead of 100.

Questions Pile

What questions did you have about samples that were difficult to understand?	I have a number of questions to follow up on: • Zach's screen shot from the SimCalc station shows the elevator at the 11th floor and nothing else. I have no idea how he made it do that or what sense he made of it since all he wrote was, "It's on the 11 floor." • Chris drew an oval for the race problem with a big "12" in the center but nothing else. Is the oval a racetrack? Did he just not know how to go further? • Junie was able to print an accurate screenshot of the elevator problem. He circled the 11th floor and wrote, "24." He was unable to do very much with the other problems. Is this an issue with English?
What (if any) common misconceptions appeared in the work?	The most common difficulty students had was being thrown off by the constant. I think this element made the problems unrecognizable as proportional problems for almost everyone.
Did students show any indicators of cognitive difficulties, such as memory difficulties, attention challenges, or anxiety? If so, who and what were the indicators?	Jocelyne didn't get finished at any of the stations. This is fairly typical of her work. I'm not sure if there is an issue but it deserves some investigation. Junie seemed to have some difficulty with the language of the problems. His English in class is pretty good so I often forget that he is still learning English. I should have read the problems to him or had him work with Jaime (so they could speak about the contexts in Spanish) to be sure he understood what he was supposed to do.
Anything else discovered with this assessment?	Next time I give it, I should remember to have an activity for students who finish early. Several students were sitting around waiting for us to change stations. Waiting is not a good use of their time.

Collaborative Study: Template

Student's name: _____ Student's grade: _____

Student's teacher: _____

Date of referral for collaborative study: _____

Who made the referral? _____

Has proper consent[1] been given to gather and share this information?

      _____ yes   _____ no

      By whom? _____ Date _____

What behavior/performance prompted a desire for collaborative study?

On which particular math content is this study focused?

I. Student History

- Impressions from the math teacher

  Report important comments from the student's math teacher about both performance/behavior on the targeted math area and overall impressions in class. Please collect samples of student work to share at the collaborative study meeting.

- Math report card assessment (and/or grades) over time

  Report student's report card assessments over the last three years. Note any patterns that exist.

- Standardized Test Scores

Years				
Results				

[1]The required consent will vary depending on student's IEP or 504 status, the information gathered, and state and local policies and statutes. Please consult with school leaders to be sure what constitutes proper consent.

- Other relevant information on the student's math history?

II. Setting Up the Collaborative Study

- Who will attend?

  (Suggestions: student's math teacher, school leader, math specialist, another math teacher)

- Who will notify attendees?

- Who will facilitate the meeting?

- When and where will the meeting take place?

  Date: _____

  Time: _____

  Location: _____

III. Meeting and Intervention

1. Identify a specific concern about the student.
2. Give background on the student (allow members to ask clarifying questions).
3. Share recent student work.
4. Brainstorm theories that might account for the student's struggles.
5. Create an action plan to test the group's theories.

- What theories does the group have about the student's difficulties?
  (Be sure to connect the theories to evidence.)

(continued)

- What interventions might be used to test these theories?

  Theory 1:

  Theory 2:

  Theory 3:

- Who will implement these interventions and gather data/impressions on their effectiveness?

  Theory 1:

  Theory 2:

  Theory 3:

- Follow-up meeting to review results:

  Theory 1:

  Theory 2:

  Theory 3:

IV. Results and Recommendations

- Report results of intervention:

- Recommendations of the collaborative study committee:

Planning a Student Interview: Template

Student's name: _____ Student's grade: _____

Student's teacher: _____

Has proper consent[1] been given to gather and share this information?

_____ yes   _____ no

By whom? _____ Date _____

On which particular math content is this interview focused?

I. Student History

- Impressions from the math teacher

  Report important comments from the student's math teacher about both performance/behavior on the targeted math area and overall impressions in class. Please collect samples of student work to share at the collaborative study meeting.

- Math report card assessment (and/or grades) over time

  Report student's report card assessments over the last three years. Note any patterns that exist.

- Standardized Test Scores

Years				
Results				

- Conversation with a parent or guardian

  Report impressions/information that the student's parent or guardian has about the student's math learning.

[1]The required consent will vary depending on student's IEP or 504 status, the information gathered, and state and local policies and statutes. Please consult with school leaders to be sure what constitutes proper consent.

(continued)

From *Solving for Why: Understanding, Assessing, and Teaching Students Who Struggle with Math, Grades K–8* by John Tapper. © 2012 Houghton Mifflin Harcourt Publishing Company. Permission granted to photocopy for nonprofit use in a classroom or similar place dedicated to face-to-face educational instruction.

- Other relevant information on the student's math history?

II. Problems to Use for the Interview

- Math focus for problems for the interview:
- Approximate grade level of student on this topic (your estimation):
- Problems at grade level:

  Problem 1:

  Problem 2:

  Problem 3:

- Problems one grade below grade level:

  Problem 1:

  Problem 2:

- Problems two grades below grade level:

  Problem 1:

  Problem 2:

- Problems one grade above grade level:

  Problem 1:

  Problem 2:

III. Setting Up the Student Interview

Make sure that the classroom teacher has advanced notification.
Try to avoid removing the student from favorite activities, like recess.
Is the interview space appropriate? Are you unlikely to be interrupted?

Date: _____

Time: _____

Location: _____

Conducting a Student Interview: Template

Student's name: _____ Student's grade: _____

Student's teacher: _____

Remember that the goal is to understand student thinking, not to teach.

Recording time will help you find places of interest in the interview more easily.

Begin Recording

Recording Time: 00:00

- Introductions

Create an informal and supportive atmosphere with a conversation about the student's interests. Be sure to get the student's impressions of why the interview is taking place and let him/her know what he/she might expect. Emphasize that you are more interested in thinking than in correct answers. For this reason it will be helpful to you if the student can think aloud while working.

Recording Time:

- Problem 1:

Read the problem <u>together</u>. Begin by asking the student to tell you what the problem is asking you to find out. As the student works and thinks aloud, record impressions below as well as follow up questions. The ➥ prompt is a space for you to record questions you want to remember to ask the student.

➥ Remember to ask:

Impressions:

Save student sample for Problem 1.

(continued)

Recording Time:

- Problem 2:

  Read the problem <u>together</u>. Begin by asking the student to tell you what the problem is asking you to find out. As the student works and thinks-aloud, record impressions below as well as follow up questions. The ➺ prompt is a space for you to record questions you want to remember to ask the student.

➺ Remember to ask:

Impressions:

Save student sample for Problem 2.

Recording Time:

- Problem 3:

  Read the problem <u>together</u>. Begin by asking the student to tell you what the problem is asking you to find out. As the student works and thinks-aloud, record impressions below as well as follow up questions. The ➺ prompt is a space for you to record questions you want to remember to ask the student.

➺ Remember to ask:

Impressions:

Save student sample for Problem 3.

Recording Time:

- Problem 4:

  Read the problem <u>together</u>. Begin by asking the student to tell you what the problem is asking you to find out. As the student works and thinks-aloud, record impressions below as well as follow up questions. The ➡ prompt is a space for you to record questions you want to remember to ask the student.

➡ Remember to ask:

Impressions:

Save student sample for Problem 4.

Continue template as needed for subsequent problems.

Analyzing a Student Interview: Template

Student's name: _____ Student's grade: _____

Student's teacher: _____

I. Prepare for Analysis

Gather the following:

- Recording of interview
- Interview template recording sheets (see Reproducible 6.2)
- Student history (see Reproducible 6.1)

II. Listen to Interview Recording

- Listen to the interview, making frequent stops to add more insights to the "Impressions" section of the Student Interview template for each problem.
- Supplement your on-the-spot impressions with connections to the Student History.

III. Develop Theories

Below articulate theories that might explain student difficulty with the target math concept. Using the learner, content, and instruction frames (see Chapter 3) may help. Evidence should link directly to <u>quotes from the interview</u> (the time on the recording is helpful), <u>impressions you recorded</u>, <u>student history</u>, or <u>examples from the student work</u>.

Theory 1:

Evidence:

Intervention that could test this theory:

Theory 2:

Evidence:

Intervention that could test this theory:

Theory 3:

Evidence:

Intervention that could test this theory:

Parent Consent Form

Dear (Parent's or Guardian's name),

I have noticed that your child, _____, has had some difficulty with math this year. Since our school wants every child to be successful, we would like to help your child by finding out more about his/her math thinking. To do this, we would like to have _____ (interviewer's name) interview _____ (child's name) to learn more about the way (s)he understands math.

I would be happy to meet with you to explain the interview process and show you what _____ (child's name) can expect during the interview. If there is any part of the process that makes you uncomfortable, I am happy to talk about it with you. We encourage you to ask questions if you have any. Your child's participation in this interview is voluntary; however, we believe he/she will enjoy the process and benefit from it. Our hope is that the interview with your child will give us information that we can use to teach him/her more successfully.

The interview will take place on _____, at _____. It will last for about an hour. We welcome the opportunity to meet with you after the interview to discuss what we have found and to get your take on our findings.

If you have any questions about this process, please do not hesitate to contact me.

_____ (interviewer's name)

_____ (school phone number)

_____ (email address)

I _____ (parent's name) give permission for my child to be interviewed by _____ (interviewer's name) for the purpose of understanding his/her mathematical thinking. I understand that this interview may be audio/videotaped for the purpose of review. I understand that recordings of the interview will be used by (here list everyone who may be involved in analysis). Any recordings of this interview will be destroyed by the end of the year.

_____ (parent's name)

_____ (date)

Main Lesson—Menu Lesson Plan: Template

Main Lesson—Menu Lesson Plan		
BIG IDEA/FOCUS		
Launch (5–10 minutes) *Think:* *How will this activate prior knowledge <u>and engage every student</u>?* *How will it lead into the main lesson?*	*Inquiry or problem for the launch:*	*Ask:*
Explore/Main Lesson (about 20 minutes) *Think:* *How can I provide opportunities for students to talk to each other about their math thinking during this lesson? How will I support all students to be part of this experience?* *Are the students doing the math work—or am I doing it for them?*	*Inquiry or problem for the main lesson:*	*Ask:*

Menu (about 30 minutes)

Think:

How will I differentiate this menu work for the variety of learners in my class?

How will I collect and respond to this work?

• Follow up from main lesson:	• Number and operations work:	• Problem to solve:
	(empty grid table) *Note:* Students choose one or the other. One dot is easier and two dots is more challenging.	*Note:* Students choose one or the other. One dot is easier and two dots is more challenging.
• Game to reinforce or investigate the big idea:	• Math Journal:	

Closure (about 10 minutes) *Think:* *What question can I ask, or problem can I pose, to focus attention and discussion on the work from the last hour?* *What do I want students to remember about this lesson?* *How will I record student thinking?*	*Ask:*	

Main Lesson—Menu Lesson Plan Example: First Grade

Main Lesson—Menu Lesson Plan		
BIG IDEA/FOCUS *comparing two or more numbers less than 20*		
Launch (5–10 minutes) *Think:* *How will this activate prior knowledge <u>and engage every student</u>?* *How will it lead into the main lesson?*	*Inquiry or problem for the launch:* *Stickies graph for boys/girls (different color for each—let them put their sticky in the right column)*	*Ask:* *Are there more boys or girls in our class? How can you tell? (turn and talk, then whole group)*
Explore/Main Lesson (about 20 minutes) *Think:* *How can I provide opportunities for students to talk to each other about their math thinking during this lesson? How will I support all students to be part of this experience?* *Are the students doing the math work—or am I doing it for them?*	*Inquiry or problem for the main lesson:* *Put students into groups of 4 (make sure there's a mixed group for the math coach to work with today)* *Each group gets 17 red cubes, 12 blue cubes, and 9 orange cubes. Don't stack beforehand.*	*Ask:* *1. Which has more, red or blue? How many more? How do you know? (small group, whole group: record on chart paper)* *2. Which has more, orange or blue? How many more? How do you know? (same)* *3. Put these in order. How do you know it's the right order? (Have groups show their results)*

(continued)

Menu (about 30 minutes)

Think:

How will I differentiate this menu work for the variety of learners in my class?

How will I collect and respond to this work?

• Follow up from main lesson:	• Number and operations work:	• Problem to solve:
• Optional (for those who want a challenge) How many <u>more</u> cubes (all together) would you need so that everyone in our cubes problem would have the same amount of cubes?	<table><tr><td>•</td><td>17 – 12 =</td><td>••</td><td>17 – 9 =</td></tr><tr><td></td><td>17 – 9 =</td><td></td><td>27 – 9 =</td></tr><tr><td></td><td>12 – 9 =</td><td></td><td>37 – 9 =</td></tr><tr><td></td><td>10 + 7 =</td><td></td><td>24 + 26 =</td></tr><tr><td></td><td>12 + 9 =</td><td></td><td>23 + 27 =</td></tr></table> **Note:** *Students choose one or the other. One dot is easier and two dots is more challenging.*	*One dot:* Tim has 8 pennies. Sam has 11 pennies. Who has more? How many more? Use numbers, words, and pictures. *Two dots:* Jose has 28 pennies. Karen has 9 pennies. Who has more? How many more? Use numbers, words, and pictures. **Note:** *Students choose one or the other. One dot is easier and two dots is more challenging.*
• Game to reinforce or investigate the big idea:	• Math Journal:	
Red and black with no face cards. Players divide the deck among them evenly. Any extra cards are discarded (as are face cards). Aces are "one." Each player puts the top car in their hand in play. Whoever has the highest card wins all the cards played. If there is a tie, players put another card down and the highest card wins all the cards out. Play continues until one player has all the cards.	Put a picture of a bar graph in the journals. One bar with 8 squares, one with 5 squares. Prompt below graph: Which has more? How many more? How do you know? Remember to read this for the students who can't do it alone. Transcribe for Edith and Jerome.	

Closure (about 10 minutes)

Think:

What question can I ask, or problem can I pose, to focus attention and discussion on the work from the last hour?

What do I want students to remember about this lesson?

How will I record student thinking?

Ask:

How can you tell when one group has more than another? (Write down ideas for this)

If possible, highlight any connections with subtraction that they make.

How might counting help you with knowing if one group has more?

Use chart paper to record student thinking.

Main Lesson—Menu Lesson Plan Example: Third Grade

Main Lesson—Menu Lesson Plan		
BIG IDEA/FOCUS multiplying numbers greater than 10		
Launch (5–10 minutes) *Think:* *How will this activate prior knowledge <u>and engage every student</u>?* *How will it lead into the main lesson?*	*Inquiry or problem for the launch:* What does the equation, 16 X 5 mean?	*Ask:* Focus on getting students to make connections so they know that 16 X 5 is not too different from 10 X 5 and 6 X 5.
Explore/Main Lesson (about 20 minutes) *Think:* *How can I provide opportunities for students to talk to each other about their math thinking during this lesson? How will I support all students to be part of this experience?* *Are the students doing the math work—or am I doing it for them?*	*Inquiry or problem for the main lesson:* Start with: A <u>gross</u> is a dozen dozens. How many is that? Follow up with: How many eggs would be in 24 dozens?	*Ask:* Be sure to mix the groups up so the students can help each other if they get stuck. Small group first, then big group sharing. Make sure to have counters out for the students who want to use them. Maybe egg cartons, too?

Menu (about 30 minutes)

Think:

How will I differentiate this menu work for the variety of learners in my class?

How will I collect and respond to this work?

• Follow up from main lesson:	• Number and operations work:	• Problem to solve:

There are 14 candies in every roll of candies.

How many rolls of candies would we have to buy for everyone to get one?

•	6 X 7 =	••	10 X 6 =
	10 X 4 =		12 X 5 =
	8 X 6 =		7 X 12 =
	83 – 17 =		350 – 147 =
	100 – 35 =		400 – 189 =

Note: Students choose one or the other. One dot is easier and two dots is more challenging.

• Rugs are $10 a square foot. If I want to buy a rug that is 6 feet by 4 feet, how much will it cost?

•• Rugs are $117 a square foot. How much would it cost to put a rug in this room?

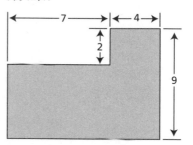

Note: Students choose one or the other. One dot is easier and two dots is more challenging.

• Game to reinforce or investigate the big idea:	• Math Journal:	

Double Dice:
Each player rolls her dice at the same time as her opponent. When the dice hit the table, the players multiply their dice together. Whoever has the higher total, wins. Graph paper is used to verify solutions when there is a dispute. For example, if one player rolls a 6 and a 4 and the other player rolls two 5s, the players may have to draw rectangles (something they learned in the main lesson) to determine which roll (6 times 4 or 5 times 5) is higher. Players play until one player has won ten rolls.

How is multiplying by numbers greater than 10 the same or different than multiplying by numbers less than 10?

> Make sure to check in with Ben and Ashley to be sure they don't need help with the writing.

Closure (about 10 minutes)

Think:

What question can I ask, or problem can I pose, to focus attention and discussion on the work from the last hour?

What do I want students to remember about this lesson?

How will I record student thinking?

Ask:

What did you find out about multiplying by numbers bigger than 10? Try to get them to focus on decomposition.

How is multiplying by numbers over 10 "different" than times tables?

Record student thinking where everyone can see it.

Main Lesson—Menu Lesson Plan Example: Fifth Grade

Main Lesson—Menu Lesson Plan		
BIG IDEA/FOCUS using equivalent fractions to add or subtract fractions with unlike denominators		
Launch (5–10 minutes) *Think:* *How will this activate prior knowledge <u>and engage every student</u>?* *How will it lead into the main lesson?*	*Inquiry or problem for the launch:* How many different ways can you write $1/2$? Have students make a list and then share. Keep a running list on the board.	*Ask:* Probe for a general rule for how to know if a fraction is another way to write $1/2$.
Explore/Main Lesson (about 20 minutes) *Think:* *How can I provide opportunities for students to talk to each other about their math thinking during this lesson? How will I support all students to be part of this experience?* *Are the students doing the math work—or am I doing it for them?*	*Inquiry or problem for the main lesson:* Heather and Brenan are eating a pan of brownies. Heather ate $1/4$ of the brownies. Brenan at $5/8$ of the brownies. Did they eat the whole pan of brownies? Students should work in table groups to come up with an answer. (Everyone must be able to explain the group answer.) One member should put their solution (and evidence) up on the board. Apply any of the strategies that groups used individually for: Tina said she ate $9/16$ of the cake. Al said he ate $2/3$ of the cake. Could they both be telling the truth? Did they eat the whole cake? Who ate more? Let students get started on this before starting menu so anyone who is stuck at the beginning can be helped.	*Ask:* Whole group debrief: What strategies did groups use for this problem? How are they the same (different)? What did you notice in another group's approach that was interesting? (If needed, ask each group to come up with something.)

(continued)

Menu (about 30 minutes)

Think:

How will I differentiate this menu work for the variety of learners in my class?

How will I collect and respond to this work?

• Follow up from main lesson:	• Number and operations work:	• Problem to solve:
Tina said she ate $9/16$ of the cake. Al said he ate $2/3$ of the cake. Could they both be telling the truth? Did they eat the whole cake? Who ate more?	(table below)	• Wai walks on a mile-long path near her house. On Monday she walked 0.3 miles. On Tuesday she walked 0.4 miles. Is her total walking closer to a half mile or a mile? Explain your answer.

Number and operations work table:

•		••	
$1/4 + 2/4 =$		$1/4 + 1/2 =$	
$1/5 + 3/5 =$		$1/6 + 1/2 =$	
$18 \times 6 =$		$327 \times 42 =$	
$83 \div 7 =$		$253 \div 14 =$	

Note: *Students choose one or the other. One dot is easier and two dots is more challenging.*

•• Wai walks on a mile-long path near her house. Every day she walks $2/3$ of the path before going home. After five days, how far has she walked?

Note: *Students choose one or the other. One dot is easier and two dots is more challenging.*

• Game to reinforce or investigate the big idea:	• Math Journal:
NCTM Illuminations Fractions Game http://illuminations.nctm.org /activitydetail.aspx?id=18[1]	Post the following prompt:

• Game to reinforce or investigate the big idea:

NCTM Illuminations Fractions Game
http://illuminations.nctm.org/activitydetail.aspx?id=18[1]
> no more than four at a time
> game only!

The object of the game is to get all of the markers to the right side of the game board, using as few cards as possible.

Click on the pile to turn over one card. This is your target fraction. Move the markers so that the sum of your moves is a fraction that is less than or equal to the target fraction.

For example, if the first card turned over is $4/5$, you could move the fifths marker to $3/5$ and the tenths marker to $2/10$, because $3/5 + 2/10 = 3/5 + 1/5 = 4/5$.

• Math Journal:

Post the following prompt:

How many different fractions are the same (equivalent) to $1/4$? How can you be sure there are that many? What makes them equivalent to $1/4$?

Remind the class that their journals must contain some answer and the evidence for it. If they don't have an answer, they should write about their current thinking and where they are stuck. (> Check on these before the end of the week. Be sure to meet with kids who have difficulty with this)

Closure (about 10 minutes)

Think:

What question can I ask, or problem can I pose, to focus attention and discussion on the work from the last hour?

What do I want students to remember about this lesson?

How will I record student thinking?

Ask:

What strategies help compare two fractions? Give examples from your work today where you used these strategies.
(If time, get some thinking about this)
How might you compare $\frac{1}{3}$ and $\frac{1}{5}$?

That creating equivalent fractions helps for comparing them.

Use the SMARTboard capture for this discussion for the students who are out today.

Main Lesson—Menu Lesson Plan Example: Seventh Grade

<table>
<tr><td colspan="3" align="center">Main Lesson—Menu Lesson Plan</td></tr>
<tr><td colspan="3">BIG IDEA/FOCUS
using unit rate to solve a proportion</td></tr>
</table>

Launch (5–10 minutes) *Think:* *How will this activate prior knowledge <u>and engage every student</u>?* *How will it lead into the main lesson?*	*Inquiry or problem for the launch:* If Herbert uses 12 ounces of nectar in his hummingbird feeder to feed 4 hummingbirds, how much nectar will he need to feed 7 hummingbirds?	*Ask:* If the students don't figure the amount/bird, move them in that direction with a question.
Explore/Main Lesson (about 20 minutes) *Think:* *How can I provide opportunities for students to talk to each other about their math thinking during this lesson? How will I support all students to be part of this experience?* *Are the students doing the math work—or am I doing it for them?*	*Inquiry or problem for the main lesson:* Herbert buys his nectar from 3 different stores. Figway sells nectar for $2.56/gallon. Tramway sells nectar for $1.00/liter. BirdsRus sells nectar for $1.00/quart. 1. Start by having groups discuss where there might be problems. 2. Have a whole-group discussion on where there might be problems and how groups are planning to attack them. If the unit of measurement issue comes up, tell them they can use the computer to find equivalence—or any other means they might have. 3. Solve and then report results and thinking. Closing problem to take to menu: How many hummingbirds could Herbert feed with that gallon of nectar?	*Ask:* I want students to focus on the cost/unit. It would be great if they found a common unit since this will allow them to compare the ratios.

Menu (about 30 minutes)

Think:

How will I differentiate this menu work for the variety of learners in my class?

How will I collect and respond to this work?

• Follow up from main lesson:	• Number and operations work:	• Problem to solve:
How many hummingbirds could Herbert feed with that gallon of nectar?	<table><tr><td>•</td><td>$2/3 + 4/5 =$</td><td>••</td><td>$4/7 \div 1/3 =$</td></tr><tr><td></td><td>$0.45 + 0.026 =$</td><td></td><td>$4^3/5 \times 1/2 =$</td></tr><tr><td></td><td>$3^1/4 \div 3/4 =$</td><td></td><td>$0.34 \times 0.2 =$</td></tr><tr><td></td><td>Put in order 0.081, 1/8, 0.8, 8/100</td><td></td><td>$1.25 \div 0.25 =$</td></tr></table> *Note: Students choose one or the other. One dot is easier and two dots is more challenging.*	• If 12 butterflies eat 60 grams of food, how much does each eat? •• If 4 butterflies eat 18 grams of food, how much does each eat? *Note: Students choose one or the other. One dot is easier and two dots is more challenging.*
• Game to reinforce or investigate the big idea:	• Math Journal:	
Play Paper Pool (make sure materials are available) http://illuminations.nctm.org/Lessons /imath/Pool/pool1b.html[1] How to Play Paper Pool • The lower-left corner is always corner A, and the labeling continues counterclockwise with B, C, and D. • The ball always starts in corner A. • The ball is hit with an imaginary cue (a stick for hitting a pool ball) so that it travels at a 45° diagonal across the grid. • If the ball hits a side of the table, it bounces off at a 45° angle and continues its travel. • The ball continues to travel until it hits a pocket.[1]	Today we worked on helping Herbert buy nectar. You found out the cost of nectar in units. In what other ways do you use units to compare things? Think about shopping, traveling, and measuring.	

[1]National Council of Teachers of Mathematics, retrieved from: http://illuminations.nctm.org/activitydetail.aspx?id=18

(continued)

Closure (about 10 minutes)

Think:

What question can I ask, or problem can I pose, to focus attention and discussion on the work from the last hour?

What do I want students to remember about this lesson?

How will I record student thinking?

Ask:

How is finding the amount per measure related to multiplication or division?

Do a pair/share before the final discussion.

Finding the unit rate will help compare ratios.

Use the SMARTboard. Save the class ideas to post on the class website.

If this is too challenging, try:

When we found out which nectar was a better bargain, how did we use multiplication or division? How could we use them in problems that were like Herbert's problem?

References

Allsopp, D., M. M. Kyger, and L. A. H. Lovin. 2007. *Teaching Mathematics Meaningfully: Solutions for Reaching Struggling Learners*. Baltimore: Paul H. Brookes.

Ashlock, R. B. 2010. *Error Patterns in Computation: Using Error Patterns to Help Each Student Learn*. Boston: Allyn & Bacon.

Baker, S., R. Gersten, and D. S. Lee. 2002. "A Synthesis of Empirical Research on Teaching Mathematics to Low-Achieving Students." *The Elementary School Journal* 103 (1).

Ball, D. L., H. C. Hill, and H. Bass. 2005. "Knowing Mathematics for Teaching: Who Knows Mathematics Well Enough to Teach Third Grade, and How Can We Decide?" *American Educator* (fall): 14–22.

Bamberger, H. J., C. Oberdorf, and K. Schultz-Ferrell. 2010. *Math Misconceptions: PreK–Grade 5: From Misunderstanding to Deep Understanding*. Portsmouth, NH: Heinemann.

Barlow, A. T., and M. R. McCrory. 2011. "3 Strategies for Promoting Math Disagreements." *Teaching Children Mathematics* 17 (9): 530–39.

Baroody, A. 2006. "Why Children Have Difficulties Mastering the Basic Number Combinations and How to Help Them." *Teaching Children Mathematics* 13 (1): 22.

Berch, D. B., and M. M. M. Mazzocco. 2007. *Why Is Math So Hard for Some Children? The Nature and Origins of Mathematical Learning Difficulties and Disabilities*. Baltimore: Paul H. Brookes.

Blanchett, W., V. Mumford, and F. Beachum. 2005. "Urban School Failure and Disproportionality in a Post-Brown Era." *Remedial and Special Education* 26 (2): 70–81.

Booth, J. L., and R. S. Siegler. 2008. "Numerical Magnitude Representations Influence Arithmetic Learning." *Child Development* 79 (4): 1016–31.

Borasi, R. 1996. *Reconceiving Mathematics Instruction: A Focus on Errors*. Norwood, NJ: Ablex.

Bright, G. W., M. J. Behr, T. R. Post, and I. Wachsmuth. 1988. "Identifying Fractions on Number Lines." *Journal for Research in Mathematics Education* 19 (3): 215–32. Universität Bielefeld.

Bryan, T., and J. Bryan. 1991. "Positive Mood and Math Performance." *Journal of Learning Disabilities* 24 (8): 490–94.

Burns, M. 1992. *About Teaching Mathematics: A K–8 Resource*. Sausalito, CA: Marilyn Burns Education Associates.

———. 2001. *Lessons for Introducing Multiplication: Grade 3*. Sausalito, CA: Math Solutions.

———. 2007. *About Teaching Mathematics: A K–8 Resource*. 3rd ed. Sausalito, CA: Marilyn Burns Education Associates.

Caine, G., and R. Nummela-Caine. 1997. *Education on the Edge of Possibility*. Alexandria, VA: Association for Supervision and Curriculum Development.

Caine, G., R. Nummela-Caine, and S. Crowell. 1999. *Mindshifts: A Brain-Based Process for Restructuring Schools and Renewing Education*. 2nd ed. Tucson, AZ: Zephyr Press.

Campbell, P. F., T. E. Rowan, A. R. Suarez, and National Council of Teachers of Mathematics. 1998. *What Criteria for Student-Invented Algorithms?* 1998 Yearbook. Reston, VA: National Council of Teachers of Mathematics.

Carpenter, T. P. 1999. *Children's Mathematics: Cognitively Guided Instruction*. Portsmouth, NH: Heinemann.

Carpenter, T. P., D. A. Carey, and V. L. Kouba. 1990. "A Problem-Solving Approach to the Operations." In *Mathematics for the Young Child*, edited by J. N. Payne. Reston, VA: National Council of Teachers of Mathematics.

Carpenter, T. P., E. Fennema, P. L. Peterson, and D. A. Carey. 1988. "Teachers' Pedagogical Content Knowledge of Students' Problem Solving in Elementary Arithmetic." *Journal for Research in Mathematics Education* 19 (5): 385–401.

Chapin, S. H., N. C. Anderson, and M. C. O'Connor. 2003. *Classroom Discussions: Using Math Talk to Help Students Learn, Grades 1–6*. Sausalito, CA: Math Solutions.

Choppin, J. M. 2007. "Teacher-Orchestrated Classroom Arguments." *Mathematics Teacher* 101 (4): 306–10.

Clark, F., and C. Kamii. 1996. "Identification of Multiplicative Thinking in Children Grades 1–5." *Journal for Research in Mathematics Education* 27 (January): 41–51.

References

Clarke, B., S. Baker, K. Smolkowski, and D. Chard. 2008. "An Analysis of Early Numeracy Curriculum-Based Measurement." *Remedial and Special Education* 29 (1): 46–57.

Cobb, P., and H. Bauersfeld. 1995. *The Emergence of Mathematical Meaning: Interaction in Classroom Cultures.* Hillsdale, NJ: Lawrence Erlbaum Associates.

Cockburn, A., G. H. Littler. 2008. *Mathematical Misconceptions: A Guide for Primary Teachers.* Los Angeles: SAGE.

Colvin, G. 2008. *Talent Is Overrated: What Really Separates World-Class Performers from Everybody Else.* New York: Portfolio.

Confrey, J. 1995. "A Theory of Intellectual Development." *For the Learning of Mathematics* 15 (1) 38–48.

Cowan, N. 2008. "What Are the Differences Between Long-Term, Short-Term, and Working Memory?" *Progress in Brain Research* 169 (April 3): 323–38.

Cramer, K., and T. Post. 1993. "Connecting Research to Teaching Proportional Reasoning." *Mathematics Teacher* 86 (5): 404–07.

Crawford, J. 2011. *Why Can't I Have Everything? Teaching Today's Children to Be Financially and Mathematically Savvy.* Sausalito, CA: Math Solutions.

Easton, F. 1997. "Educating the Whole Child, 'Head, Heart, and Hands': Learning from the Waldorf Experience." *Theory into Practice* 36 (2): 87–94.

Fennema, E., and M. L. Franke. 1992. "Teachers' Knowledge and Its Impact." In *Handbook of Research on Mathematics Teaching and Learning: A Project of the National Council of Teachers of Mathematics,* edited by D. Grouws, 147–64. New York: Macmillan.

Fosnot, C. T., and M. L. A. M. Dolk. 2001a. *Young Mathematicians at Work: Constructing Multiplication and Division.* Portsmouth, NH: Heinemann.

———. 2001b. *Young Mathematicians at Work: Constructing Number Sense, Addition, and Subtraction.* Portsmouth, NH: Heinemann.

Fuchs, L. S., and D. Fuchs. 2002. "Mathematical Problem-Solving Profiles of Students with Mathematics Disabilities with and Without Comorbid Reading Disabilities." *Journal of Learning Disabilities* 35 (6): 563–73.

Fuchs, L. S., D. Fuchs, and K. Prentice. 2004. "Responsiveness to Mathematical Problem-Solving Instruction: Comparing Students at Risk of Mathematics Disability with and Without Risk of Reading Disability." *Journal of Learning Disabilities* 37: 293–306.

Fuchs, L. S., D. Fuchs, K. Prentice, C. L. Hamlett, R. Finelli, and S. J. Courey. 2004. "Enhancing Mathematical Problem Solving Among Third-Grade Students with Schema-Based Instruction." *Journal of Educational Psychology* 96 (4): 635–47.

Gersten, R., S. Beckmann, B. Clarke, A. Foegen, L. Marsh, J. R. Star, and B. Witzel. 2009. *Assisting Students Struggling with Mathematics: Response to Intervention (RtI) for Elementary and Middle Schools* (NCEE 2009-4060). Washington, DC: National Center for Education Evaluation and Regional Assistance, Institute of Education Sciences, U.S. Department of Education. Retrieved from http://ies.ed.gov/ncee/wwc/publications/practiceguides/.

Gersten, R., N. Jordan, and J. Flojo. 2005. "Early Identification and Interventions for Students with Mathematics Difficulties." *Journal of Learning Disabilities* 38 (4): 293–304.

Ginsburg, H. P. 1997. *Entering the Child's Mind: The Clinical Interview in Psychological Research and Practice.* Cambridge: Cambridge University Press.

Good, T. L. 1981. "Teacher Expectations and Student Perceptions: A Decade of Research." *Educational Leadership* 38 (5): 415–22.

Hallowell, E. M., and J. J. Ratey. 1994. *Answers to Distraction.* New York: Pantheon Books.

Hanich, L. B., N. C. Jordan, D. Kaplan, and J. Dick. 2001 "Performance Across Different Areas of Mathematical Cognition in Children with Learning Difficulties." *Journal of Educational Psychology* 93 (3): 615–26.

Harel, G., and J. Confrey. 1994. *The Development of Multiplicative Reasoning in the Learning of Mathematics.* Albany: State University of New York Press.

Hartman, H. J. 2001. *Metacognition in Learning and Instruction: Theory, Research, and Practice.* Dordrecht, Netherlands: Kluwer Academic.

Hiebert, J., and D. Wearne. 1993. "Instructional Tasks, Classroom Discourse, and Students' Learning in Second-Grade Arithmetic." *American Educational Research Journal* 30 (2): 393–425.

Hill, H. C., S. G. Schilling, and D. L. Ball. 2004. "Developing Measures of Teachers' Mathematics Knowledge for Teaching." *Elementary School Journal* 105: 11–30.

Kamii, C., and F. B. Clark. 1995. "Equivalent Fractions: Their Difficulty and Educational Implications." *Journal of Mathematical Behavior* 14 (4): 365–78.

Kilpatrick, J., C. Hoyles, O. Skovsmose, and P. Valero. 2005. *Meaning in Mathematics Education.* (Springer e-books.) Boston: Springer Science+Business Media.

Lawton, C. A. 1993. "Contextual Factors Affecting Errors in Proportional Reasoning." *Journal for Research in Mathematics Education* 24 (5): 460–66.

Lesh, R., T. Post, and M. Behr. 1988. "Proportional Reasoning." In *Number Concepts and Operations in the Middle Grades,* edited by J. Hiebert and M. Behr, 93–118. Reston, VA: Lawrence Erlbaum & National Council of Teachers of Mathematics.

Levine, M. D. 2002. *A Mind at a Time*. New York: Simon & Schuster.

Linchevski, L., and B. Kutscher. 1998. "Tell Me with Whom You're Learning, and I'll Tell You How Much You've Learned: Mixed-Ability Versus Same-Ability Grouping in Mathematics." *Journal for Research in Mathematics Education* 29 (5): 533–54.

Littleton, K., and C. Howe. 2010. *Educational Dialogues: Understanding and Promoting Productive Interaction*. London: Routledge.

Lobato, J., A. B. Ellis, R. I. Charles , and R. M. Zbiek. 2010. *Developing Essential Understanding of Ratios, Proportions, and Proportional Reasoning for Teaching Mathematics: Grades 6–8*. Reston, VA: National Council of Teachers of Mathematics.

Mayo, M. J. 2009. "Video Games: A Route to Large-Scale STEM Education?" *Science* 323 (5910): 79–82.

Mazzocco, M. M. M. 2007. "Defining and Differentiating Mathematical Learning Disabilities and Difficulties." In *Why Is Math So Hard for Some Children? The Nature and Origins of Mathematical Learning Difficulties and Disabilities*, edited by D. B. Berch and M. M. M. Mazzocco. Baltimore: Paul Brooks.

McKeough, A., J. L. Lupart, and A. Marini. 1995. *Teaching for Transfer: Fostering Generalization in Learning*. Mahwah, NJ: Lawrence Erlbaum Associates.

McNamara, J. 2010. *Beyond Pizzas & Pies: 10 Essential Strategies for Supporting Fraction Sense, Grades 3–5*. Sausalito, CA: Math Solutions.

Misailidou, C., and J. Williams 2003. Measuring Children's Proportional Reasoning, The "Tendency" for an Additive Strategy and the Effect of Models. PME Conference, January.

Montague, M. 1997. "Cognitive Strategy Instruction in Mathematics for Students with Learning Disabilities." *Journal of Learning Disabilities* 30 (2): 164.

National Center for Education Statistics. 2006. *The Condition of Education 2006*. NCES 2006-071. Washington, DC: U.S. Government Printing Office.

National Council of Teachers of Mathematics. 2000. *Principles and Standards for School Mathematics*. Reston, VA: National Council of Teachers of Mathematics.

———. 2006. *Curriculum Focal Points for Prekindergarten Through Grade 8 Mathematics: A Quest for Coherence*. Reston, VA: National Council of Teachers of Mathematics.

Orton, A. 2004. *Learning Mathematics: Issues, Theory, and Classroom Practice*. London: Continuum.

Otto, A. D., and National Council of Teachers of Mathematics. 2011. *Developing Essential Understanding of Multiplication and Division for Teaching Mathematics in Grades 3–5*. Reston, VA: National Council of Teachers of Mathematics.

Petit, M. M., R. E. Laird, and E. L. Marsden. 2010. *A Focus on Fractions: Bringing Research to the Classroom*. New York: Routledge.

Piaget, J., and M. Cook. 1977. *The Origin of Intelligence in the Child*. Harmondsworth, England: Penguin.

Prediger, S. 2008. "Discontinuities of Mental Models: A Source for Difficulties with the Multiplication of Fractions." Retrieved from: www.mathematik. uni-dortmund.de/~prediger/veroeff/08-ICME11-TSG10-Fractions.pdf.

Ramani, G. B., and R. S. Siegler. 2008. "Promoting Broad and Stable Improvements in Low-Income Children's Numerical Knowledge Through Playing Number Board Games." *Child Development* 79: 375–94. doi: 10.1111/j.1467-8624.2007.01131.x

Reid, R., A. L. Trout, and M. Schartz. 2005. "Self-Regulation Interventions for Children with Attention Deficit/Hyperactivity Disorder." *Exceptional Children* 71 (4): 361.

Richardson, K. 1999. *Developing Number Concepts: Book 2*. White Plains, NY: Dale Seymour.

Richardson, K. 2003. Assessing Math Concepts Series. Bellingham, WA: Mathematical Perspectives.

Ryan, J., and J. Williams. 2007. *Children's Mathematics 4–15: Learning from Errors and Misconceptions*. Maidenhead, England: McGraw-Hill/Open University Press.

Schoenfeld, A. H. 1994. *Mathematical Thinking and Problem Solving*. Hillsdale, NJ: Lawrence Erlbaum Associates.

Sheffield, S. 2001. *Teaching Arithmetic: Lessons for First Grade*. Sausalito, CA: Math Solutions.

Smith, M. S., and M. K. Stein. 2011. *5 Practices for Orchestrating Productive Mathematics Discussions*. Reston, VA: National Council of Teachers of Mathematics.

Sousa, D. 2011. *How the Brain Learns*. 4th ed. Thousand Oaks, CA. Corwin Press.

Steinbring, H., B. M. G. Bartolini, and A. Sierpinska. 1998. *Language and Communication in the Mathematics Classroom*. Reston, VA: National Council of Teachers of Mathematics.

Steiner, R. 2003. *What Is Waldorf Education? Three Lectures*. Great Barrington, MA: Steiner Books.

Stewart, I. 2006. *Letters to a Young Mathematician*. New York: Basic Books.

Swanson, H. L., K. R. Harris, and S. Graham. 2003. *Handbook of Learning Disabilities*. New York: Guilford Press.

References

Tank, B., and L. Zolli. 2001. *Teaching Arithmetic: Lessons for Addition and Subtraction: Grades 2–3*. Sausalito, CA: Math Solutions.

Tapper, J. R., and R. J. Tobias. 2009. Measuring School Success: An Analysis of Elementary School Mathematics Performance Based on Regression to Poverty. Conference proceedings, American Evaluation Association, Atlanta, Georgia.

Tate, W. F. 1997. "Race-Ethnicity, SES, Gender, and Language Proficiency Trends in Mathematics Achievement: An Update." *Journal for Research in Mathematics Education* 28 (6): 652–79.

Tobey, C. R., and L. Minton. 2011. *Uncovering Student Thinking in Mathematics, Grades K–5: 25 Formative Assessment Probes for the Elementary Classroom*. Thousand Oaks, CA: Corwin Press.

Tournaki, N. 2003. "The Differential Effects of Teaching Addition Through Strategy Instruction Versus Drill and Practice to Students with and Without Learning Disabilities." *Journal of Learning Disabilities* 36 (5): 449–458.

Tzur, R., Y. P. Xin, L. Si, R. Kenney, and A. Guebert. 2010. Students with Learning Disability in Math Are Left Behind in Multiplicative Reasoning? Number as Abstract Composite Unit Is a Likely "Culprit." Paper presented at the Annual Meeting of the Americal Educational Research Association, Denver, Colorado. April 30–May 4.

Van De Walle, J. A., K. S. Karp, and J. M. Bay-Williams. 2009. *Elementary and Middle School Mathematics: Teaching Developmentally*. Boston: Allyn & Bacon.

Vergnaud, G. 1988. "Multiplicative Structures." In *Number Concepts and Operations in the Middle Grades*, edited by J. Hiebert and M. Behr, 141–61. Hillsdale, NJ: Lawrence Erlbaum.

Vinner, S. 1997. "The Pseudo-Conceptual and the Pseudo-Analytical Thought Processes in Mathematics Learning." *Educational Studies in Mathematics* 34 (2): 97–129.

Vygotsky, L. S., and A. Kozulin. 1987. *Thought and Language*. Cambridge, MA: MIT Press.

Whitman, C. 2011. *It's All Connected: The Power of Proportional Reasoning to Understand Mathematics Concepts: Grades 6–8*. Sausalito, CA: Math Solutions.

Wickett, M., and M. Burns. 2003. *Lessons for Extending Division: Grades 4–5*. Sausalito, CA: Math Solutions.

Wright, R. J. 1994. "A Study of the Numerical Development of 5-Year-Olds and 6-Year-Olds. *Educational Studies in Mathematics* 26 (1): 25–44.

Wright, R. J., J. Martland, and A. K. Stafford. 2006. *Early Numeracy: Assessment for Teaching and Intervention*. London: Paul Chapman.

Wright, R. J., G. Stanger, A. K. Stafford, and J. Martland. 2006. *Teaching Number in the Classroom with 4–8 Year-Olds*. London: Sage.

Yasutake, D., and T. Bryan. 1995. "The Influence of Affect on the Achievement and Behavior of Students with Learning Disabilities." *Journal of Learning Disabilities* 28 (6): 329–34.

Zimmerman, B. J. 2001. "Theories of Self-Regulated Learning and Academic Achievement: An Overview and Analysis." In *Self-Regulated Learning and Academic Achievement: Theoretical Perspectives*, edited by B. J. Zimmerman and D. H. Schunk, 1–65. Mahwah, NJ: Lawrence Erlbaum Associates.

Index